POSTCARD HISTORY SERIES

Carteret County

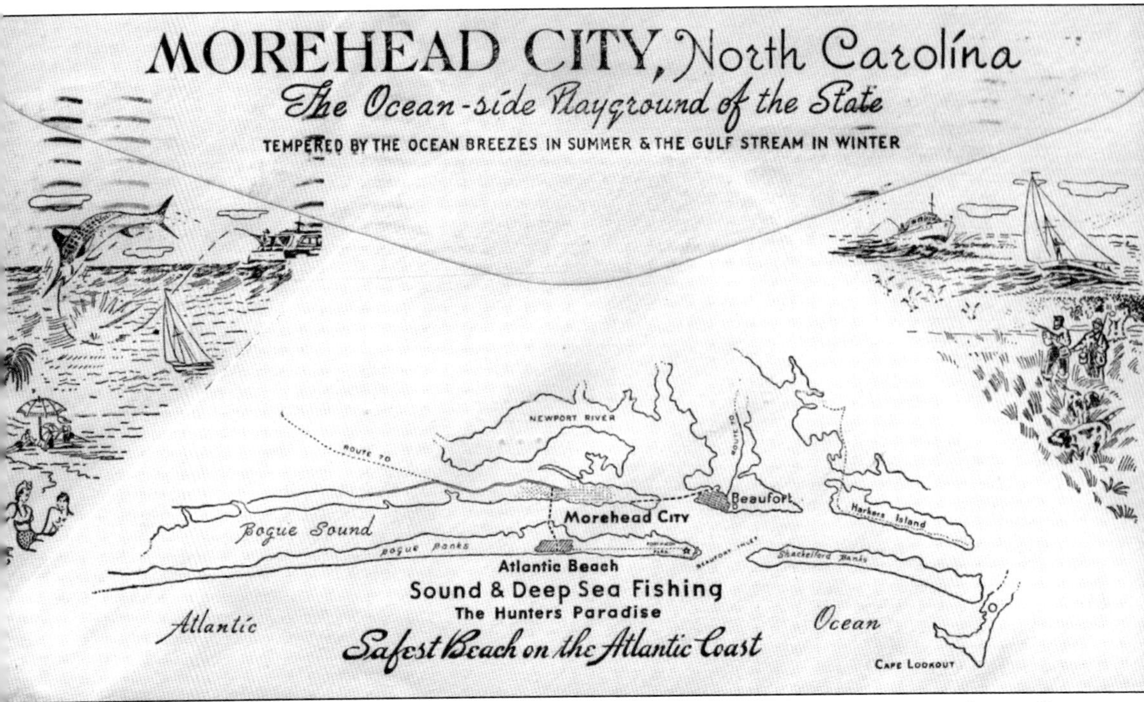

CARTERET COUNTY. Carteret County stretches across North Carolina's central coastline. Western Carteret County includes the communities of Morehead City, Newport, and Cape Carteret. In the east lie the county seat of Beaufort and the 13 communities collectively known as "Down East." Several beach communities are located on Bogue Banks, while the Cape Lookout National Seashore is home to one of North Carolina's first lighthouses.

ON THE FRONT COVER: The Morehead City Boating Club was founded in 1934, sponsoring such races as the Shanghai Trophy, the Gib Arthur Memorial Trophy, and the D. G. Bell Memorial Trophy. The flag called Old Mullet, designed by D. G. Bell, distinguished the boats. The club also sponsored the Junior Boat Club. These clubs were active until World War II put a stop to pleasure boating. (Courtesy of the author.)

ON THE BACK COVER: In the late 1800s, resort hotels in Morehead City and Beaufort began ferrying patrons to Bogue Banks for picnicking and surf bathing. Bathhouses were added, and soon a pavilion and hotel followed. In 1928, a bridge connected the island to Morehead City, and in 1937, Atlantic Beach was born. (Courtesy of the author.)

POSTCARD HISTORY SERIES

Carteret County

Linda Sadler and Kevin Jenkins

ARCADIA PUBLISHING

ISBN 978-0-7385-4448-9

Published by Arcadia Publishing
Charleston SC, Chicago IL, Portsmouth NH, San Francisco CA

Printed in the United States of America

Library of Congress Catalog Card Number: 2007924362

For all general information contact Arcadia Publishing at:
Telephone 843-853-2070
Fax 843-853-0044
E-mail sales@arcadiapublishing.com
For customer service and orders:
Toll-Free 1-888-313-2665

Visit us on the Internet at www.arcadiapublishing.com

To Neal and Evelyn,
who instilled in us a love for local history and family heritage.

For Gerry, Holly, Nathan, and Noah,
whose love and support have made this book possible.

Contents

ACKNOWLEDGMENTS

There are a number of people who truly helped make this book a reality. We would like to thank Shannon, Whitney, and Holly Jenkins for providing editing and wordsmithery assistance. Their suggestions helped clear our minds to focus on providing legible captions that effectively convey meaning to our readers.

A sincere thank you goes to Mickey Weeks of Cary, North Carolina, and Gail Barnes and Helen Chappell of Beaufort for sharing their personal postcard collections. Without their contributions, we would not have been able to cover such a wide range of worthy topics. All other postcards are from Linda Sadler's collection.

We utilized many more references than space allowed us to cite in the bibliography. We applaud all of the local authors and historians who are working to keep the county's heritage alive.

Finally, we would like to acknowledge the History Place and Beaufort Historical Association for their dedication to preserving the history of the county; the Carteret County Public Library for providing access to so many microfilms of old newspapers; and the many newspaper editors, photographers, and writers who have given us a record of historical events as they happened.

Introduction

Sparkling waters and miles of sandy beaches characterize the Crystal Coast of Carteret County. This unspoiled stretch of coastland offers an abundance of natural beauty, but it is also rich in history. The area was one of the first to be explored in the state. With its wealth of natural resources and excellent natural harbor, it was settled by the early 18th century. Visitors can still see glimpses of those early days. Quaint fishing villages dot the eastern part of the county, 300-year-old homes are on tour, and wild ponies race across undeveloped beaches. It is no wonder that the Crystal Coast has grown to become one of the state's most popular vacation destinations.

Part of the area's appeal can be attributed to its relaxed pace and simple way of life. For 200 years, Beaufort and the eastern portion of the county were isolated from most of the state. The waterways surrounding the area provided for its economy but hampered its growth. Aside from Newport, settled in the early 1700s, western Carteret County was relatively undeveloped until the mid-1800s. Morehead City was organized and chartered in 1857 as an attempt to capitalize on the newly planned coastal railroad. The railroad reached Shepard's Point in 1858, ushering in a new era for the small county.

The coming of the train brought with it new avenues of trade and industry. It was the influx of visitors, however, that really changed the landscape and history of the area. For the first time, the county's beauty and tranquility could be shared on a grand scale. Seaside resort hotels, such as the Ocean House in Beaufort and Hotel Charles in Morehead City, opened to great fanfare. The luxurious Atlantic Hotel became known as the summer capital of the state and played host to tourists from all over the country.

Around that same time, postcards came into vogue. In 1898, Congress allowed private printers to sell "Private Mailing Cards." Publishers placed illustrations on the front, leaving a small border for short messages because the backs of cards could not be written on. Real black-and-white photographs began showing up on cards shortly thereafter. In 1907, the concept of a divided back provided for messages on the back and therefore better art on the front. That change brought a boom to the postcard industry, and over the next few years, half a billion postcards were printed and mailed in the United States. The hobby of collecting picture postcards swept the nation and became the biggest collectible hobby in the world. In the 1930s, a new technique of printing postcards on linen stock was developed, allowing the use of dyes to color pictures. By 1940, however, real color, high-quality photo cards, known as photochromes, replaced all others as the most popular type of card.

The heyday of the postcard corresponds to the transformation that was taking place in Carteret County. No longer simply a community of fishermen, farmers, and whalers, the county was experiencing newfound growth and spreading out into new industries and commercial endeavors. Picture postcards captured those changes as they were occurring.

Beaufort's excellent harbor was the primary reason that it was the third established town in the state. Many of the town's early residents rose to prominence in state government and the military. Trade between Beaufort and the major colonies of Boston and Baltimore flourished, although Beaufort's remoteness soon overshadowed the advantage that its port provided. The lack of an easy overland route to the interior of the state stymied its growth. Beaufort, once envisioned to outshine Boston, had peaked.

In November 1906, Beaufort's savior arrived. The railroad bridge connecting Morehead City and Beaufort was completed, and the first passenger train pulled into the station. The Beaufort-Western Railroad brought a new prosperity to the historic town. The fish and shellfish industry grew as fish houses had an easy means of sending their goods to market. The menhaden industry exploded and gave rise to many fish factories supported by hundreds of vessels. A multitude of vacationers spent their summers at the Inlet Inn, Manson House, and Davis Hotel. The railroad had such an impact on the local economy that in June 1907, a weeklong festival was held. In 1927, a causeway and automobile bridge built over Gallants Channel forever linked Beaufort to the outside world.

Pier One, the wharf at Shepard's Point, helped jump-start Morehead City's growth in the mid-1800s. The new railroad, ending at the wharf, enhanced shipping. Lots were divided and sold to new settlers, and the town was incorporated. The Civil War temporarily halted progress as Federal troops seized control of Morehead City's shipping operations. The damage from the occupation was minor and, in fact, may have spurred future growth. The war gave Northerners a look at the area, and many returned to open businesses. Former Union soldiers from Rhode Island were responsible for establishing Carteret County's menhaden industry. Many others spread the word about the area's splendor, sending wealthy vacationers to the "South's most beautiful vacationland."

The label "sportsman's paradise" was included in Morehead City's advertising brochures and newspaper articles. Indeed, the county's fishing and hunting grounds were plentiful and attracted regional attention. By the 1930s, numerous duck hunting lodges and gun clubs were established throughout the Down East communities and guided hunts were available for other game animals. Capt. Ottis Purifoy became a pioneer in sportfishing, and his Lucky 7 Fishing Fleet was well-known along the Atlantic Seaboard. Seafood restaurants were a natural extension of the charter boat business. Morehead City's most famous the Sanitary and Capt. Bill's offered patrons the freshest seafood anywhere.

Surf bathing was a newly popularized pastime in the late 1800s. Local boats ferried hotel patrons to Pivers Island, Swimming Shoal, and Bogue Banks for a day of picnicking and surf bathing. The 21-mile-long barrier island of Bogue Banks was viewed by many locals as an island desert. However, enterprising young men like J. J. Royal, Winfield Chadwick, and Alfred Cooper had other visions for the beach.

Tourists were attracted to the sand and surf, and in 1887, a small pavilion and bathhouse was built to accommodate them. By 1916, a 100-room hotel had been built on a section of the banks called Atlantic View Beach. A bridge from Morehead City, built in 1928, greatly enhanced development of the new resort area. The town of Atlantic Beach was incorporated in 1937 and has continued to grow in popularity ever since.

Carteret County itself has grown in popularity. Its natural beauty and treasure trove of resources has attracted settlers, pirates, and tourists alike. The area has undergone many changes since the 18th century's Age of Sail, though the most dramatic transformation took place between the 1880s and 1950s. That was also the time that postcards were at the height of their popularity. The cheap cards, never originally intended to be kept, have captured the images of that time period, inadvertently becoming not only souvenirs but historical records.

One

Beaufort

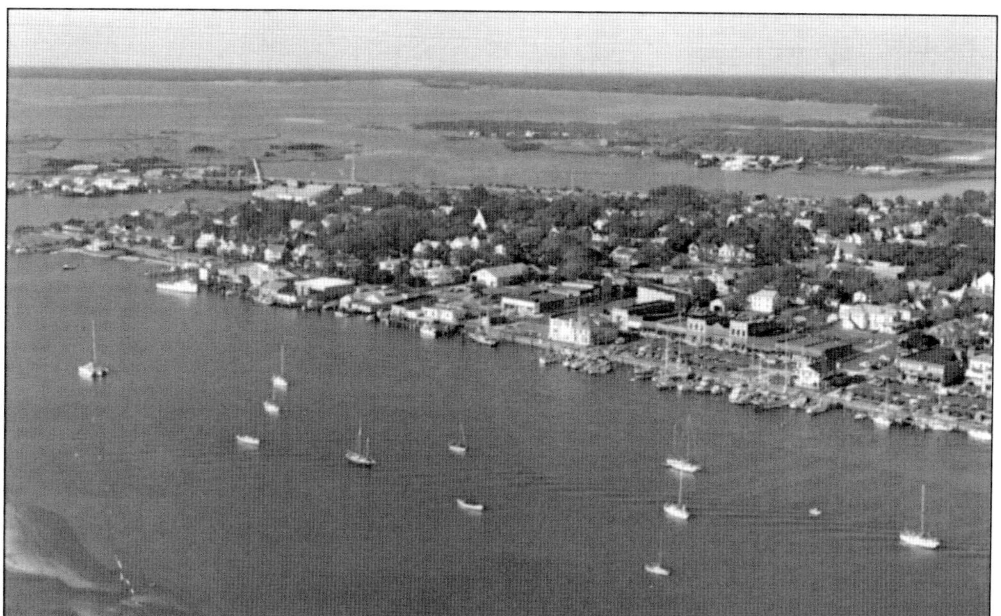

Fish Towne. Early settlers, recognizing the importance of the maritime site, originally called the settlement Fish Towne. Beaufort was laid out in 1713. As seen in this postcard, Beaufort is nearly surrounded by water. Taylor's Creek is in the foreground. Gallants Channel separates it on the west from Radio Island, while Town Creek (middle) feeds into the Newport River (top). On the eastern side, Beaufort is bordered by North River.

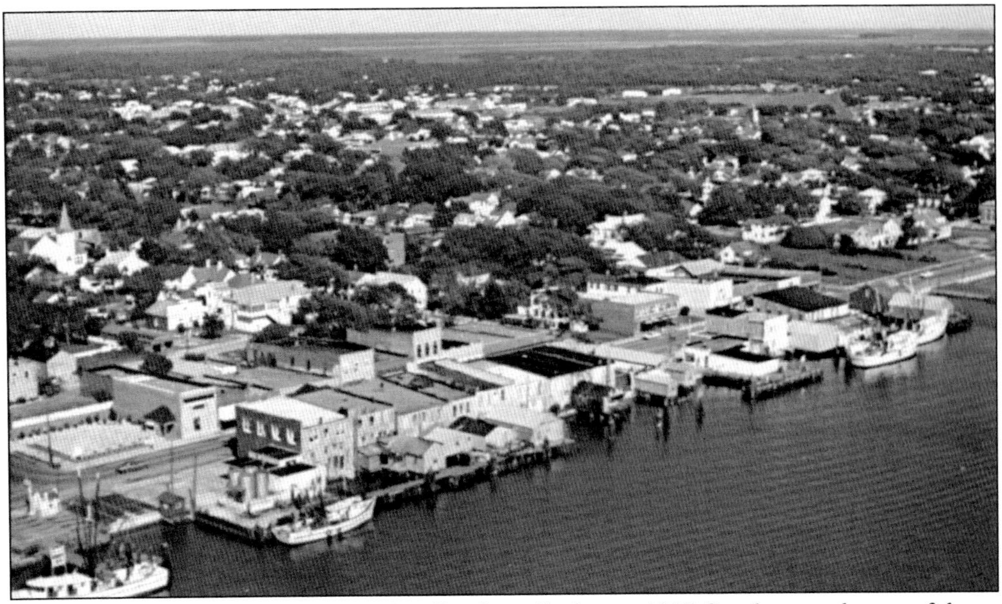

WATER FRONT. Stores were not built of brick until after an 1888 fire destroyed most of them. Later a change in the fire code required brick construction with the exception of fish houses. Because of the low crime rate, a tiny building (bottom left corner) was deemed adequate for the town's police station. Most of the buildings on the water side of Front Street were torn down for urban renewal.

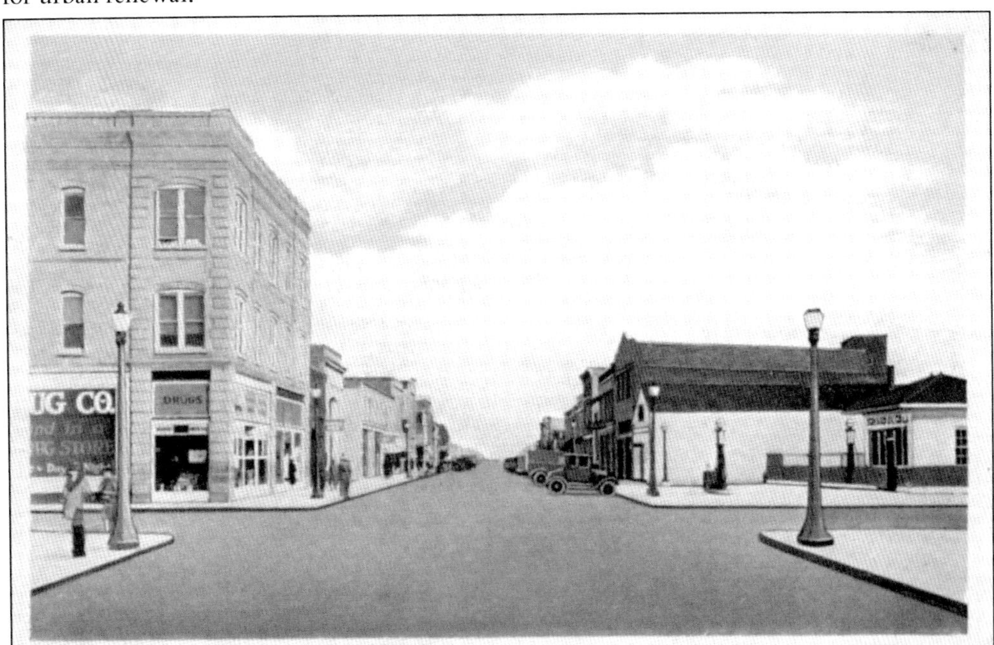

FRONT STREET LOOKING EAST. Streetlights were placed on Front Street in 1923, and nearly a mile of the street was paved in 1924. The entire length would be paved from Duncan Green to Lennoxville Road in 1937. Beaufort Drug Company gave rise to several other drugstores. Employee George Bell opened Bell's Drug Store, while employee Joe House purchased Beaufort Drug in 1924, renaming it Joe House Drug Store.

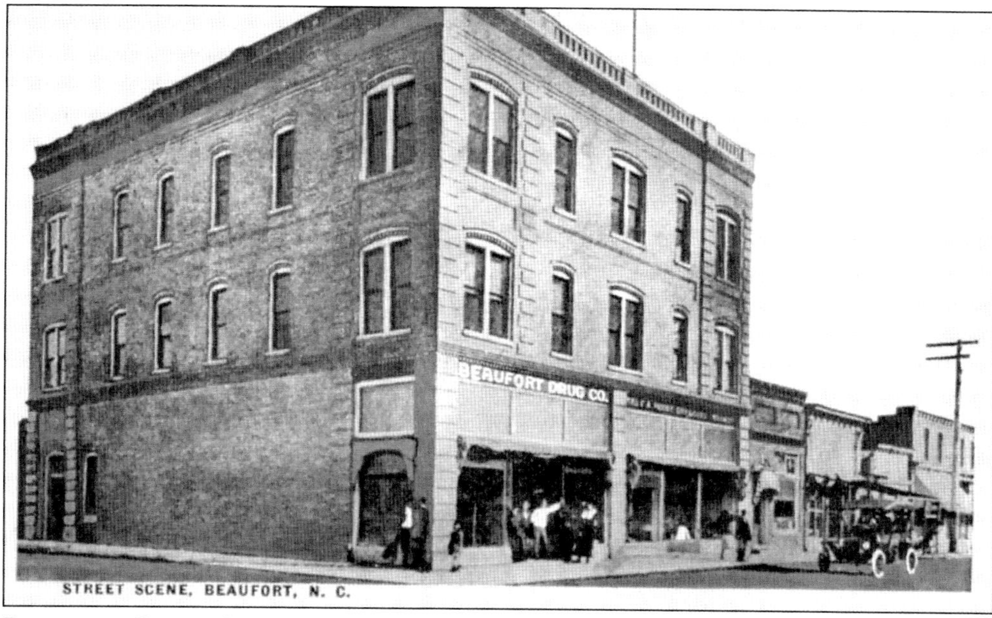

BEAUFORT DRUG COMPANY. Dr. Charles Lucas Duncan, also a pharmacist, operated his medical office and Beaufort Drug Company in the three-story building bearing his name. An obstetrician and pediatrician, Duncan is especially remembered for working tirelessly during the 1918 influenza epidemic. The Duncan Building, located on Turner and Front Streets, housed various other stores over the years, including C. A. Moore Dry Goods (shown), Lipman's Department Store, and Eastman's Furniture.

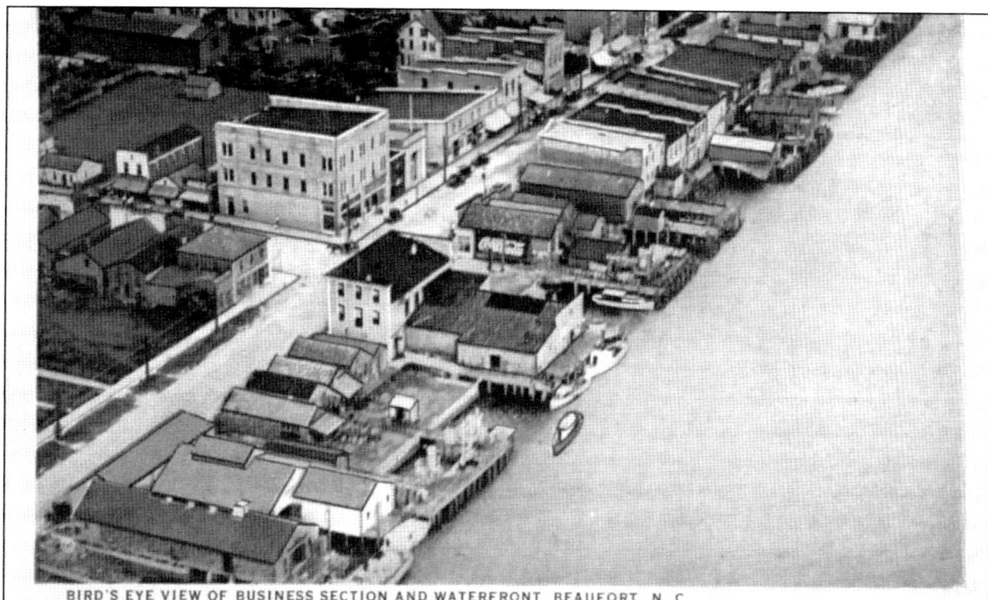

DAVIS HALL. Located on the southwest corner of Front and Turner Streets was three-story Davis Hall. In the late 1800s and early 1900s, it was the principal public hall. Davis Hall was used for political rallies, plays, and the U.S. Court. At one time, it housed a bowling alley on the second floor. The empty lot behind the Duncan Building is now home to the Beaufort Historic Grounds.

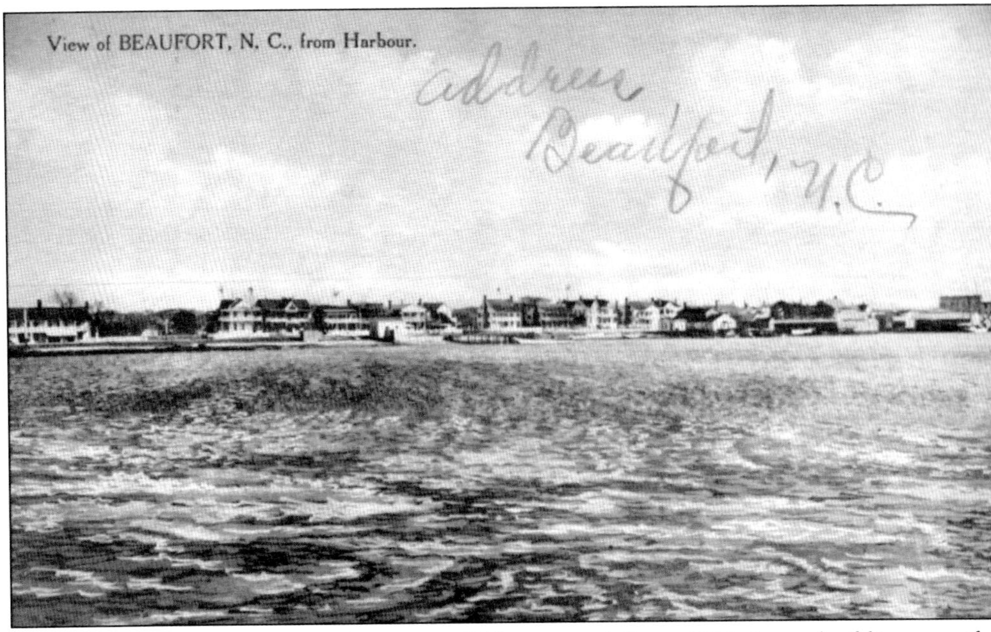

VIEW OF BEAUFORT FROM HARBOUR. This postcard from 1915 shows buildings on the water side of Front Street that no longer exist today. From left to right are the Duncan House, Manson House, Davis Hotel, Leslie Davis House, Nelson House, Jule Duncan House, and Sloo House. Note the many windmills high above the buildings. Windmills were used to draw water from wells. Previously families captured rainwater in cisterns.

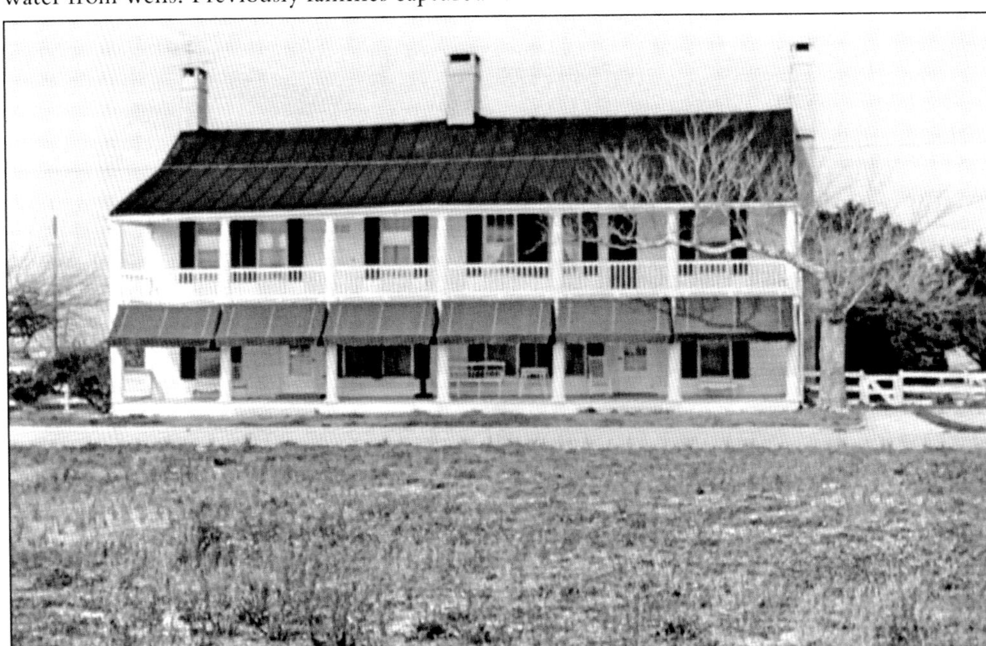

DUNCAN HOUSE. The house located at the west end of Front Street was built in 1790. Purchased by Thomas Duncan Jr. in 1805, the west end of the house was used as a ship's store. In the 1930s, it was occupied by William Blades, a local fish factory owner. Baseball legend Babe Ruth often traveled from New York to duck hunt with Blades.

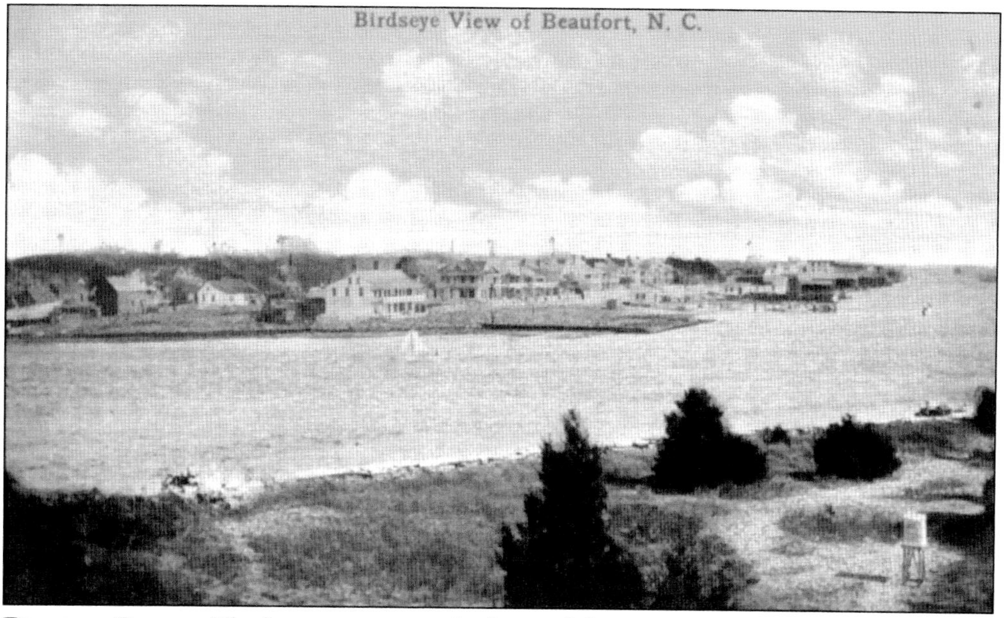

DUNCAN GREEN. The large grassy area in front of the Duncan House known as Duncan Green was used for picnics and entertaining. In the 1930s and 1940s, Capt. Jack Willis, one of the most famous sheepshead guides along the coast, operated a small fishing wharf there. Down Gallants Channel from there was a shipyard, and beyond stood one of the world's first oyster canneries, built in the 1890s.

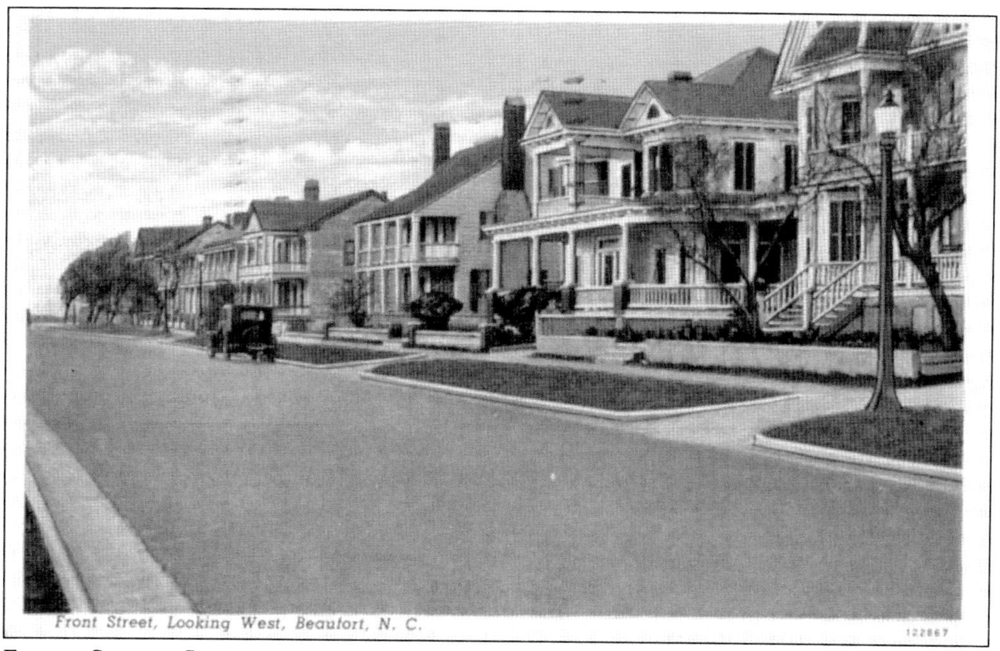

FRONT STREET LOOKING WEST. The houses pictured from left to right are the Manson, *c.* 1860; Davis House(s), *c.* 1769, 1820, 1880; Davis, *c.* 1812; Nelson, *c.* 1790; Jule Duncan, *c.* 1920; and Sloo, *c.* 1768. The Jules Duncan House replaced the 18th-century Perry House. The Perry House, originally known as the Cook House, was the birthplace of James Wallace Cook, commander of the Confederate ram *Albemarle*.

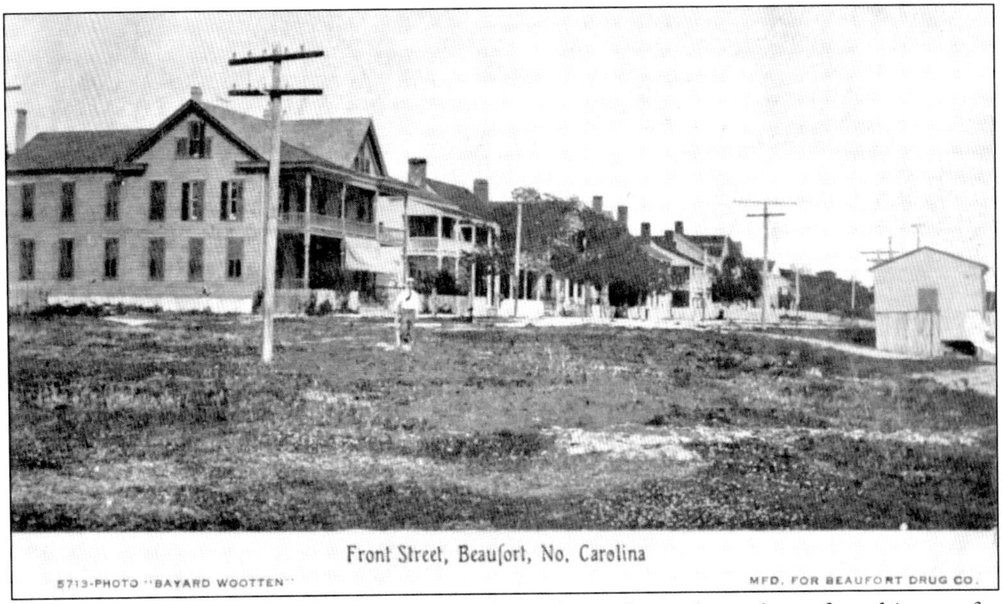

MANSON HOUSE. Thomas Duncan built the house located two doors down from his own for his daughter Esther in 1860. She married John Manson, for whom the house is named. Their daughters, Emma and Etta, later made the Manson House a famous boarding house known for good food and hospitality. Like the Davis House next door, the Manson House was a choice destination for summer tourists. (Courtesy of Mickey Weeks.)

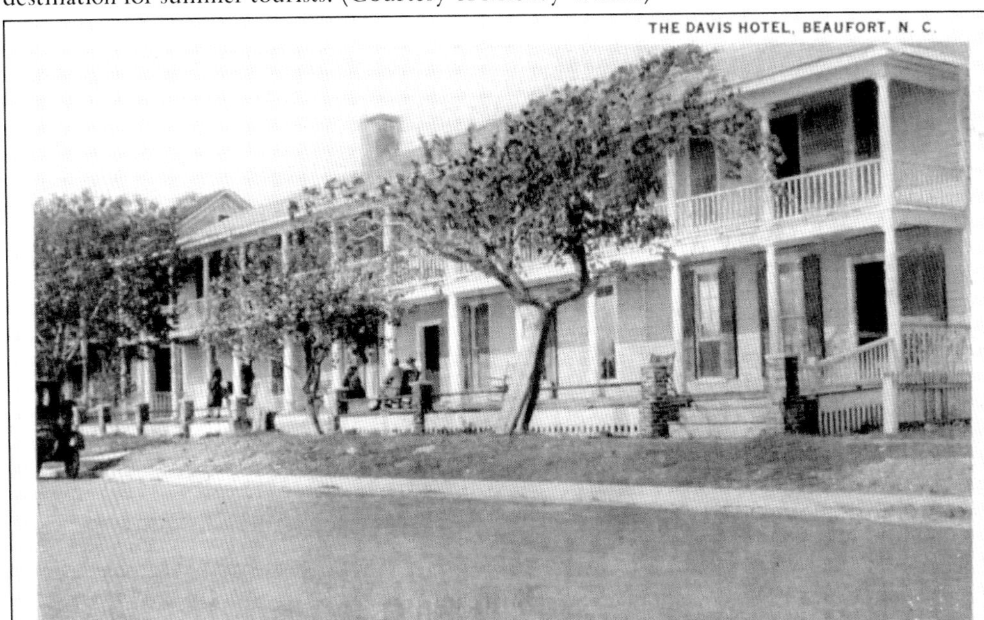

DAVIS HOTEL. This hotel was one of many that emerged during the early boom in Beaufort tourism. It was actually three separate houses joined in the 1880s by a common roof and porches. Guests arrived with their steamer trunks by boat or train and stayed for months at a time. Tup Fisher, a chambermaid at the hotel, became one of the original Fisk Jubilee Singers touring the United States and Europe.

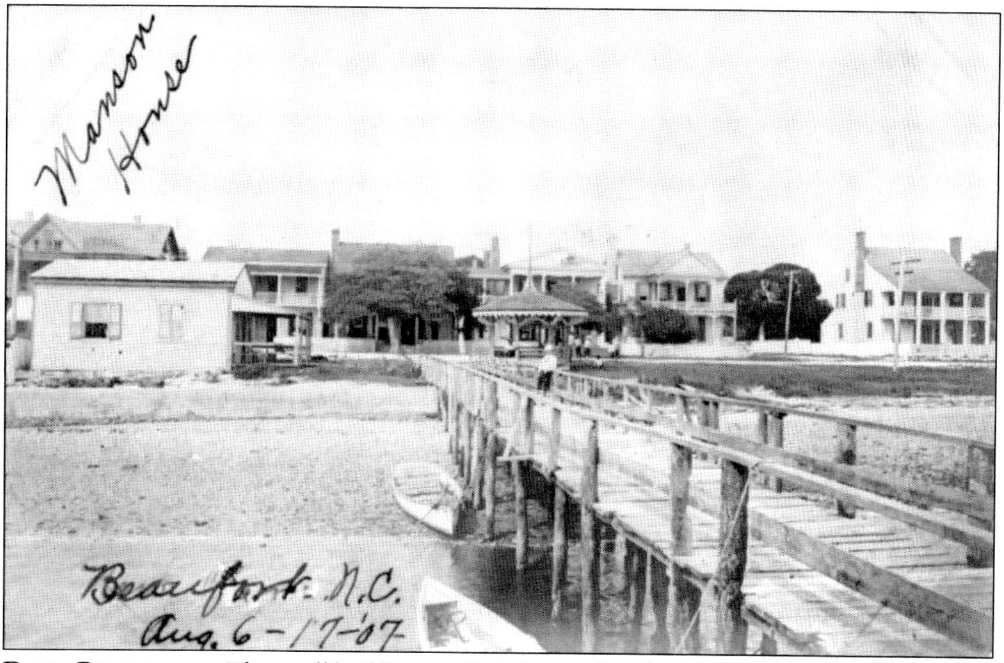

DAVIS BATHHOUSE. The small building on the left served as the Davis Hotel's bathhouse. Hotel guests would often rent bathing suits and water wings for swimming. Locals like Capt. Jack (John) Willis and his sons would be hired to row the tourists to Pivers Island and Swimming Shoal for 15¢ per round-trip. The hotel also maintained a dock and gazebo for its guests.

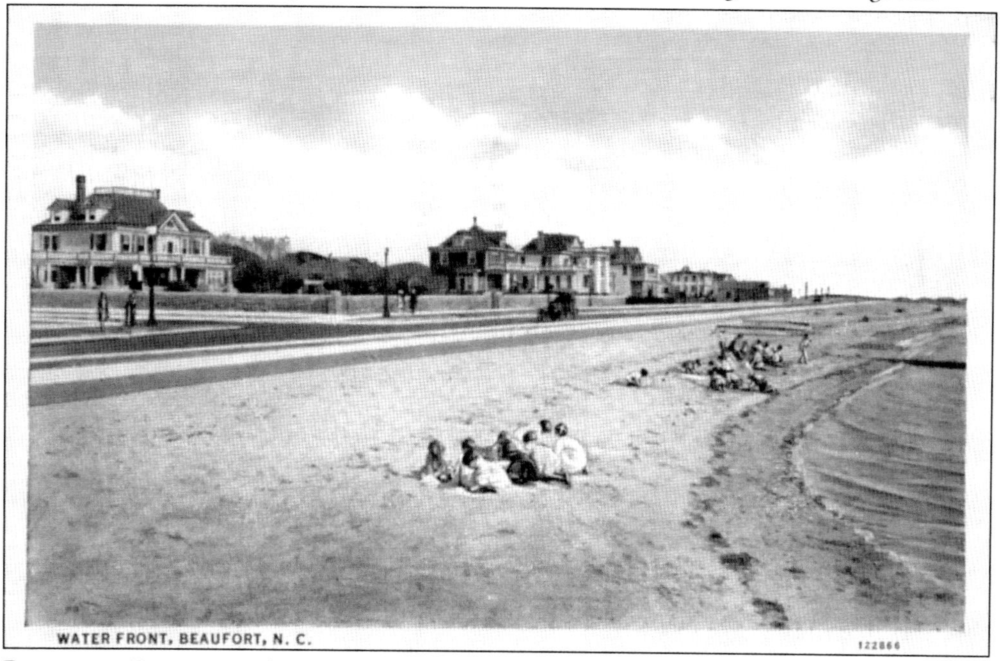

BEAUFORT BEACHES. This scene displays children playing on a sandy beach in front of the Inlet Inn. Beaufort beaches have succumbed to the changing of times and have been replaced with breakwaters and docks. Located on the corner of Pollock and Front Streets was the home (left) of Dr. Charles Duncan, a local doctor and business owner.

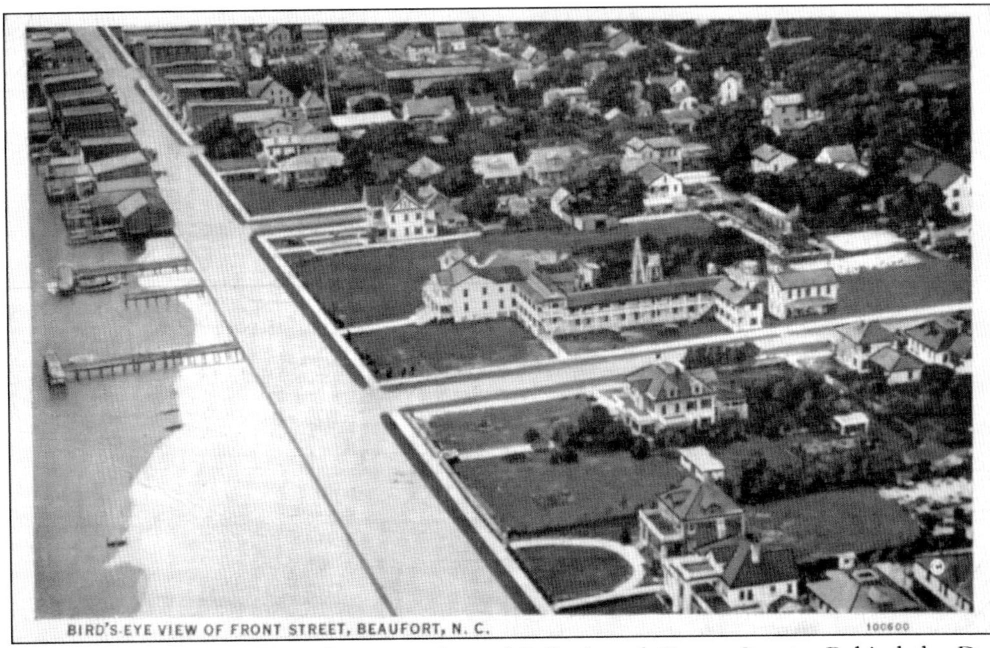

BIRD'S-EYE VIEW. This card gives a view of Pollock and Queen Streets. Behind the Dey House at 120 Queen Street is the Allen Davis House, built *c.* 1774. It served as Gen. Ambrose Burnside's headquarters during the 1862 Federal occupation. The Dill House, built *c.* 1860 at 119 Queen, served as the Methodist Parsonage. Other notables are the Hendrix House with circular drive and, on Pollock, the Tillman and Willis homes.

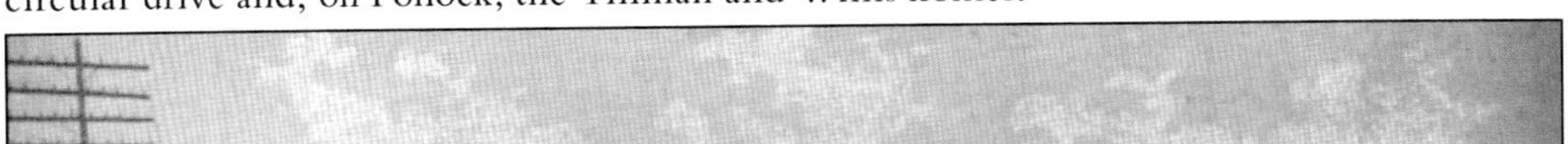

BOARD WALK EAST. Moving east from Queen Street is the C. P. Dey house, the White House or Ernest Duncan House, and the Inlet Inn. Queen Street is one of several streets named for Queen Anne. The White House is thought to have been built by the descendants of John White of Lost Colony fame. Houses connected to the boardwalk via piers; some ended with a boat landing and bathhouse.

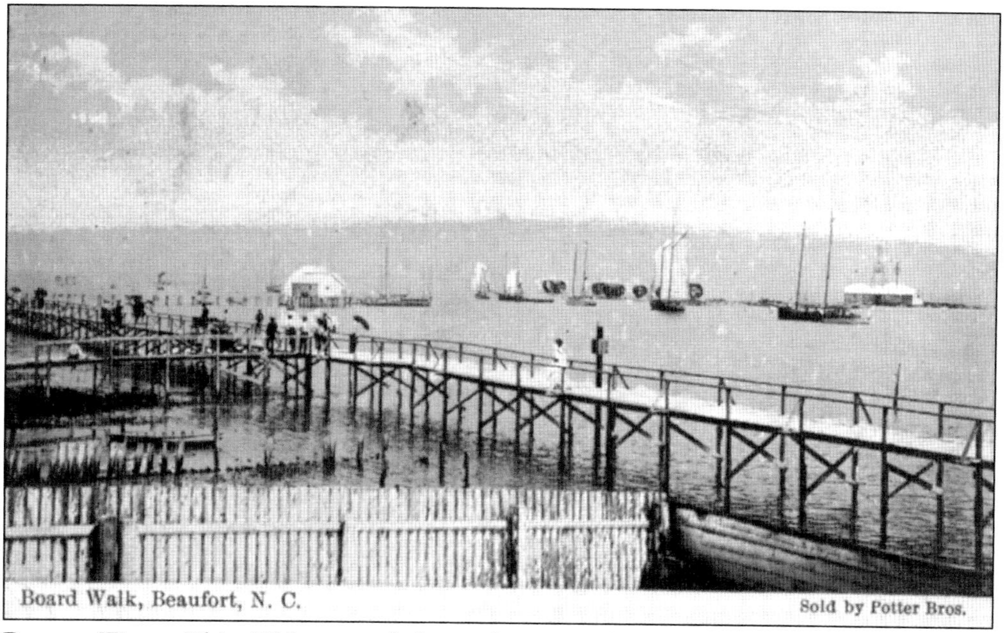

BOARD WALK. This 1906 postcard shows the original boardwalk, which extended from Craven Street to Gordon Street. The box on the pole marked the dividing line of Old Town and New Town. It replaced the original marker, Capt. Otway Burns's cannon, in 1901. The *Alphonso* (right), a cargo vessel and one-time trawler, was moved ashore and became the Whaling Museum in 1961. The boardwalk was demolished in 1913.

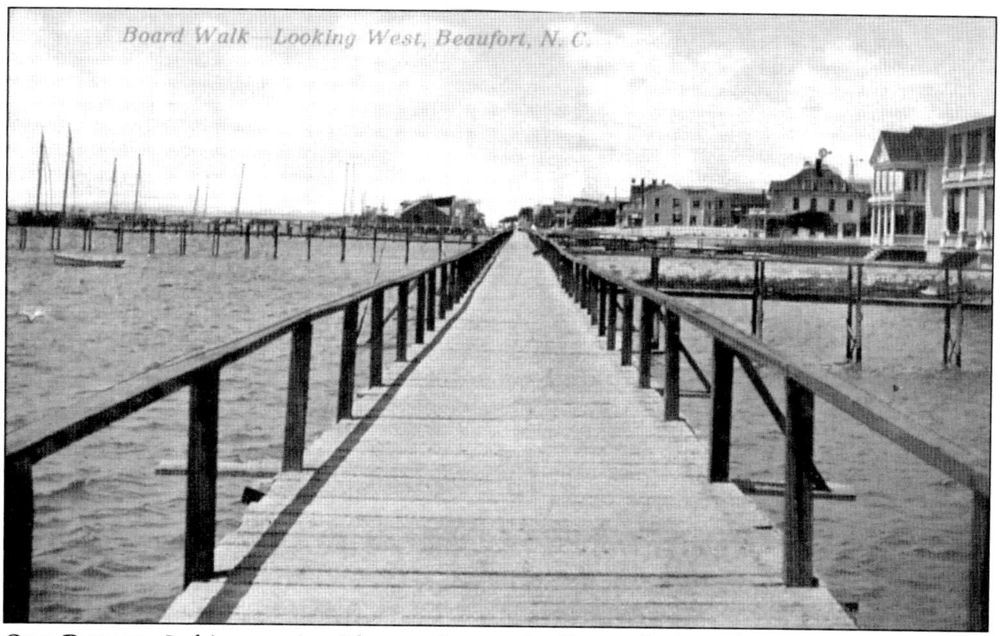

OLD BRIDGE. In his memoirs, Thomas Carrow fondly recalls the "old bridge" as "a thing of beauty with the moon full, a still southwest breeze, and the boys and girls singing and laughing as if all life was to be happy." His sister, Lutie, lived with her husband, C. D. Jones, in the house on the far right. Following to the left are the Bell House, Dr. C. L. Duncan's residence, and the Inlet Inn.

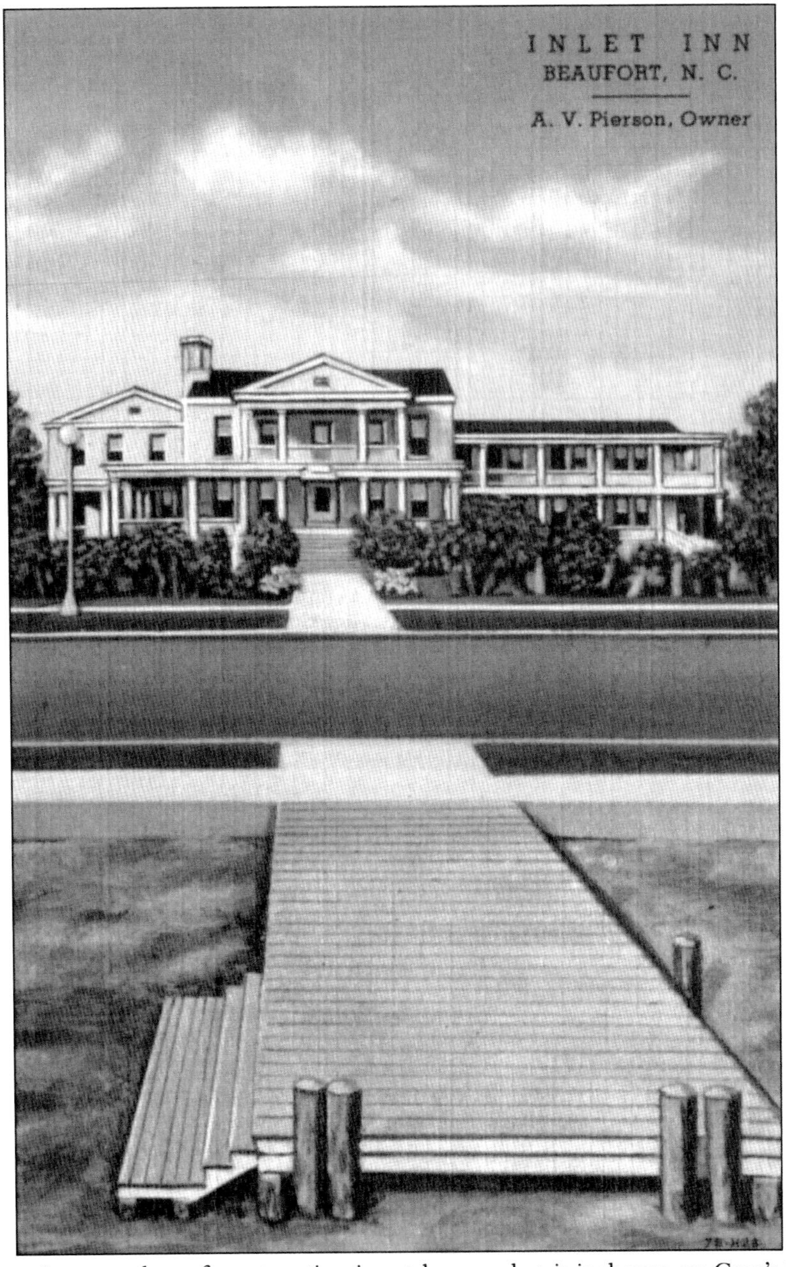

INLET INN. Its exact date of construction is not known, but it is shown on Gray's New Map of 1877 as the Lowenberg House and may have been built as early as the 1700s. It became the Morris boarding house in the early 1900s before being sold to Congressman Charles Abernathy in 1911 and renamed the Inlet Inn. It had a ballroom on the second floor where dances and social events were held. In the 1920s, the hotel offered dance lessons to teenagers conducted by an instructor from New Bern. Traveling showboats were brought in to put on shows for the hotel guests. The Original Floating Theatre (originally the James Adams Floating Theatre) docked at the Inlet Inn in 1940. It was that showboat, built in Washington, North Carolina, that inspired the book *Showboat* by Edna Ferber, later adapted into the Kerns and Hammerstein musical. The building was torn down in 1967 to make room for Branch Bank and Trust.

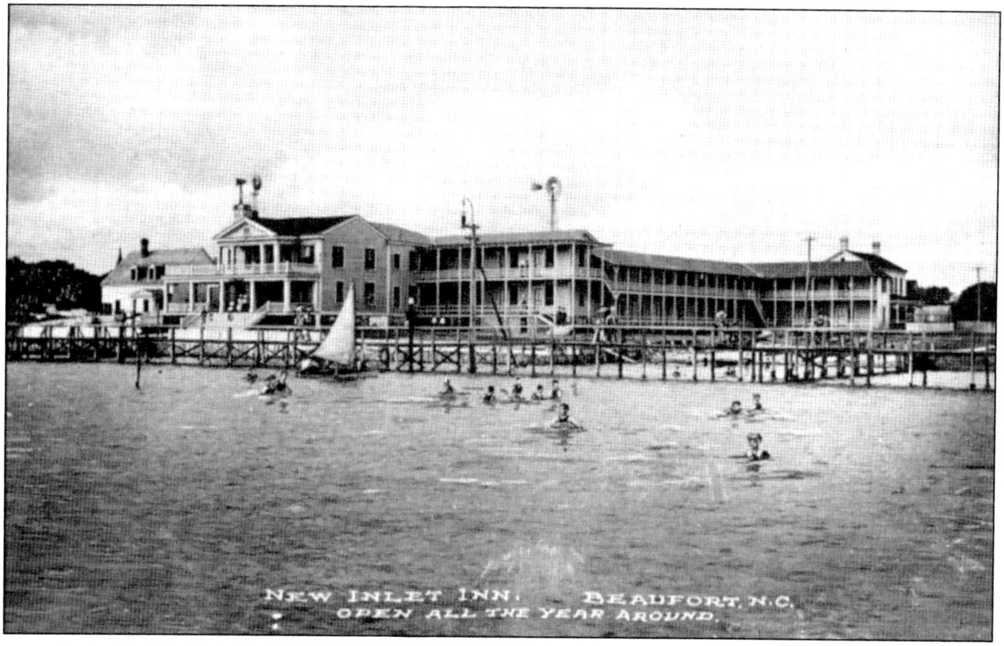

THE INLET INN. The large two-story inn was located on Front Street. Its porches were popular for the breeze from the ocean and the magnificent view of the channel. In its day, it was noted as having one of the best bathing beaches and prettiest water scenes on the Atlantic Coast. A T-shaped dock with a large covered cabana and benches was built over the water for use by hotel patrons. It was not unusual to see children diving from the top of the cabana 15 feet to the water below. Boats were not allowed to tie up to the dock as it was reserved as a swimming area. Swimming was not the only use for the dock, however, for what couple could resist the romance of a moonlit stroll on the dock above Taylor's Creek?

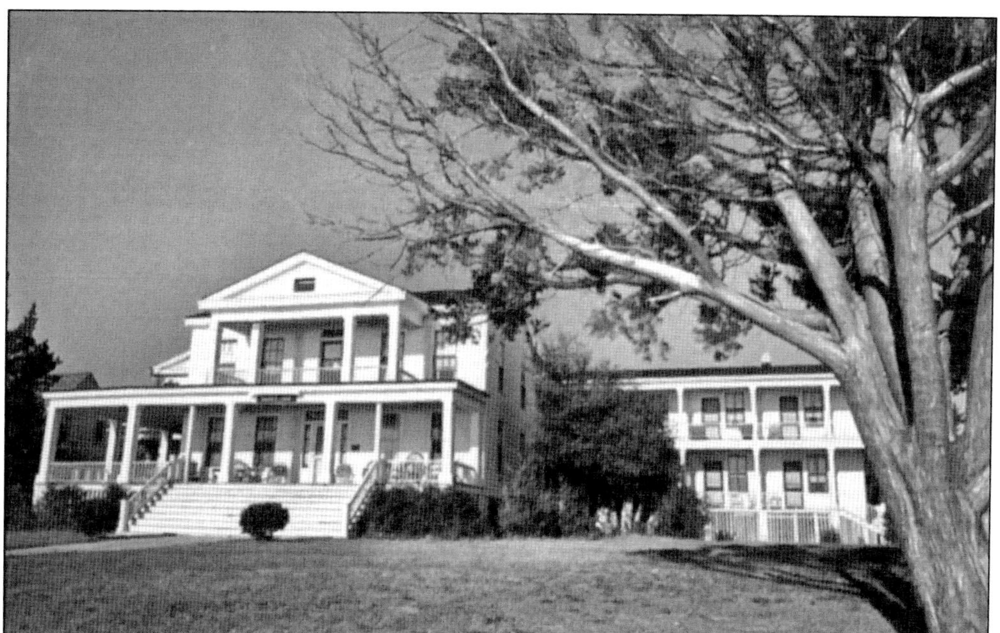

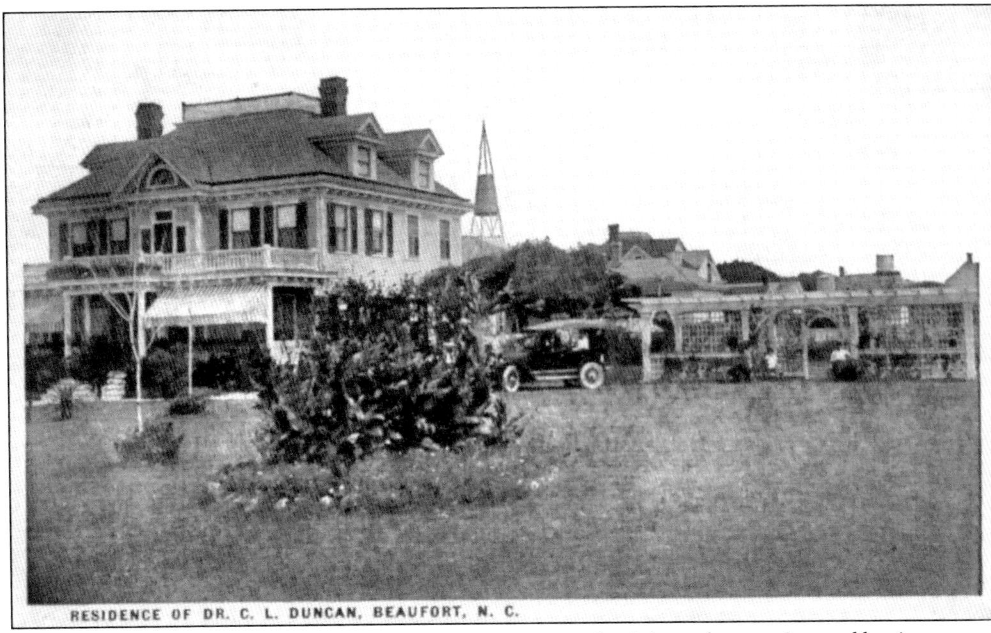

DR. CHARLES L. DUNCAN HOUSE. Dr. Duncan was a physician, pharmacist, and businessman. His dredge, the *Never Rest*, was used in 1927 to build the Beaufort–Morehead City causeway. On Craven Street, Duncan operated a diamondback terrapin hatchery, shipping terrapins to fancy Northern restaurants for turtle soup. In 1937, his house was moved by a windlass and a single donkey to make room for the new post office.

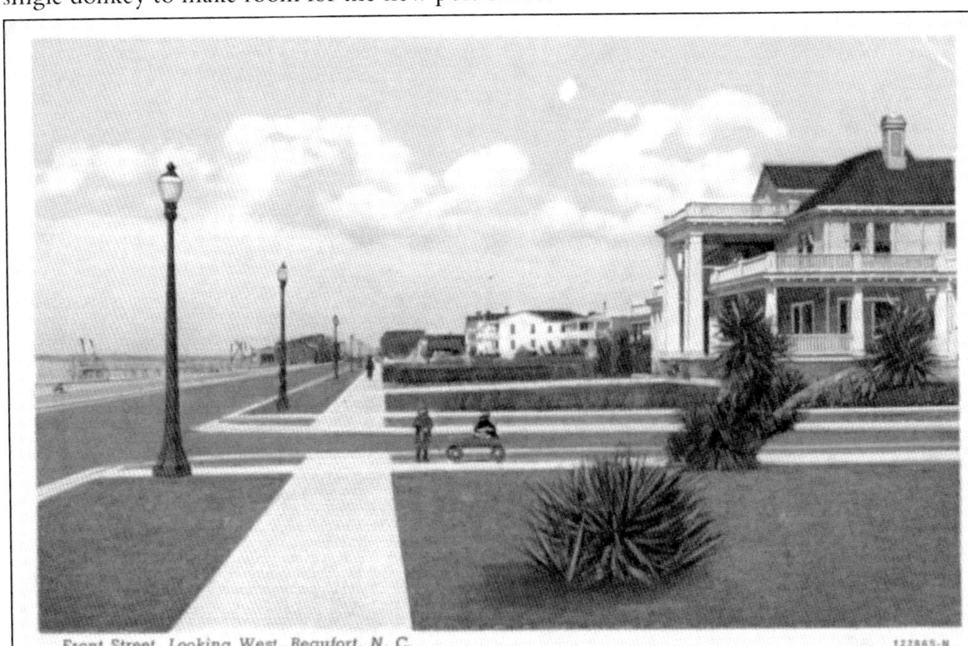

CLAUDE WHEATLY HOUSE. This 1930s postcard depicts Front Street from Marsh Street looking west toward downtown. Front Street had been paved and extended by this time, and the sidewalks and streetlights are prominently displayed in this view. The *c.* 1918 Claude Wheatly House with its columned front facade is reminiscent of the South's early antebellum homes.

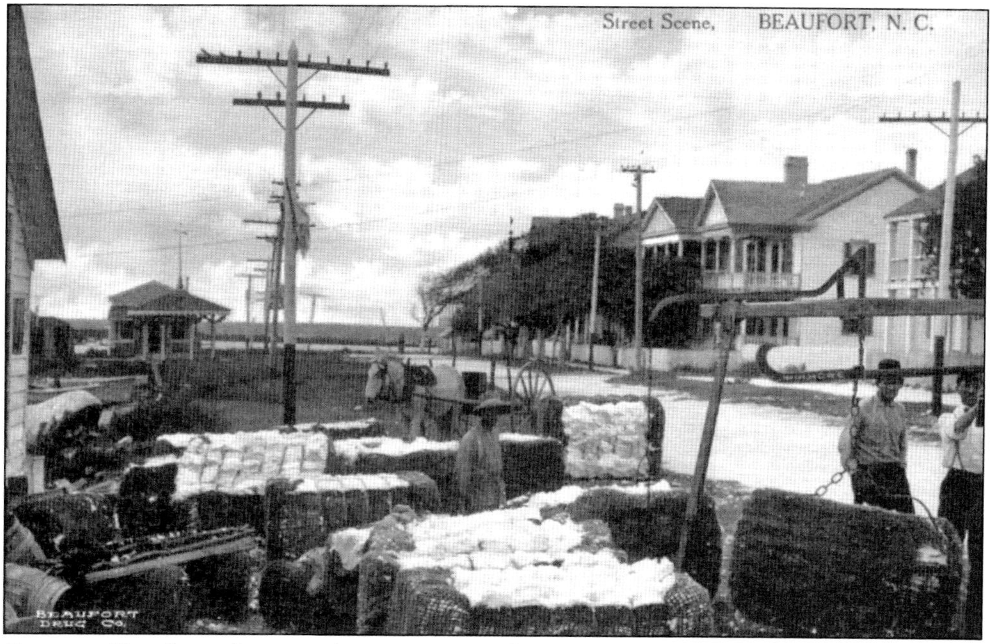

COTTON GIN. Several cotton gins were operated around Beaufort in the early 1900s. In 1912, Beaufort was credited as one of the best cotton markets in the state. Dave Sanders owned the cotton gin on Front Street. It sat over the water and used a Fairbanks Morse engine. Cotton coming in by cart or boat was processed and shipped by boat to Northern markets. (Courtesy of Mickey Weeks.)

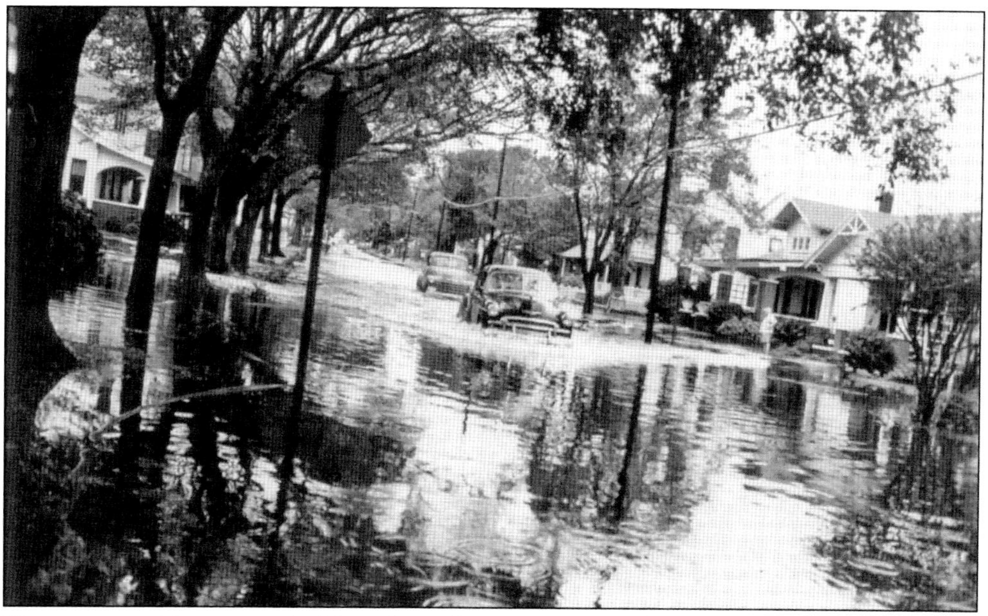

HURRICANES. This postcard of Ann Street demonstrates Beaufort's vulnerability to hurricanes. The 1933 storm was unexpected and killed several people in Merrimon and South River. Boats were thrown over the West Beaufort Bridge, and the school was so badly damaged that classes were moved to the Odd Fellows Lodge. Hurricane Hazel did extensive damage in 1954. Water on Front Street topped parking meters and flooded stores. (Courtesy of Mickey Weeks.)

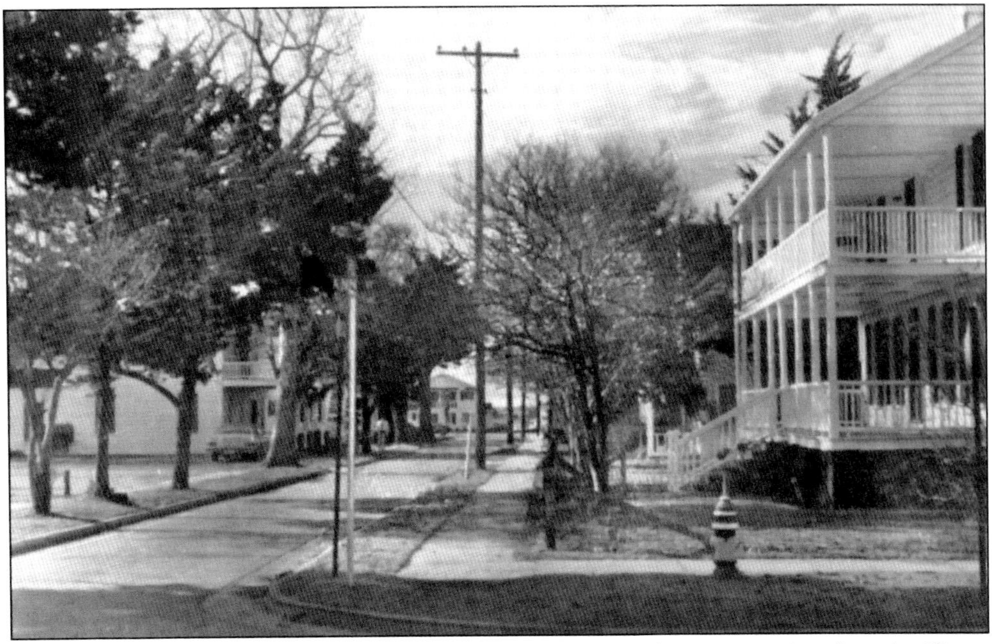

CRAVEN STREET. Pictured on the right is the 1764 Langdon House. Another significant building on Craven Street was the Potter Building, which burned in 1958. In 1927, Dr. Clarence Maxwell opened Potter's Emergency Hospital on its second floor. The 14-bed hospital, Beaufort's first and only, served the community well for 17 years. It also provided free services for the Coast Guard and other branches of the military.

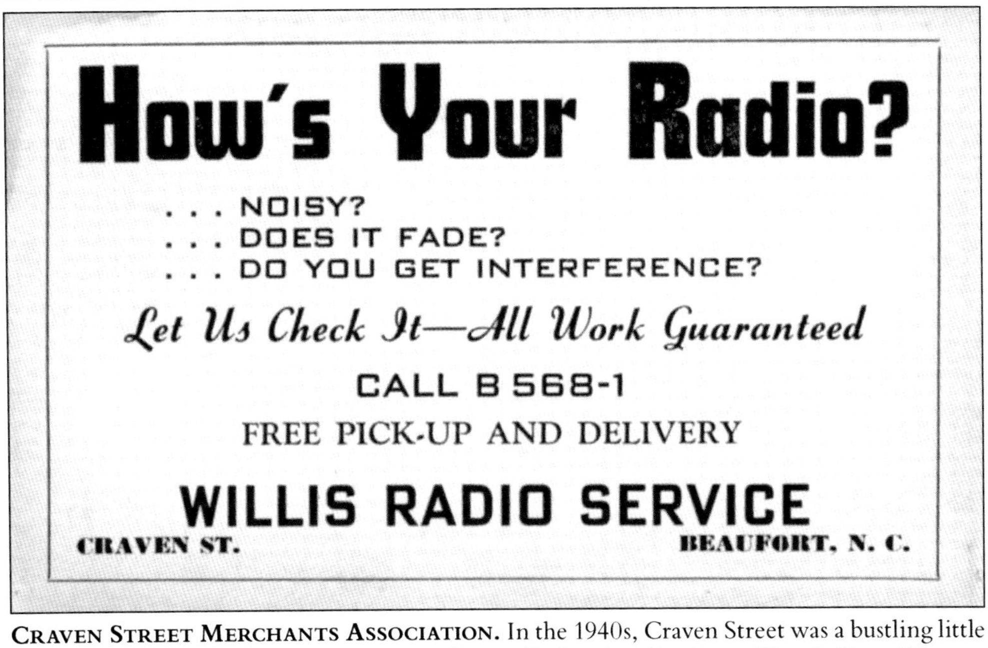

CRAVEN STREET MERCHANTS ASSOCIATION. In the 1940s, Craven Street was a bustling little business district with such businesses as Willis Radio Service, Ben Jones Bicycle Shop, Western Union, Jarvis Herring Jewelry, Beaufort News, and Bill Willis's clothing store. When selling newspaper advertisements, Ruth Peeling laughingly called them the Craven Street Merchants. The owners laughed, too, and the informal association was born.

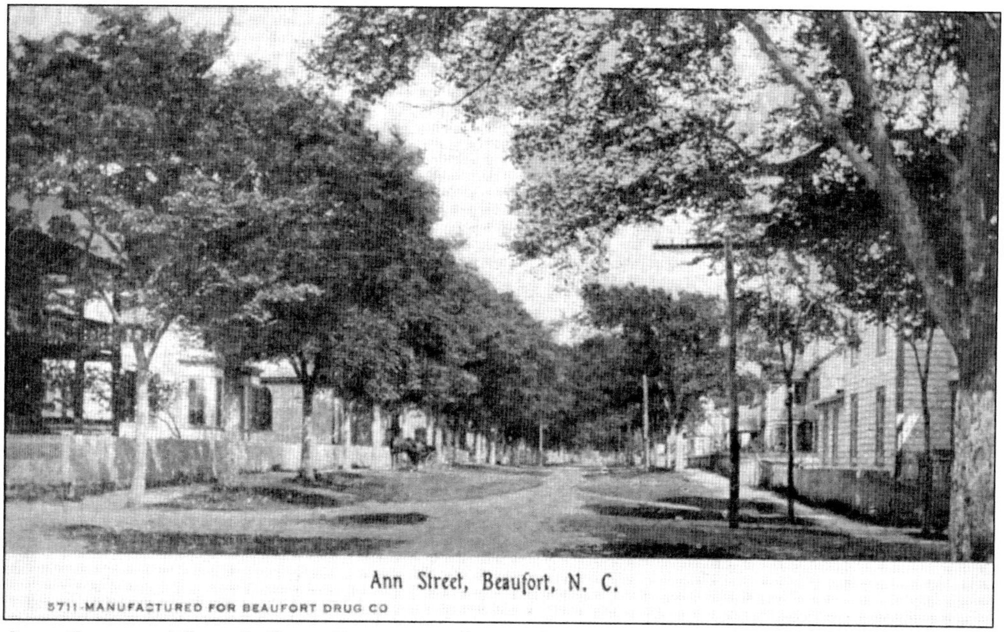

ANN STREET. Though Front Street was always the main street, after the bridge was built, Ann Street became very busy and the main link to the western part of the county. It began as a muddy path covered by logs and branches to aid traction. Later oyster shells from the oyster cannery at the west end of the street were used to build up and "pave" the road.

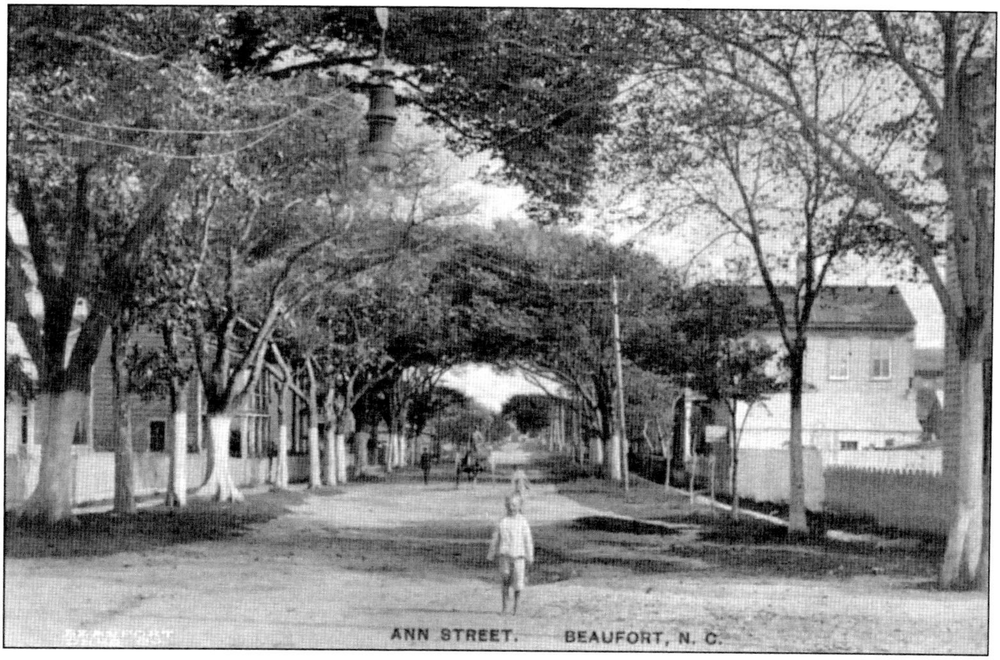

ANN STREET TREES. Lined on both sides with beautiful elm trees that form an arch overhead, Ann Street has always been one of Beaufort's most picturesque avenues. Named for Queen Anne in 1713, it is believed that the queen herself gave the elm trees to Beaufort in appreciation for having her name attached to the New World. It later became fashionable to whitewash tree trunks up to six feet high.

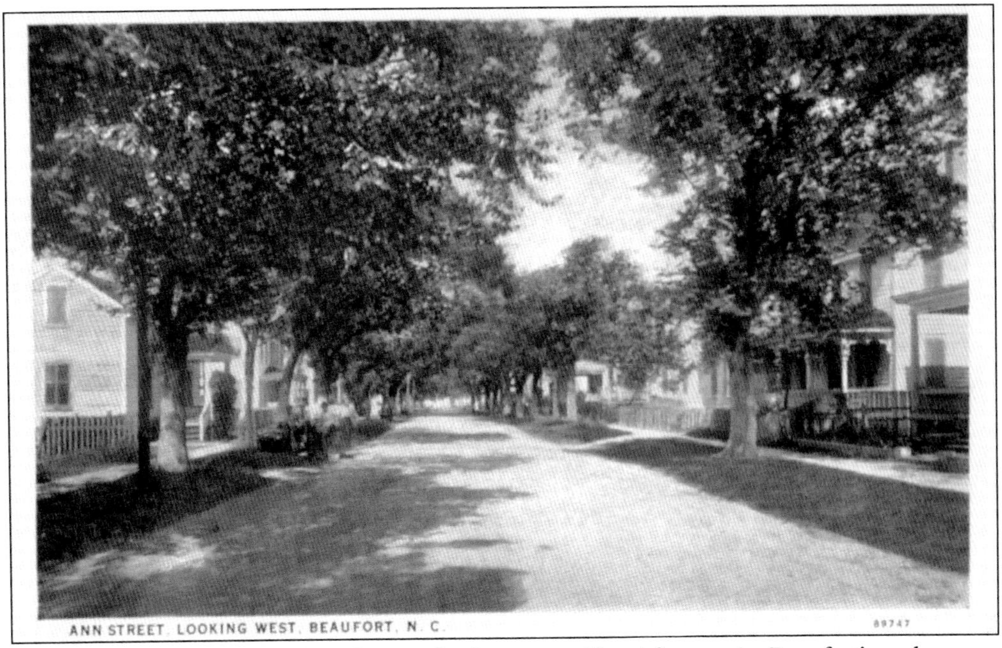

Architectural Style. Ann Street, the longest residential street in Beaufort's early years, contains a wealth of historic homes and architectural styles. Beaufort has the largest number of coastal cottages of any historic town in North Carolina. The style is characterized by an engaged porch and presence of small rear rooms located under the main roof. These often single but sometimes two-story homes display Caribbean influence. Porches, running the width of a house and used to capture the coastal breezes, add credence to the Caribbean influence since this is not generally a feature found on homes in Virginia. Examples of coastal cottages on Ann Street include the Jesse Piver House, built *c.* 1786 and the Wade House, built in 1785. Another noticeable style, Greek Revival, is seen in the trio of Leecraft homes built on west Ann Street in the 1850s.

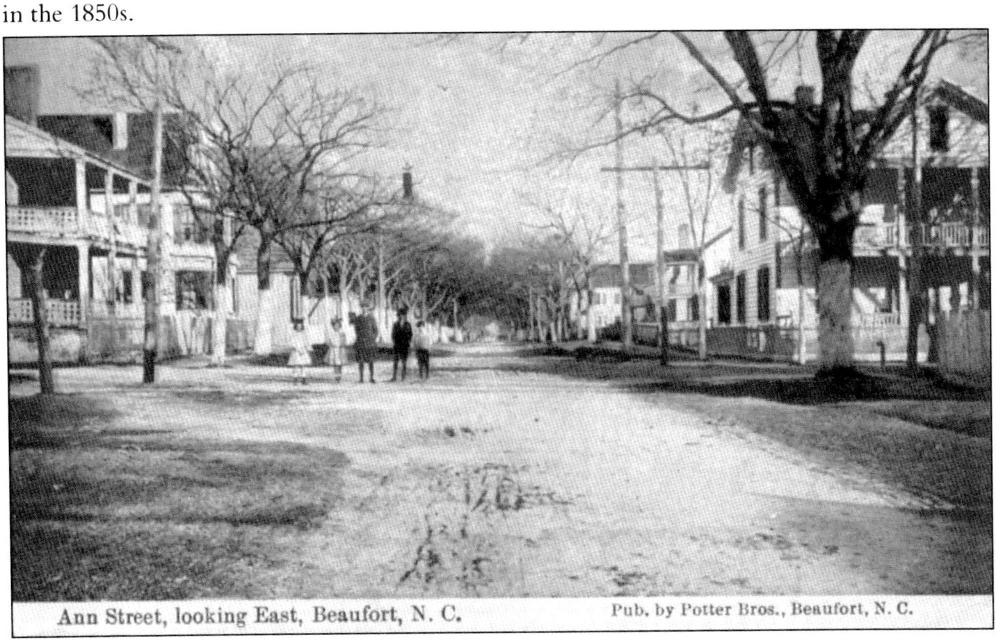

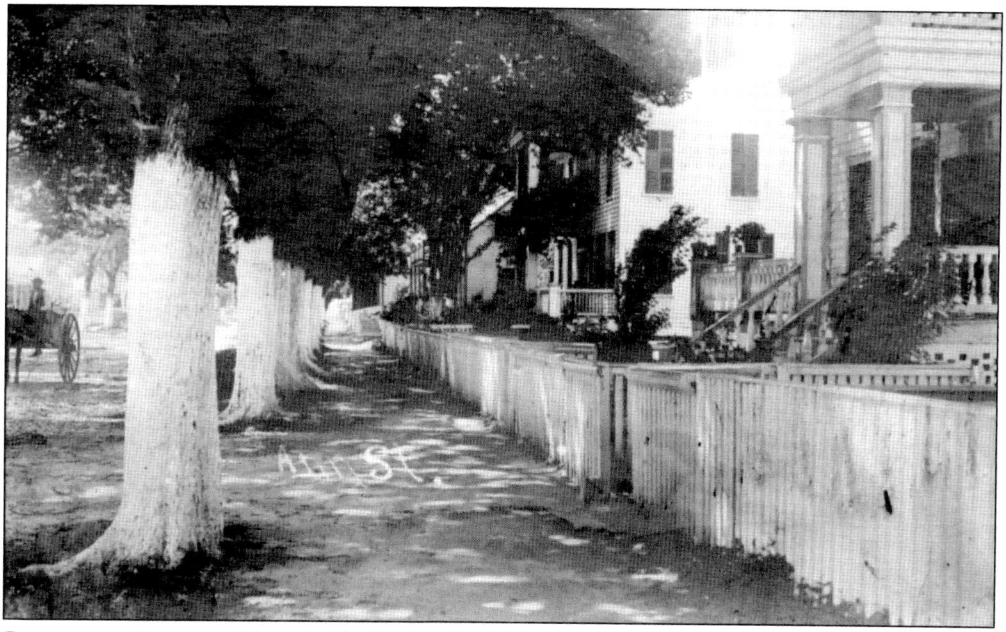

BEAUFORT FENCES. Many early homes were surrounded by wooden fences like the ones shown. This measure was taken to protect yards and gardens from domesticated animals that freely roamed the town streets. One visitor noted on this 1910 postcard that Beaufort residents "still hold on to the old fashioned idea of fences but happily they are getting modern and taking them away." (Courtesy of Mickey Weeks.)

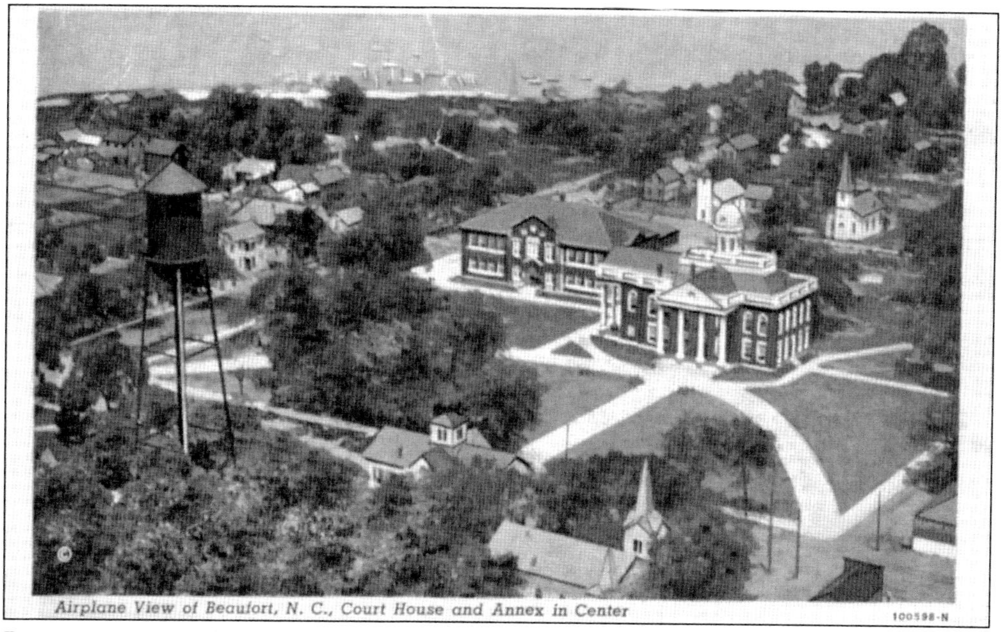

PURVIS CHAPEL. The oldest church (at the bottom) in Beaufort was built in 1820. It was named after Rev. James Purvis, who, in 1834, held a stirring revival in Beaufort. The bell, donated by Bishop Francis Asbury, was cast in Scotland in 1797. Originally the Methodist church, the building was given to the African American community in 1854. In 1863, missionary James Walker Hood enrolled it into the African Methodist Episcopal Zion denomination.

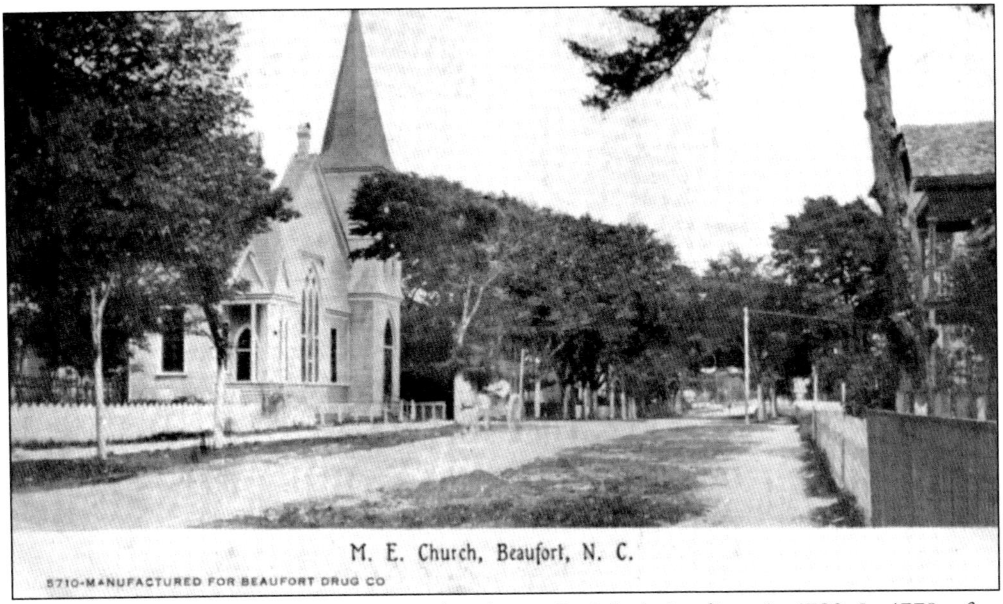

METHODIST CHURCH. Beaufort's first church was St. John's Anglican in 1723. In 1778, after the Church of England was dissolved and St. John's died out, the Methodists claimed the building. That building was also used by the court system. Bishop Francis Asbury visited twice in 1785. His initial impression was that Beaufort had little religion. Twenty-one years later, he would write, "The whole town seems to bow to the Scepter of the Lord."

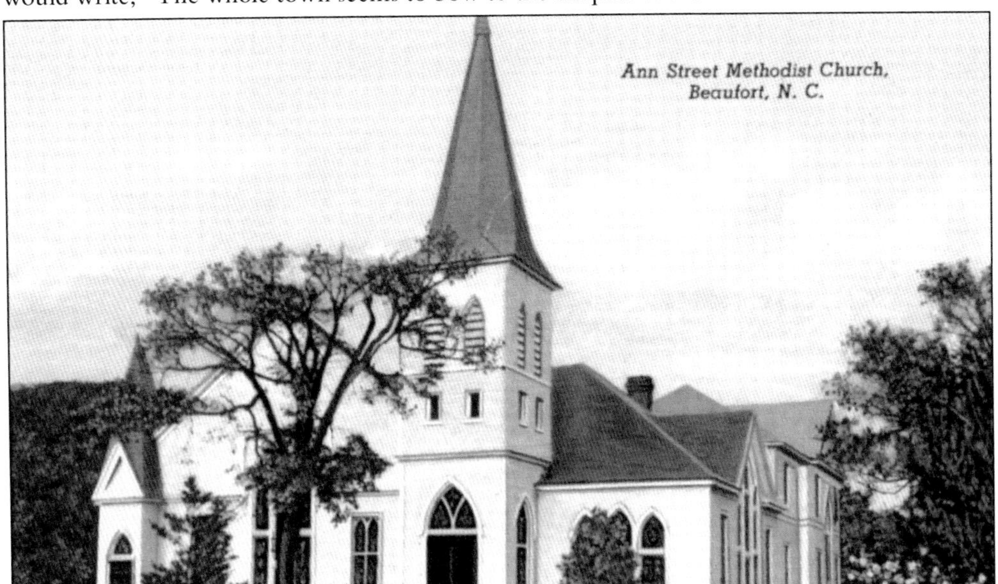

ANN STREET METHODIST. Ann Street Methodist Church was built at its present location in 1854. The Queen Anne–style building's large steeple became a landmark for sailors, according to U.S. Coast Survey Maps. When news came that Hatteras had fallen to the Union in 1862, Rev. R. G. Barrett fled town. Some felt that his departure left the church unprotected and led to its use as a Union barracks and hospital.

FIRST BAPTIST CHURCH. The Baptist congregation organized in 1851 and met in the courthouse and Odd Fellows Hall. They began construction of the original wooden church building in 1853 and moved in prior to its completion in 1854. Union soldiers commandeered the building during the Civil War, sending church members to seek other accommodations. (Courtesy of Gail Barnes.)

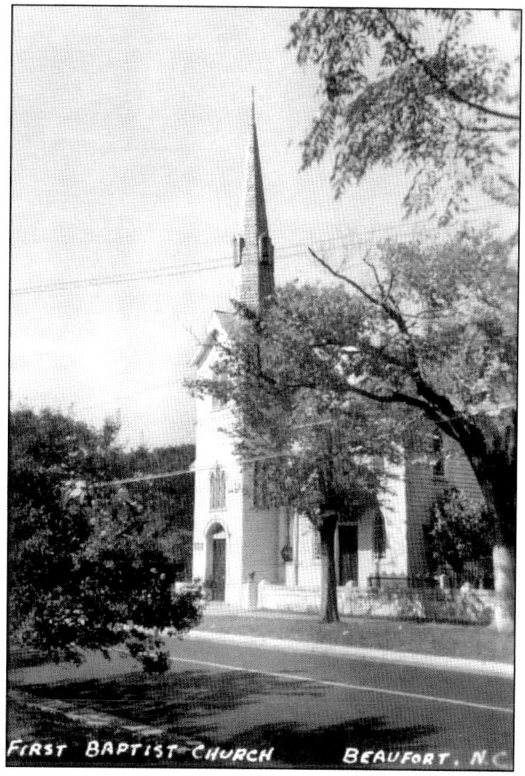

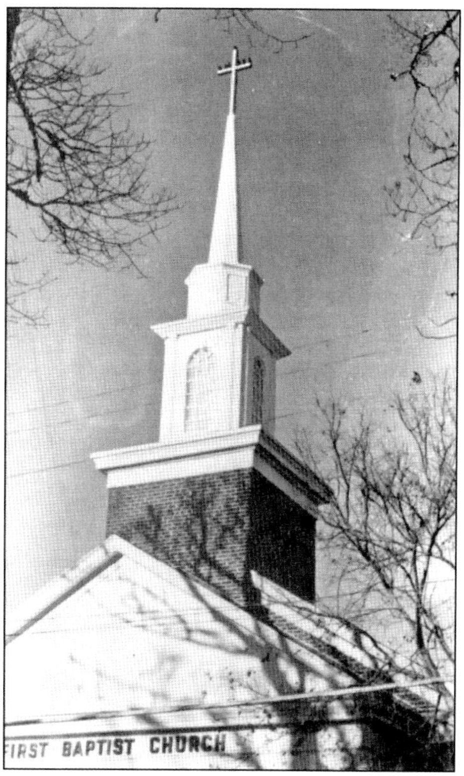

FIRST BAPTIST CHURCH. The church has undergone several expansion and beautification projects. The first began in 1887 under Rev. Duncan McLeod. Sunday school rooms were added in 1914. The 1943 expansion produced an auditorium and educational building. The largest expansion occurred in 1953 when the current brick sanctuary was built. The original building was torn down in 1960 to make room for a new educational building. (Courtesy of Mickey Weeks.)

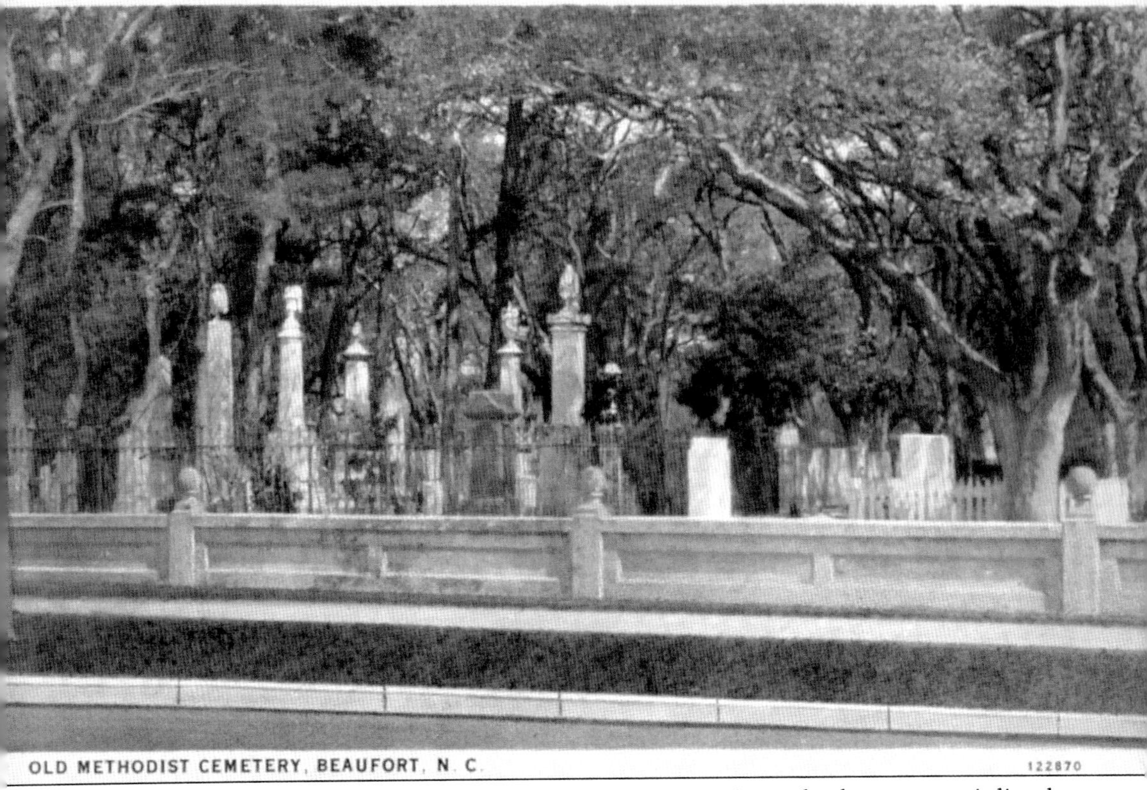

OLD METHODIST CEMETERY. Known as the Old Burying Grounds, the cemetery is listed on the National Register of Historic Places. The land was given in 1731 by the town, although burials had taken place for years before. It is situated between three churches: Purvis Chapel, Ann Street United Methodist Church, and the First Baptist Church. The earliest graves were not marked with stones. It is probable that many of those graves contained victims of the Tuscarora Indian War of 1711–1714. The headstones of the marked graves hold many interesting stories of past lives. One concerns Charlie Soong, a young Chinese runaway who served aboard the revenue cutter *Colfax*, stationed in Morehead City. He was taken in by the Chadwick family, who now rest in this cemetery. Charlie became the first international student at Trinity College, now Duke University. His daughter Soong Ch'ing-ling married Sun Yat-Sen, the "father of modern China," and his youngest daughter, Soong Mey-ling, became Madame Chiang Kai-shek.

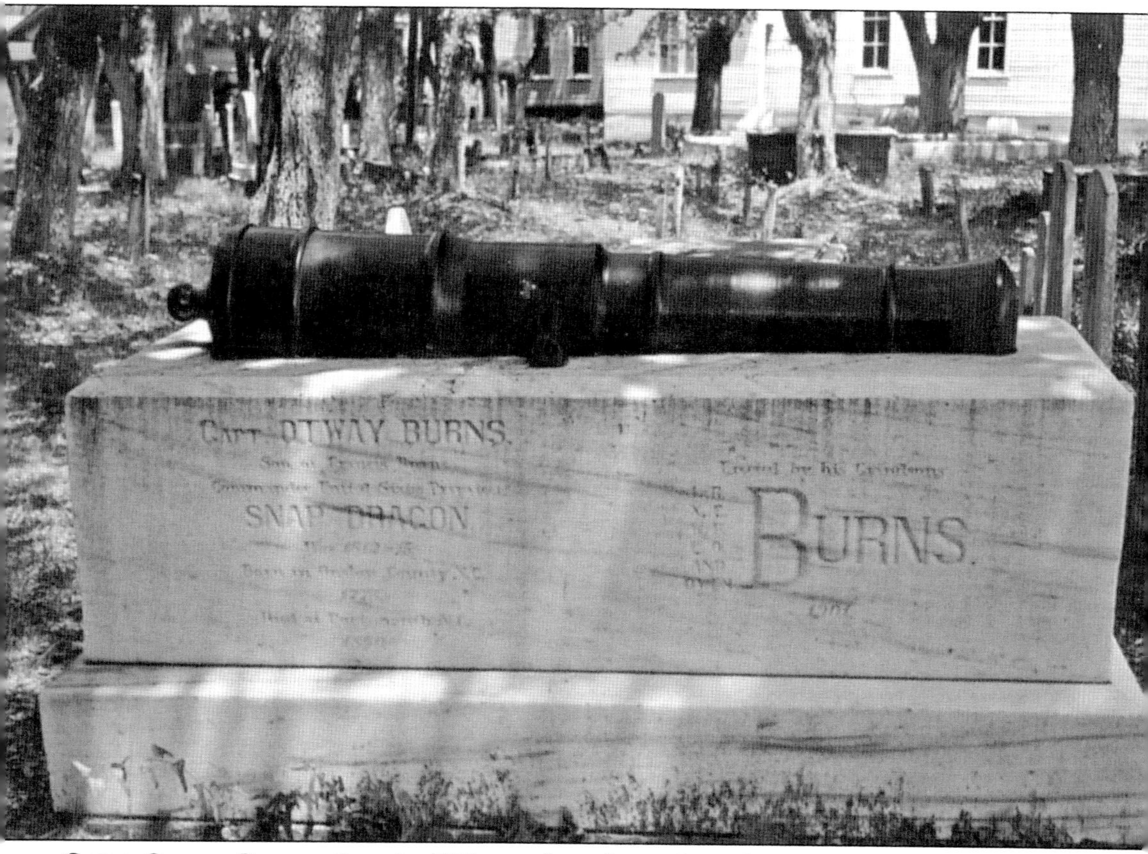

CAPT. OTWAY BURNS. Born in 1775 near Swansboro, Capt. Otway Burns became a naval hero during the War of 1812. He received Letters of Marque and Reprisal from the U.S. government and became a privateer aboard his schooner the *Snap Dragon*. The *Snap Dragon* captured 42 English vessels, 300 officers, and cargo worth $40 million. Burns was so successful that the British placed a £50,000 reward on his head. Burns, also a member of the North Carolina legislature, had two towns named for him, Burnsville in Yancey County and Otway in eastern Carteret County. On the corner of Front and Pollock Streets in Beaufort, one of the cannons from the *Snap Dragon* was stuck muzzle down in the ground, marking the dividing line between Old Town and New Town. In 1901, the cannon was moved to the Old Burying Grounds where it was attached to Burns's tomb.

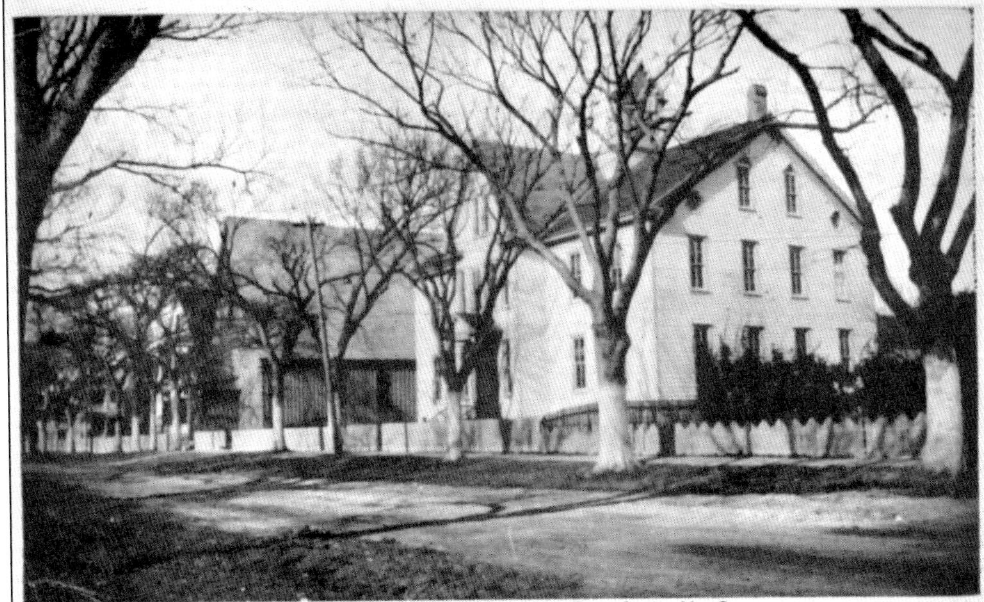

St. Paul's School, Beaufort, N. C.

ST. PAUL'S EPISCOPAL CHURCH. North Carolina was one of the last colonies to establish the Church of England as the "official" church. St. John's Parish was organized in Beaufort shortly after the town was settled, but the Revolutionary War led to the demise of the Anglican Church. In 1855, the new parish of St. Paul's Episcopal was organized by Rev. David D. Van Antwerp, a chaplain at Fort Macon. In 1857, a lot was purchased for $10 on which the church was built. Constructed by shipbuilders, it is recognized as one of 10 architecturally perfect buildings in North Carolina. The 1861 consecration by Bishop Thomas Atkinson was attended by Antwerp, a Union officer, and Rev. Alfred Augustin Watson, a Confederate officer.

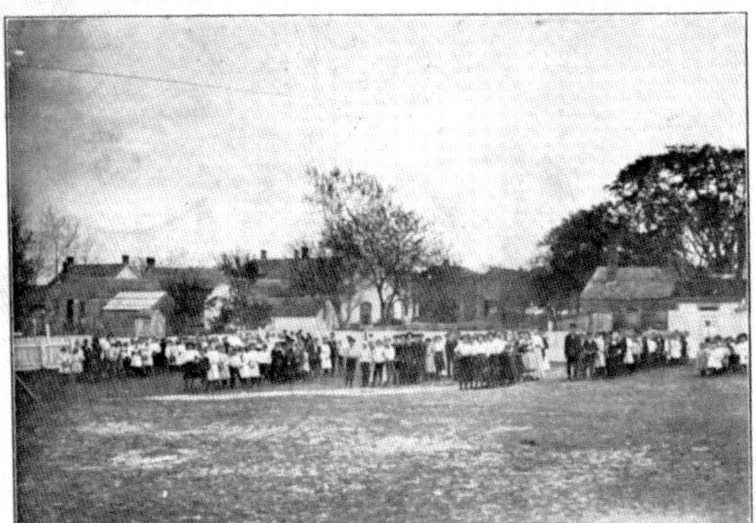

ST. PAUL'S SCHOOL ASSEMBLED ON THE GROUNDS. Beaufort, N. C.

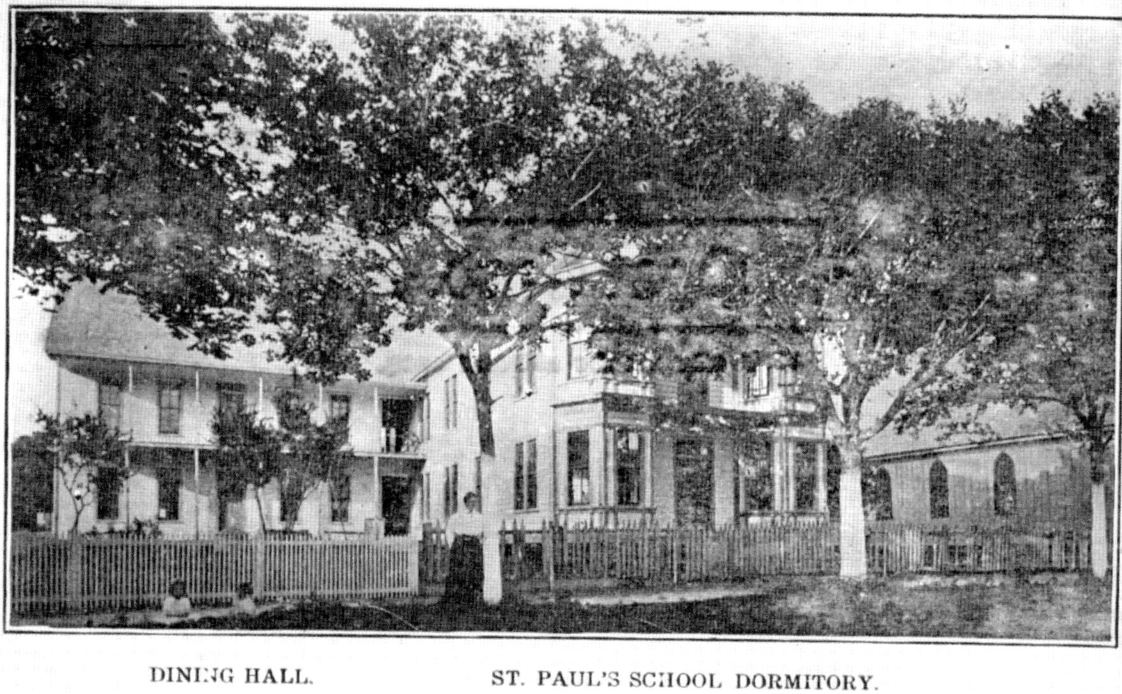

ST. PAUL'S SCHOOL. The first school was opened by Reverend Antwerp in 1858 under teachers Elizabeth Robinson and Sallie Pasteur, niece of Louis Pasteur. The school was short-lived and closed in 1867. Antwerp attributed the closure to the loss of students to the Civil War effort. He wrote, "The civil war has had a disastrous effect upon its prosperity." In 1899, a new school was established by Rev. Thomas P. Noe and Mrs. Nannie Geffory. A three-story classroom building was erected the following year, and in 1905, Watson Hall, containing a dormitory and dining hall, was built. The school's success is attributed to its headmistress, Mrs. Nannie Geffory, daughter of Sallie Pasteur. She has been described as a stern, Christian woman passionate about education. Mrs. Nannie served as superintendent, business manager, secretary, and treasurer. After her death in 1936, the school began to decline and ultimately closed two years later. The classroom building was torn down in 1951 and replaced with a new rectory, now the Parish Office. Watson Hall was razed in 1961. (Courtesy of Mickey Weeks.)

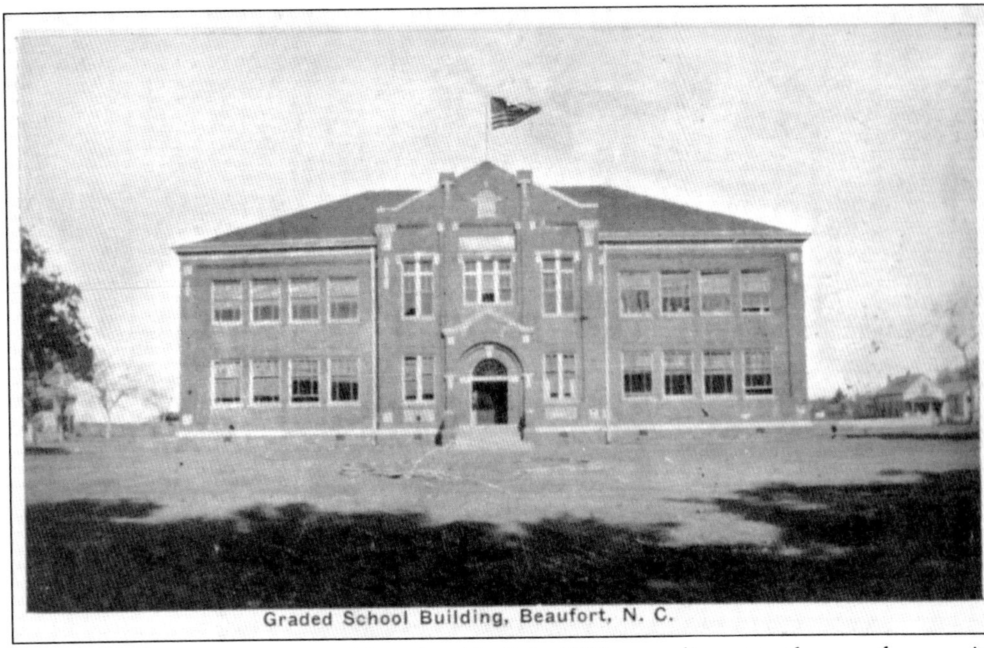

Graded School Building, Beaufort, N. C.

BEAUFORT GRADED SCHOOL. The school built in 1915 was adjacent to the courthouse with a sidewalk connecting the two buildings. A separate walk led north to bathrooms and a small playground. Between the walks was a bell tower. Each morning, David Willis, the truant officer, would pull the rope ringing the bell at 8:00 a.m. and again at 8:30 a.m. indicating tardiness. In 1925, schoolchildren were asked to bring a penny to contribute to the restoration of the USS *Constitution*, "Old Ironsides," the only surviving ship of the Revolutionary War. Each was given a pin-on button with a picture of the ship and the words "Save Old Ironsides." The next year, a new school was built on Mulberry Street, providing much-needed space for the growing school population. (Below, courtesy of Gail Barnes.)

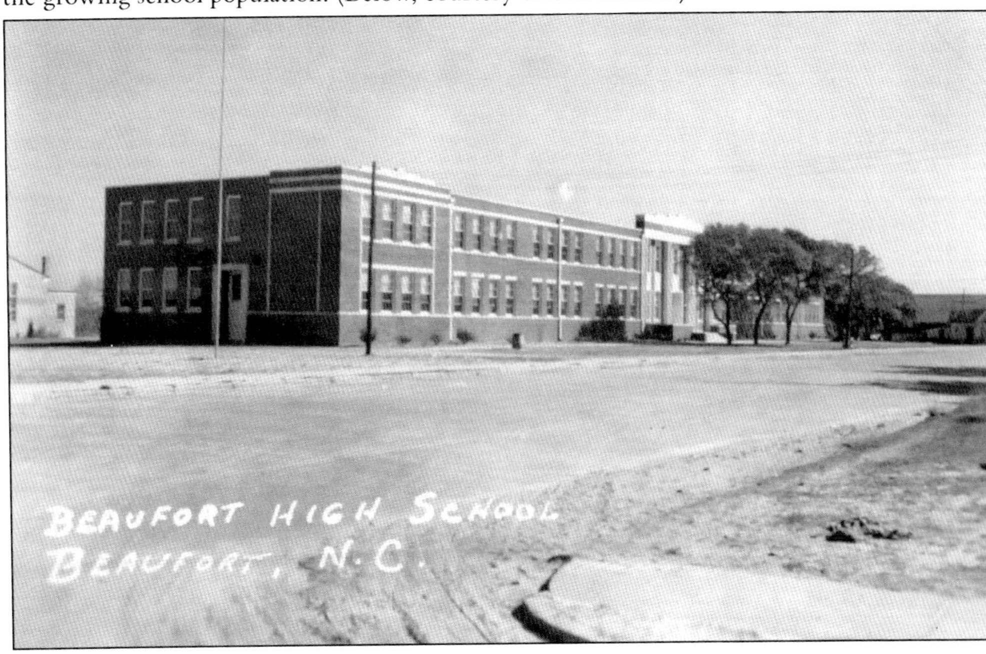

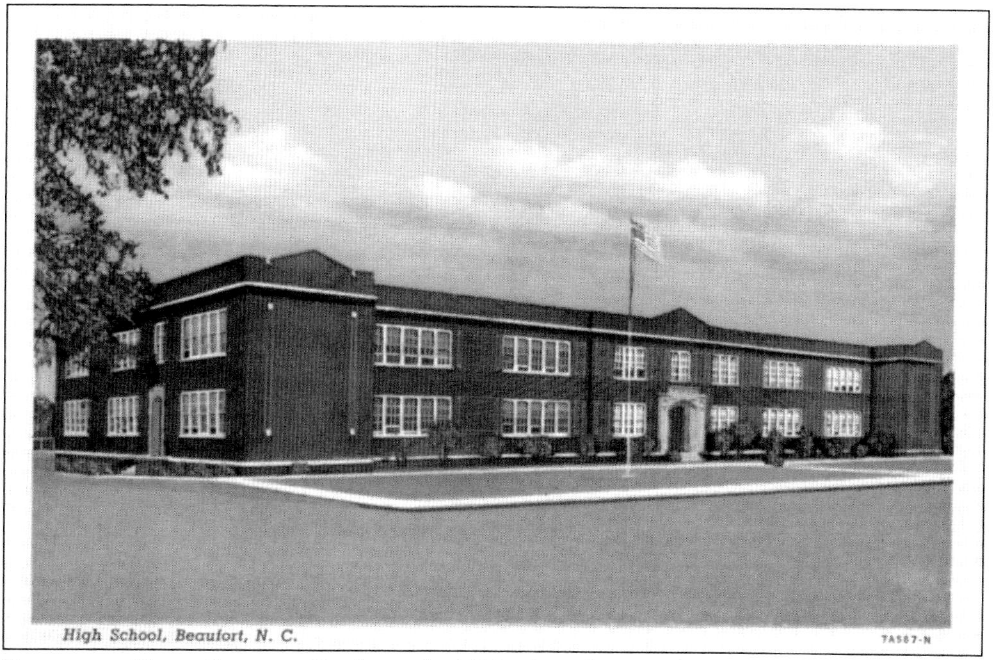

BEAUFORT HIGH SCHOOL. By the early 1920s, Beaufort Graded School was over capacity and holding classes throughout town. The problem was solved in 1926 with a new building on Mulberry Street. That school burned in 1945, again displacing students and teachers. They were reunited in 1947 with the opening of a new school on the same site. Though it was named Beaufort High School, it served grades 1 through 12.

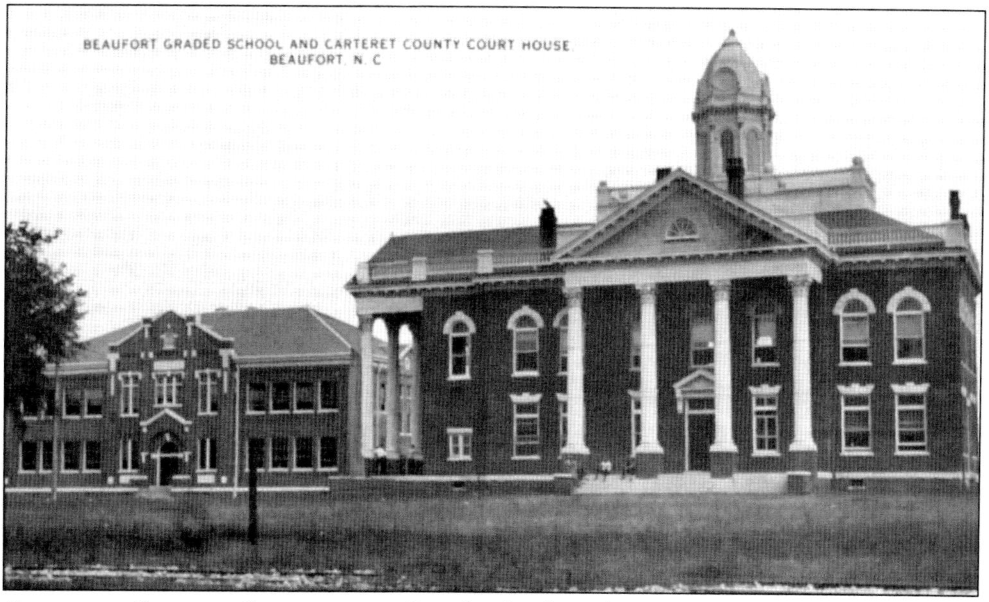

CARTERET COUNTY COURTHOUSE. Beaufort has been home to five courthouses, of which only two remain. The first burned and the second was lost to a hurricane. The third one, built in 1796, is the oldest existing wood-framed courthouse in the state. Originally located at the intersection of Ann and Turner Streets, that building was restored and relocated to the Beaufort Historic Site in 1977.

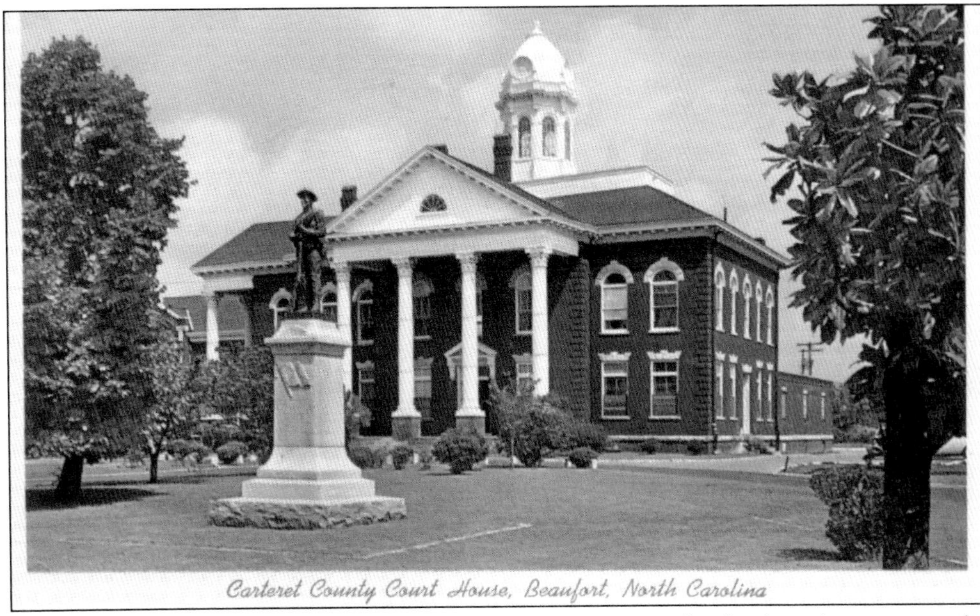

COURTHOUSE. The current courthouse was built in 1907. In the daytime, it was a popular place for children to play, while at night, the porches and live oak trees provided a romantic place for lovers. In those early days, the grounds were illuminated by globe lampposts. In 1921, the Daughters of the Confederacy erected a monument on the grounds honoring Confederate soldiers. (Courtesy of Mickey Weeks.)

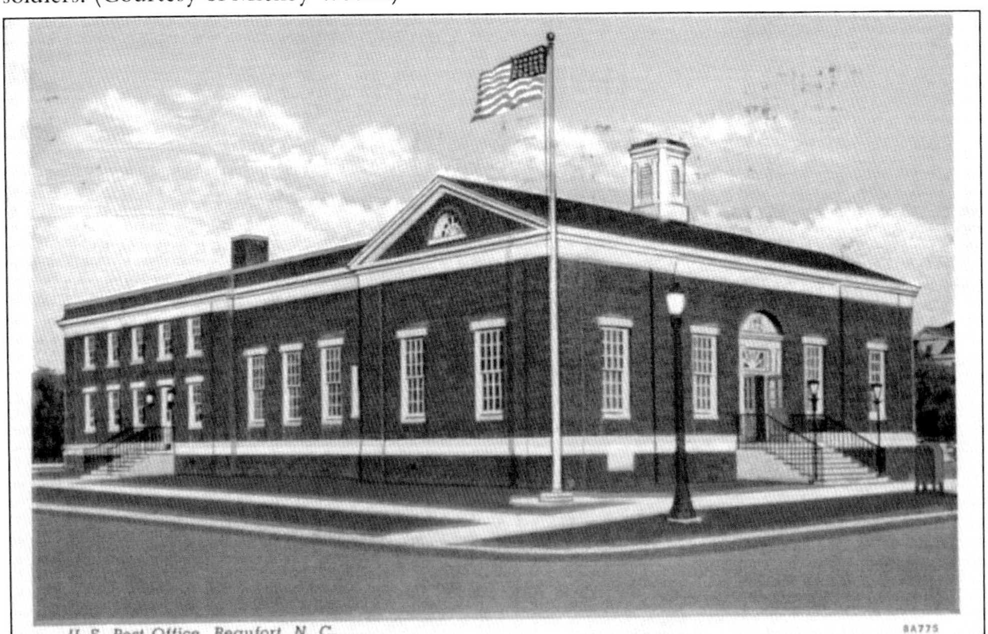

POST OFFICE. In 1937, a public works project moved Dr. Duncan's house to make room for a new post office. Simka Simkhovitch, a Russian artist, was commissioned in 1940 to paint murals for the post office walls. The murals, oil on canvas, were painted in his Connecticut studio. They depicted the *Crissie Wright*'s sinking, Cape Lookout Lighthouse, "sand ponies," and Canadian geese.

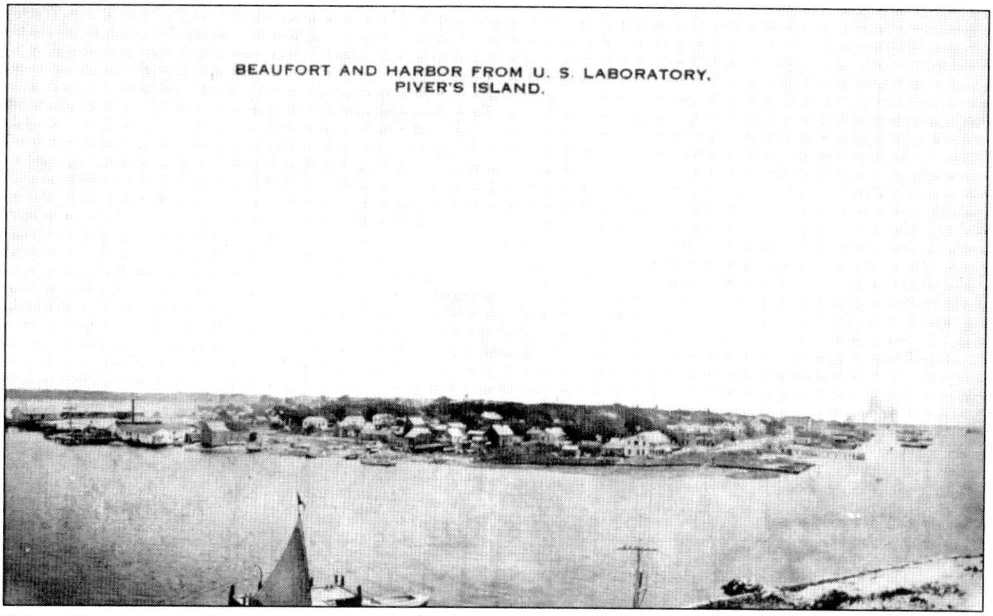

WEST BEAUFORT. Across Town Creek (back), the area of West Beaufort remained undeveloped until well after a bridge was built from Turner Street in the 1920s. Around that time, Beaufort Realty envisioned developing West Beaufort into a world-class resort and residential area anchored by a yacht club, hotel, and bathing beaches. According to their brochure, West Beaufort would rival Miami and Atlantic City. (Courtesy of Gail Barnes.)

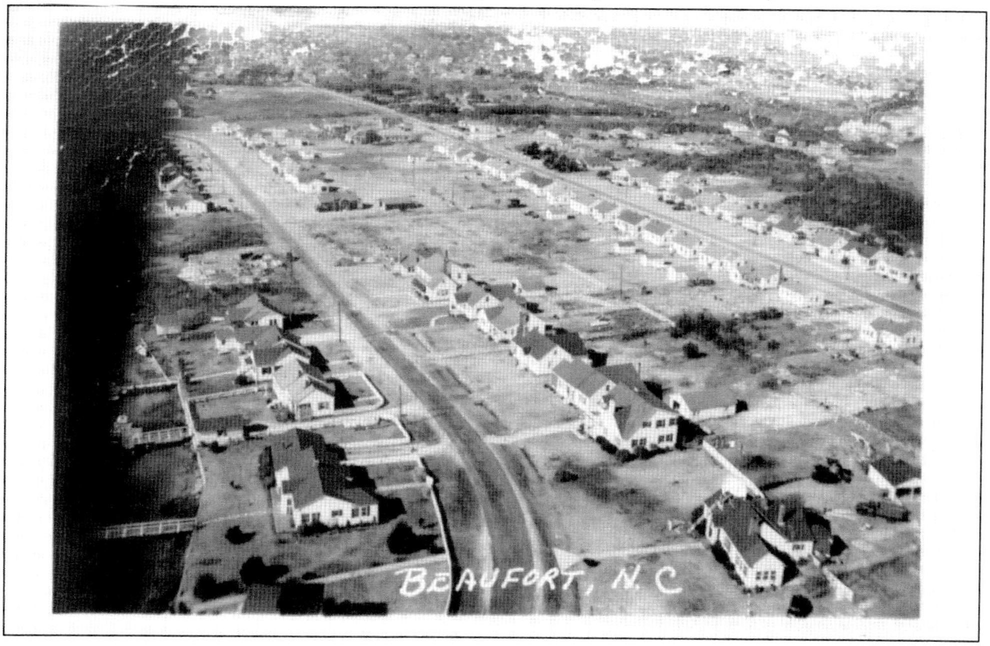

SANDWICH VILLAGE. A breakwater was constructed at the east end of Front Street in 1912, allowing for the extension of the street. In the late 1930s, Charlie Britton purchased much of the land on Front Street Extension and subdivided it into lots. To maximize the land, the lots were small. Because the resulting homes were so close together, the area became known as Sandwich Village. (Courtesy of Mickey Weeks.)

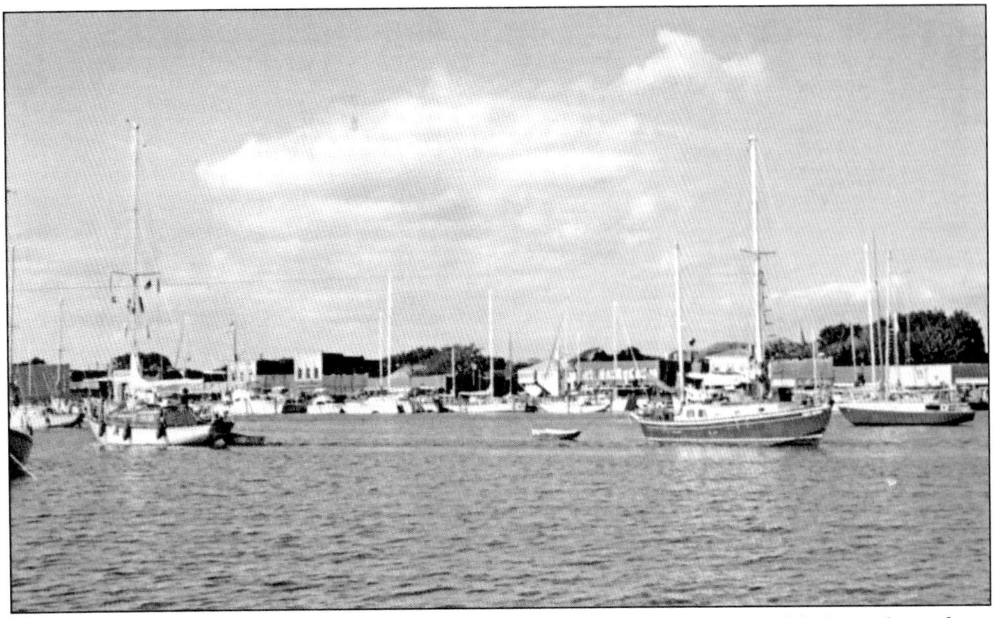

Pirate Invasions. For pirates, North Carolina's barrier islands were ideal hiding places from which to prey on shipping. Beaufort's harbor was also attractive to buccaneers like Blackbeard, who was welcomed at the Hammock House. His ship, *Queen Anne's Revenge*, was recently discovered in Beaufort Inlet. Twice in 1747, Spanish pirates invaded Beaufort. In both cases, the pirates held the town for a couple of days before being driven off.

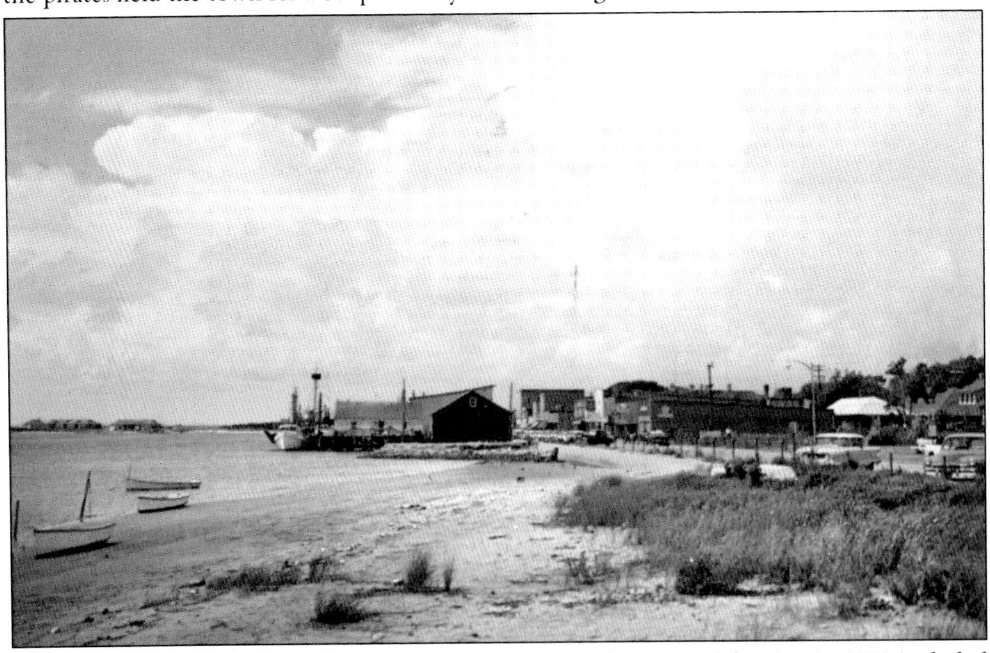

Pirate Invasion Reenactment. Beaufort's 251st anniversary celebration in 1960 included reenacting the 1700s pirate invasion. Firemen assumed the role of pirates while merchants served as town defenders. The "pirates" attacked a fort on Carrot Island then rowed across Taylor's Creek for the "invasion." The staged landing took place on the beach shown here. A battle ensued near the Inlet Inn, concluding with the pirates being carted off to jail.

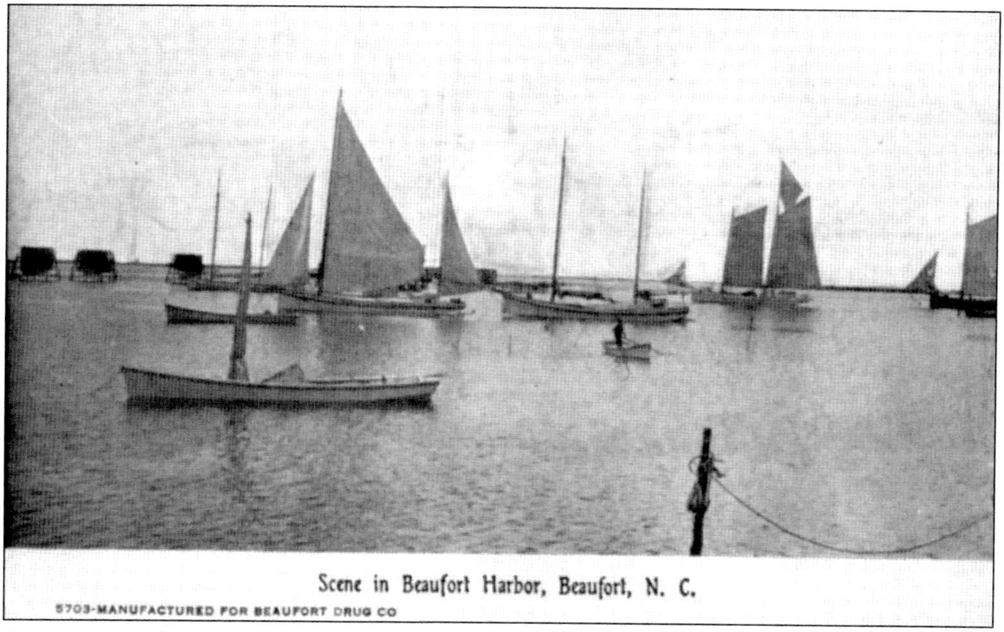

SHARPIES. Before the railroad reached Beaufort, sailboats were used to connect with the train in Morehead City. Highly dependent on the tide and wind, the trip could take anywhere between 15 minutes and 2 hours. Some of the original sharpies introduced in the 1890s were Capt. Ben Pigott's *Viola*, Capt. Frank Ellison's *S. M. Buckman*, Capt. Obit Gaskil's *Emily*, and *Ruth*, captained by Ben Franklin.

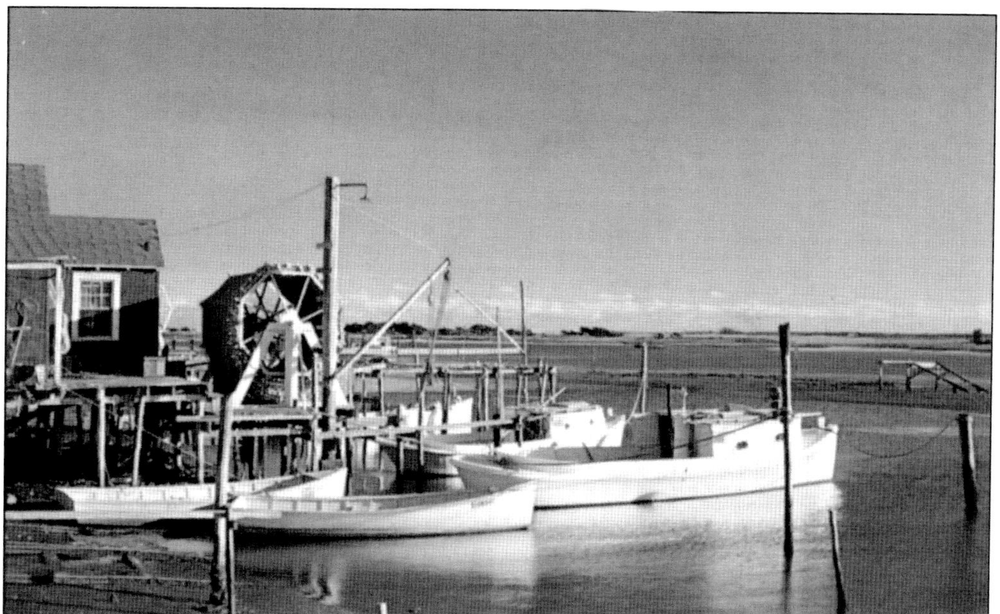

ALONG THE WATERFRONT. Boats have always been important to life in Beaufort. In the 1890s, Captain Hall operated a boat line to New Bern. His sharpie was scheduled for one trip per week—a day to go, a day to unload, and a day to return. The two-masted ship *Charles* brought merchandise from Baltimore, while a three-masted ship from Maine conveyed ice to local fish houses.

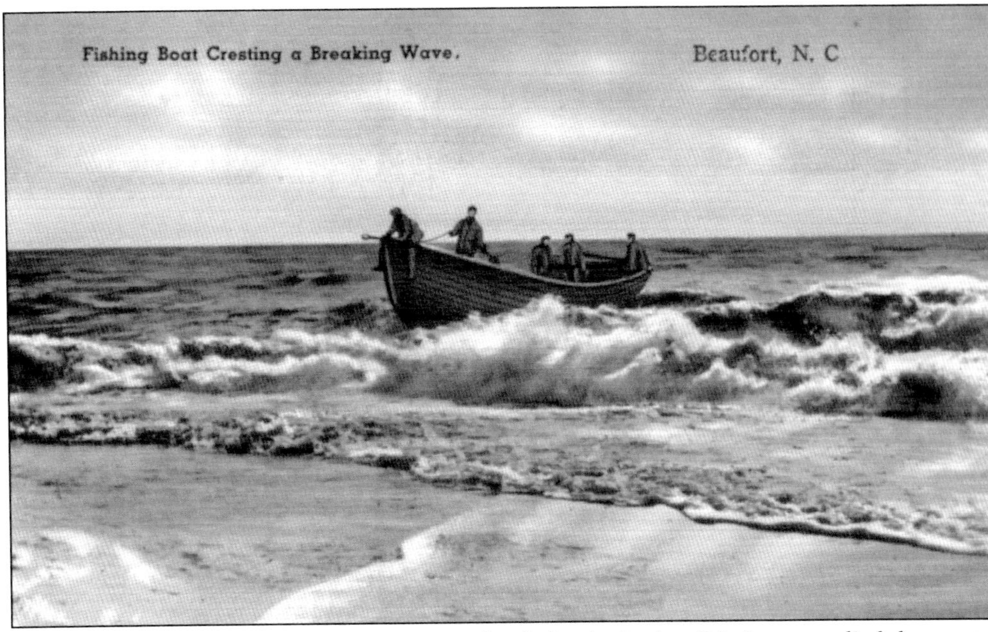

EARLY FISHING. Large fishing boats powered only by the backs of their crews plied the coastal waters. It must have been enchanting to hear the beautiful songs from the crewmen as they rowed their boats to the docks. On weekends and in bad weather, Front Street was filled with crews from not only Beaufort, but also Virginia and South Carolina.

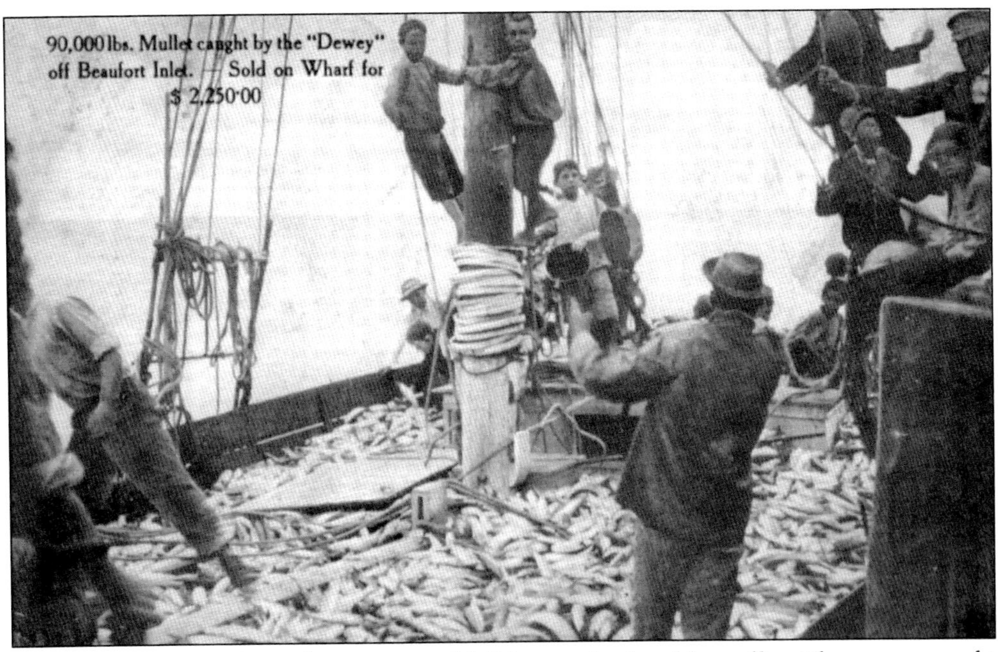

MULLET FISHING. The earliest commercial fish was the humble mullet. They were caught in seines, dragnets, and gill nets, then salted and shipped north. By the late 1800s, Carteret County's share of the mullet fishery exceeded the combined fisheries of all others on the Atlantic coast. In 1914, ninety thousand pounds of mullet caught by the *Dewey* sold on the wharf for $2,250. The average annual income at the time was $628.

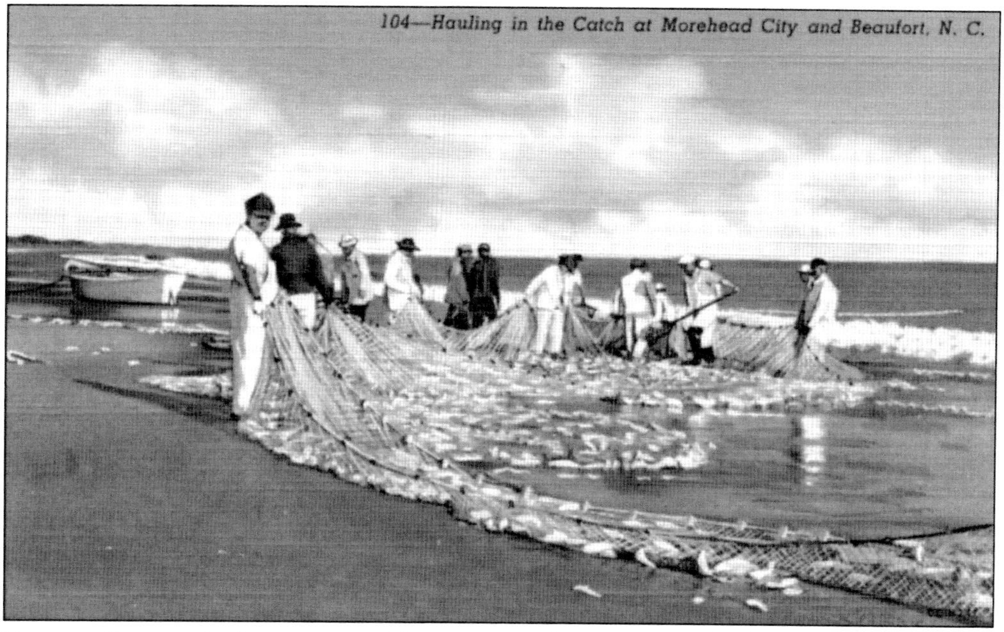

FISHING CAMPS. During summer, fisherman moved to camps on Shackleford Banks and lived in thatched huts near the fishery at Mullet Pond. From the beach, a lookout would spot for fish. Once they were discovered, a rowboat let out a seine. A group of fishermen on the bank would hold one end of the net while the boat encircled the school with the other end of the net. The catch was then hauled onto the beach.

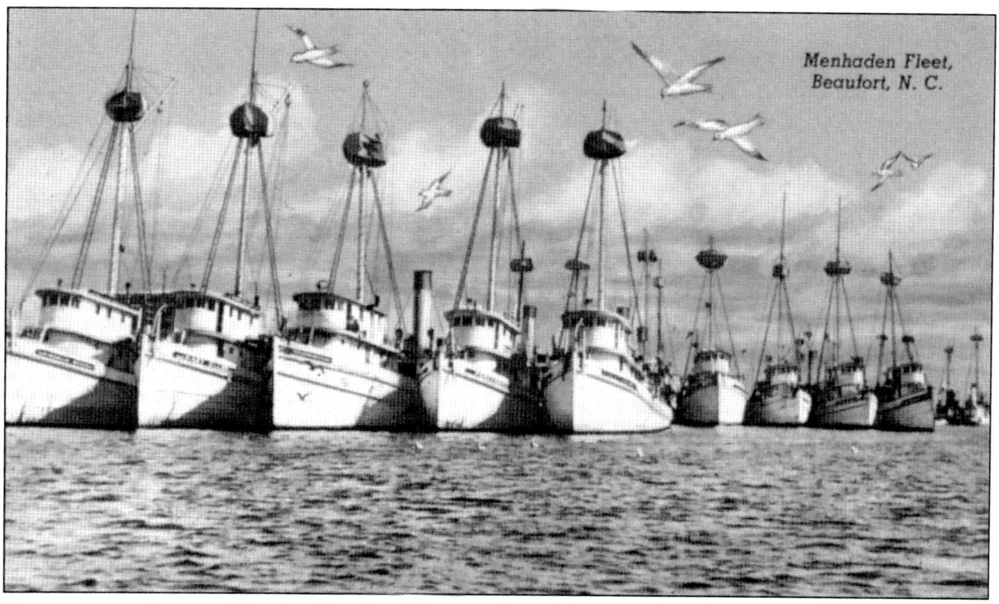

MENHADEN FLEET. Rhode Island soldiers stationed in Beaufort during the Civil War noted the abundance of oil-bearing fish in Carteret County waters. Some returned and launched the important fertilizer and fishmeal industry that thrived in Beaufort and surrounding communities. Processing factories were built on Harker's Island, in Portsmouth, and in Beaufort. The menhaden boats with their distinctive crow's nests brought in 30 million fish each year.

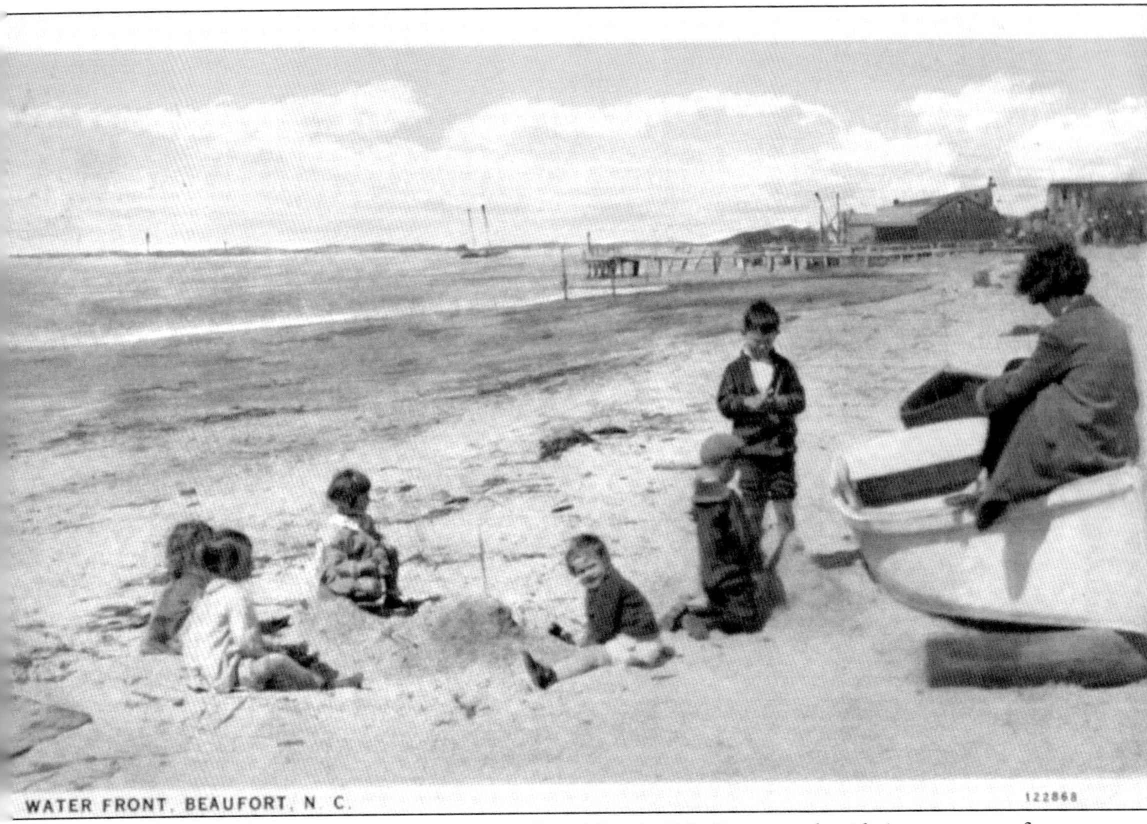

FISH HOUSES. Way's Fish House (pictured) and Davis Fish Company beside it were two of many businesses reflecting Beaufort's sea heritage. Trawlers and "by-boats" (boats that transferred fish from larger fishing boats) brought in catches to the fish houses. Like M. C. Holland's and J. H. Potter's before them, these fish houses sorted, iced, and packed mullets, croakers, trout, bluefish, spots, mackerel, oysters, scallops, and shrimp. The boxes or barrels were then shipped by train to markets in Richmond, Washington, Baltimore, and Fulton's Fish Market in New York City. Way Brothers was opened in 1913 and operated by Brady Way until his death in 1935. His son, William "Stoney" Way, took over management until it closed in the 1960s. Davis Fish Company was owned by Leslie Davis. Other fish houses were located on Gallant's Channel and Town Creek. Four small fish houses operated at the end of Pine Street or Back Landing. These one-room outfits owned by Denny Glover, Jack Parson, Benny Copeland, and Con Merrill catered to local patrons.

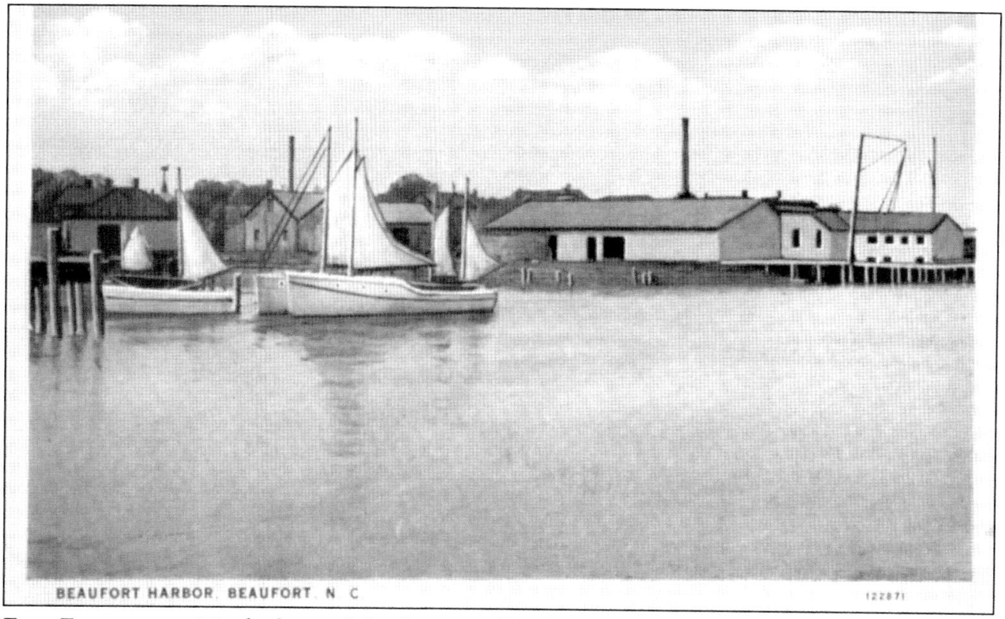

FISH FACTORIES. Menhaden or fatback are small, oily fish used in fertilizer, animal feeds, paint, linoleum, and cosmetics. Fish factories emerged in Beaufort in 1881 when C. P. Dey opened his at the end of Lennoxville Road on Taylor's Creek. Doan and Bartlett followed, building on the Newport River. Purchased in 1911 by William Blades, it was renamed Beaufort Fish Scrap and Oil Company. Other companies opened and many changed hands. Howard Smith acquired the Blades operation in 1931 and his son, Harvey, started the Fish Meal Company. Beaufort Fisheries was started in 1930 when Claude Wheatly Jr. and W. V. B. Potter acquired the assets of Taylor's Creek Fish Scrap and Oil Company. In their heyday, over 100 boats supported the factories. Due in part to foreign competition, none of the North Carolina menhaden factories remain in business.

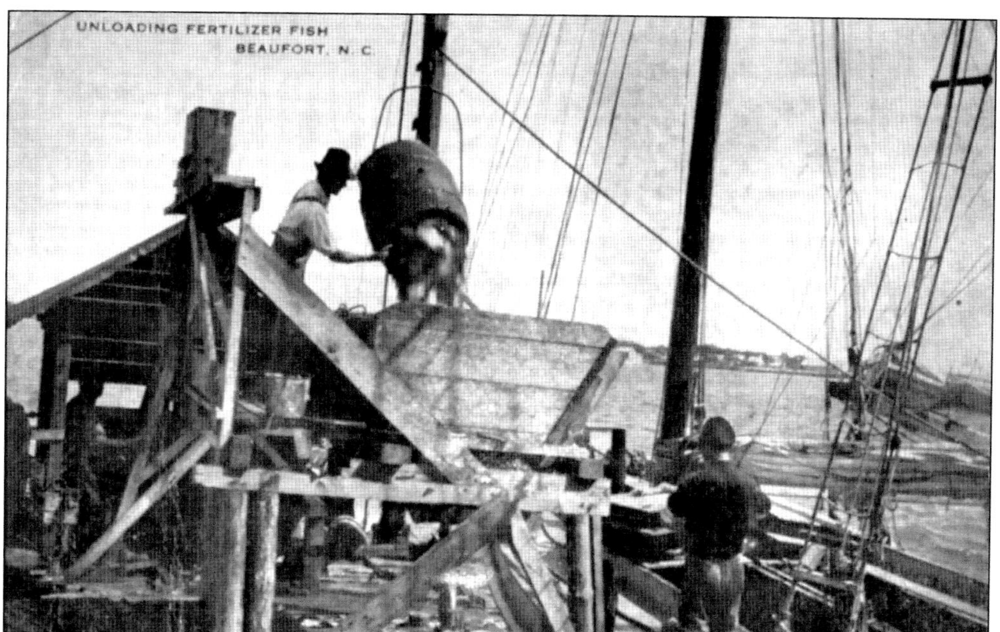

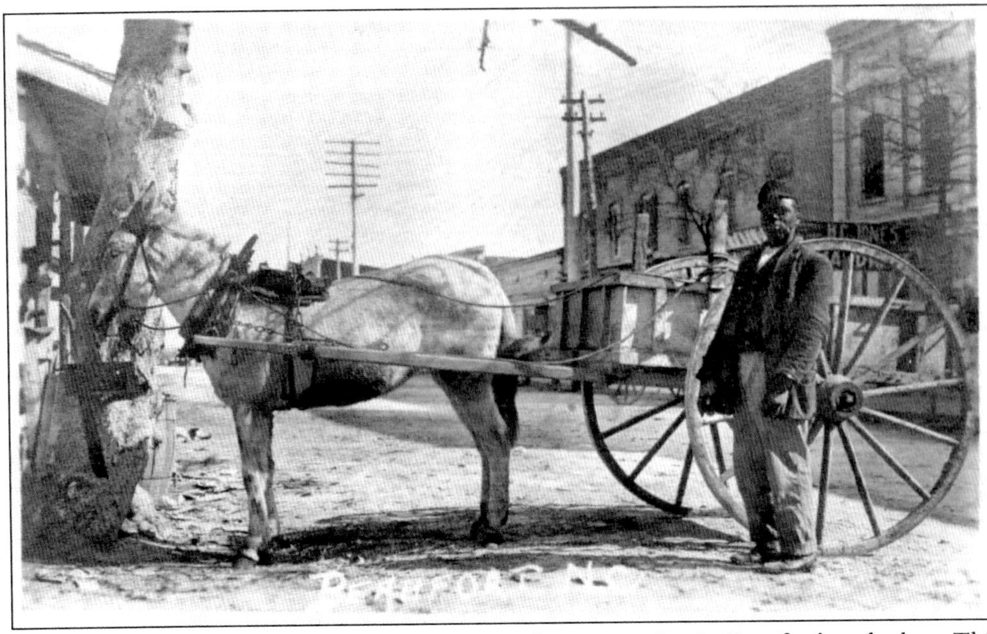

DRAYMEN. Mule and cart was a primary means of transportation in Beaufort's early days. This postcard depicts a drayman in front of H. C. Jones Hardware store around 1913. Draymen worked the town docks delivering freight and seafood to their regular customers. Local farmers like Will Smith, John Noe, and the "Cantaloupe Man," Henry Jones in Morehead City, traveled all over town selling vegetables from their carts. (Courtesy of Gail Barnes.)

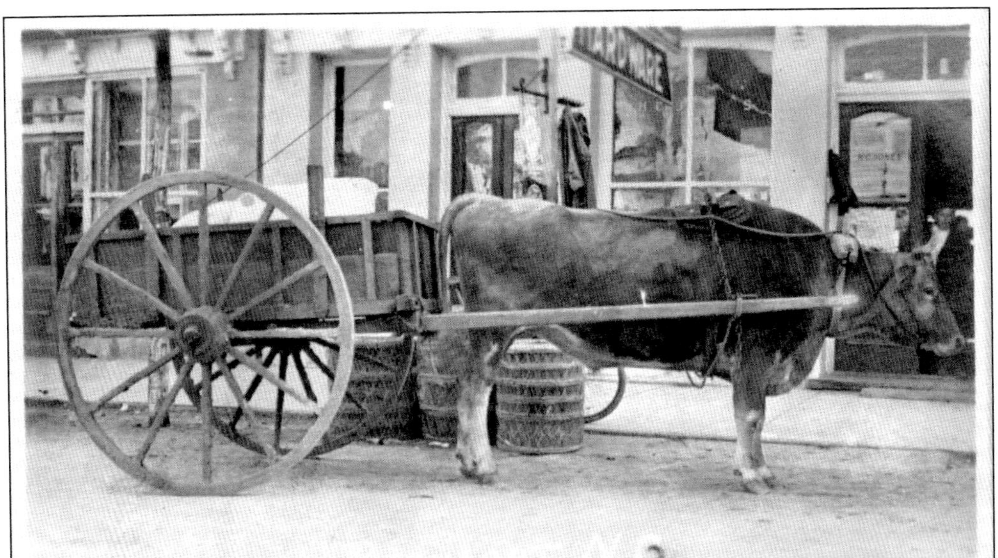

OXCART. This picture was also taken in front of H. C. Jones Hardware sometime before Front Street was paved in 1924. Most roads began as paths made by the two-wheeled oxcarts of the drayage business. The tall thin wheels cut deep tracks into the roads, making travel difficult. As a result, roads paved with oyster shell became very popular. (Courtesy of Gail Barnes.)

RAILROAD BRIDGE. The Beaufort-Western Railroad began work to connect Beaufort and Morehead City by rail in 1905. The largest obstacle was the three miles of water and marsh separating the two towns. The solution required a trestle across the Newport River from Morehead City to Radio Island and one across Gallants Channel to Beaufort. The work was completed in 1906. It is interesting to note that Beaufort did not have a turntable, so trains were backed across the railroad bridge to Beaufort's depot. When Norfolk Southern abandoned the railway in 1937, it was purchased by the Beaufort-Morehead Railroad Company. The B&M became the shortest railroad in the country to perform the four major rail functions: freight, passenger, express, and mail services. (At right, courtesy of Helen Chappell; Below, courtesy of Mickey Weeks.)

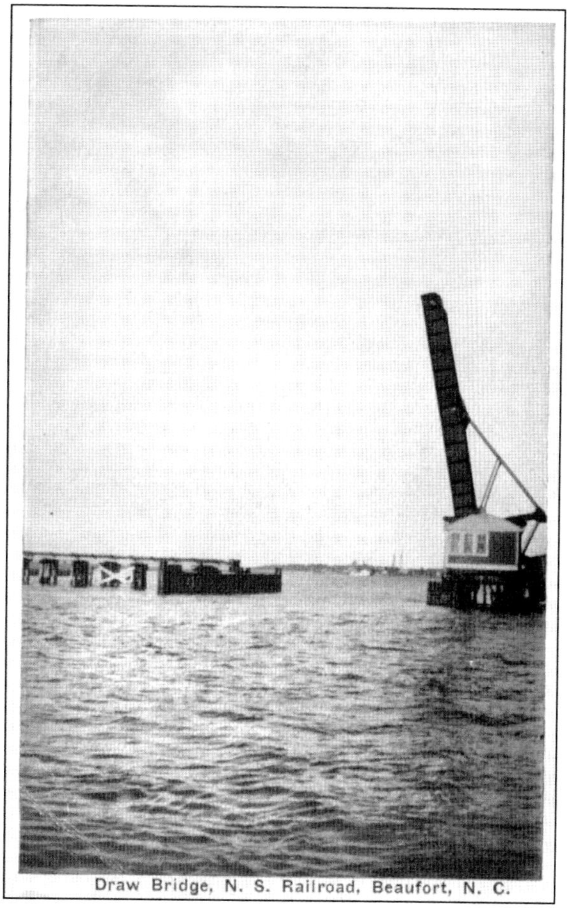

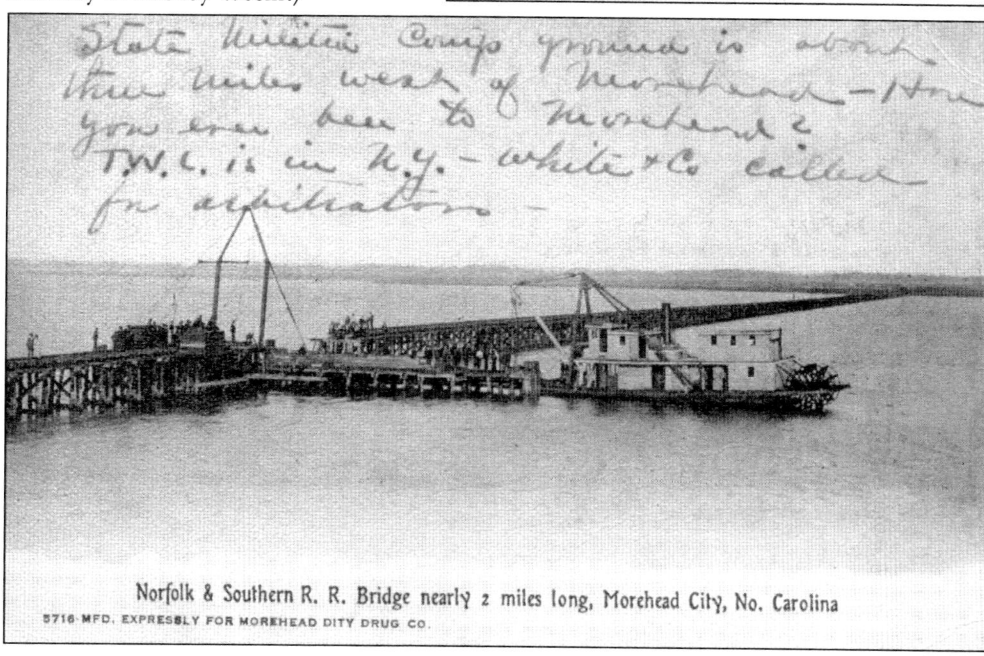

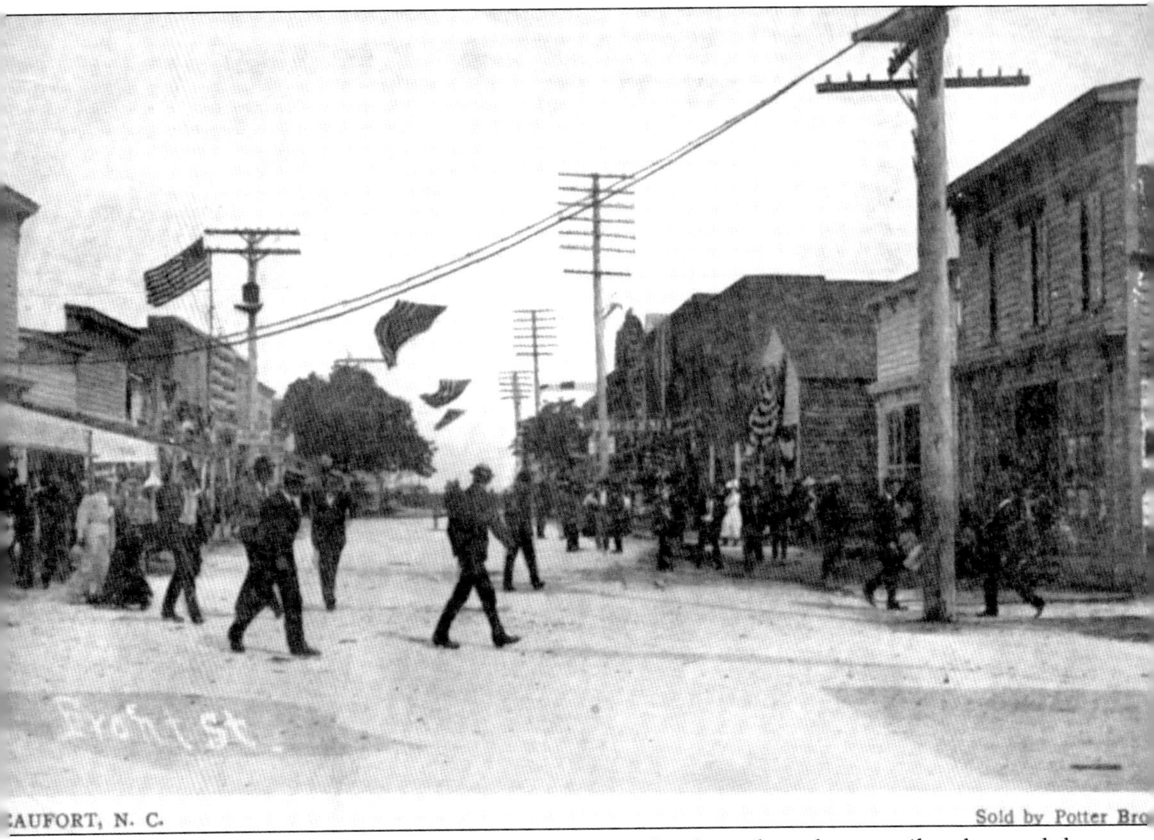

GALA WEEK. In the 1850s, Gov. John Motley Morehead sought to have a railroad extend the length of the state from the mountains to the coast. Unfortunately for Beaufort, its construction ended when it reached Morehead City in 1856. Fifty years after it was envisioned, the train finally came to Beaufort in November 1906. It brought such excitement that a weeklong celebration was held in June 1907. The people dressed in their finest clothing, bunting was placed on buildings, and a welcoming arch was erected on Turner Street. Gov. R. B. Glenn, local politicians, and railroad executives spoke from a grandstand placed at the intersection of Ann and Turner Streets. Parades, picnics, and other activities were also scheduled. The coming of the railroad brought a new economy to Beaufort by making passenger travel and the transportation of goods much easier. It was also another step toward ending Beaufort's isolation.

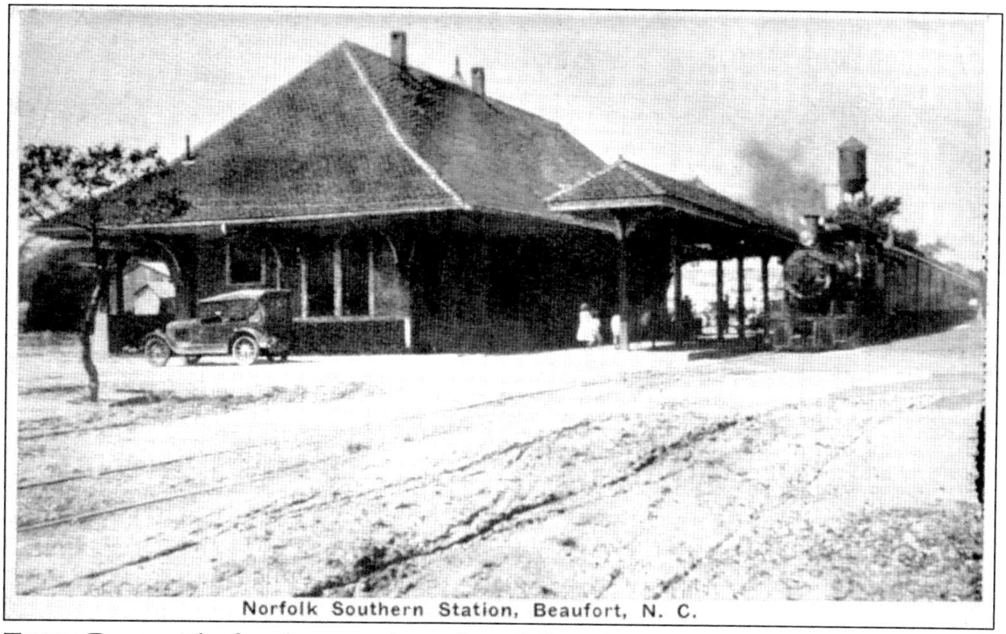

TRAIN DEPOT. The first depot was located on Gallants Point. In 1907, a new depot was built on the corner of Pollock and Broad Streets. It was characteristic of other Victorian-style depots except for its roof. The red tile roof evokes the Spanish colonial Revival style. After passenger trains ceased operation to Beaufort in the 1930s, the depot became home to the county library. (Courtesy of Mickey Weeks.)

BEAUFORT BRIDGE. Almost completely surrounded by water, Beaufort has historically been isolated from neighboring areas. That improved with the coming of the train in 1906 and construction of a bridge at Core Creek. Later a ferry capable of carrying three cars ran between Beaufort and Morehead City. However, nothing increased access more than the bridge built over Gallants Channel in 1927, forever connecting Beaufort to the outside world.

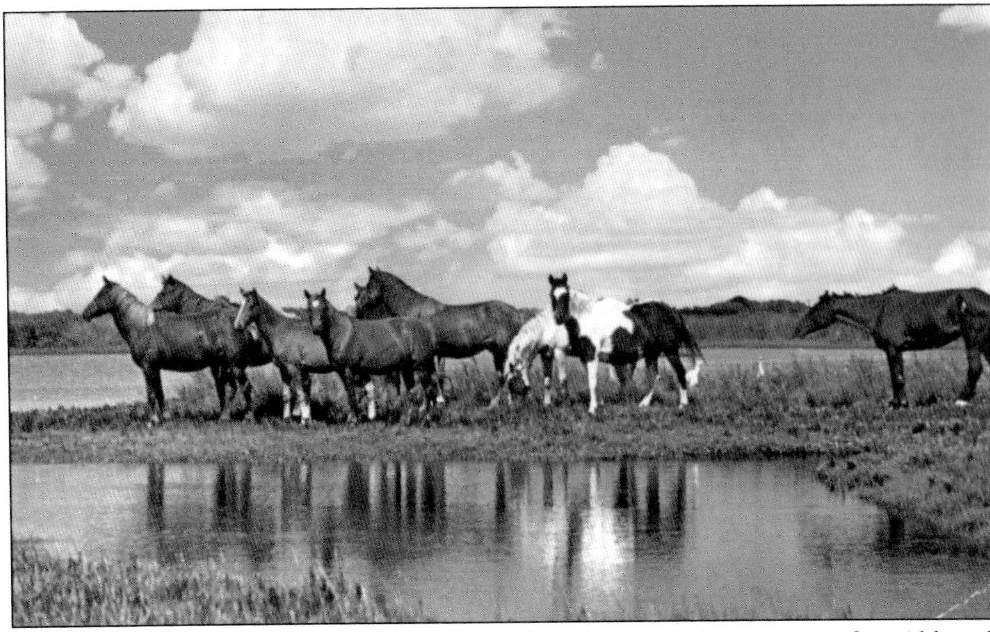

BANKER PONIES. There are two distinct herds of wild horses living near Beaufort. Although sharing some similar traits—compact with a shaggy coat and mane—they have dissimilar origins. The group on Shackleford Island (between Beaufort and Cape Lookout) is believed to be descendants of horses brought to the New World in 1526 by Spaniard Lucas Vasques de Ayllon, who established a short-lived colony at Cape Feare, now known as Cape Lookout. Another theory posits that when Sir Walter Raleigh's flagship *Tiger* ran aground near Portsmouth Island in 1585, horses were pushed overboard to lighten their load. The horses on Carrot Island (across Taylor's Creek) are descendants of domesticated horses taken to the island to graze long ago. Until the coming of the automobile, locals held annual "pony-pennings" whereby the horses were rounded up, branded, and auctioned.

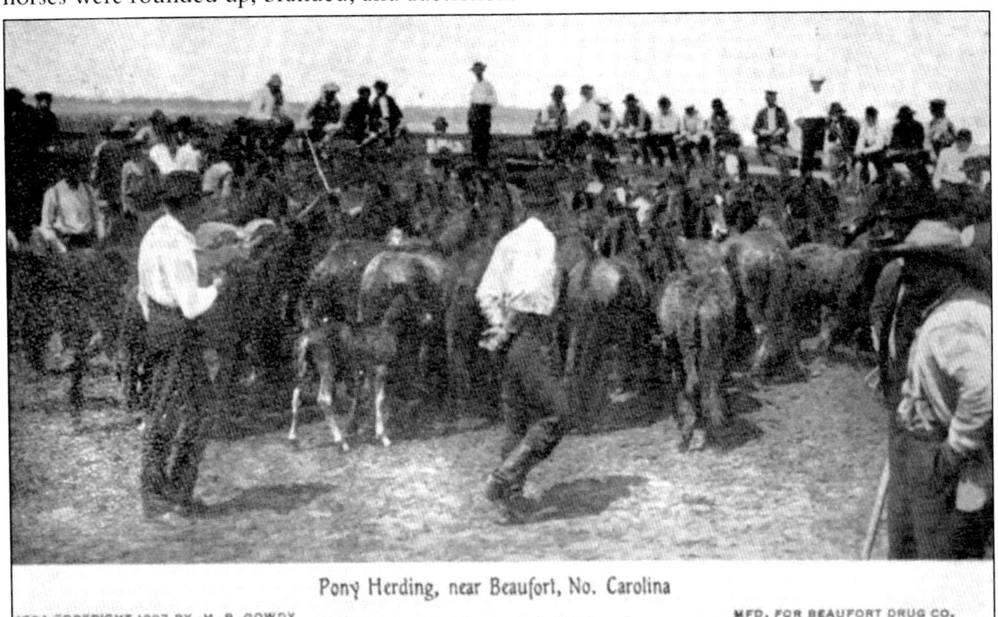

Two

Morehead City

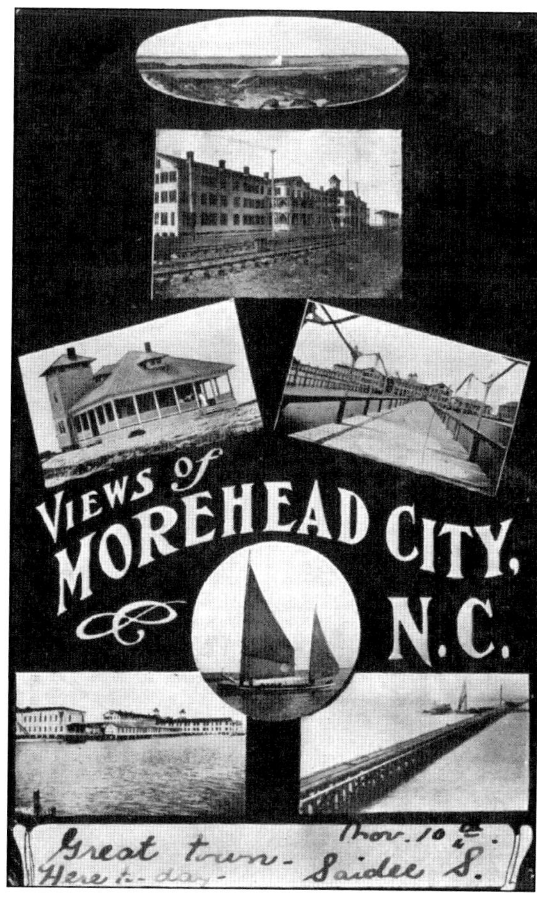

Views of Morehead City. The 1907 postcard shows a view of many of the places important to Morehead City history at the start of the 20th century. Pictured are the Atlantic Ocean (top), several pictures of the Atlantic Hotel (second from the top, third row from the top on the right, and fifth row on the left), the U.S. Lifesaving Station at Fort Macon (third row, left), sharpie boats (fourth row), and the railroad bridge joining Morehead City and Beaufort (fifth row on the right).

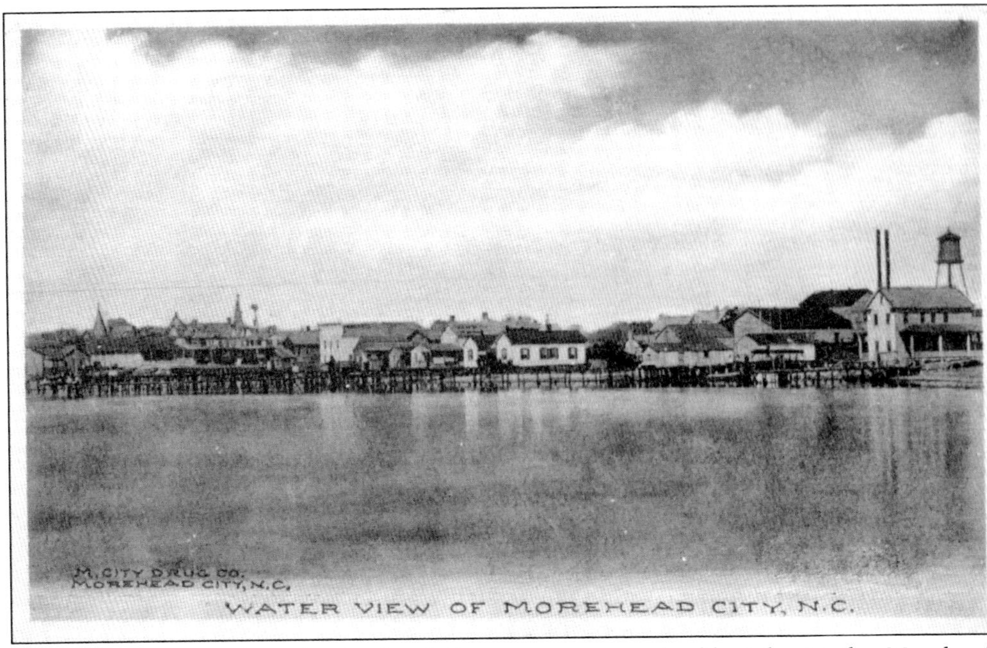

WATER VIEW. The Shepard Point Land Company was organized by John Motley Morehead, 20th governor of North Carolina, shortly after it became known that a railroad would be extended to Shepard's Point. Shepard's Point was a narrow peninsula bordered by Bogue Sound on the south, Newport River on the east, and Calico Creek on the north. Morehead City was laid it out in a grid pattern with blocks and alleys. Only six blocks wide, the original town extended from the Point to Fourteenth Street. The town was named after its founder, and the east-west streets were named for other developers and landowners. The bottom postcard shows the town as it appeared in the early 1900s, and in the distance is the Atlantic Hotel. (Above, courtesy of Mickey Weeks.)

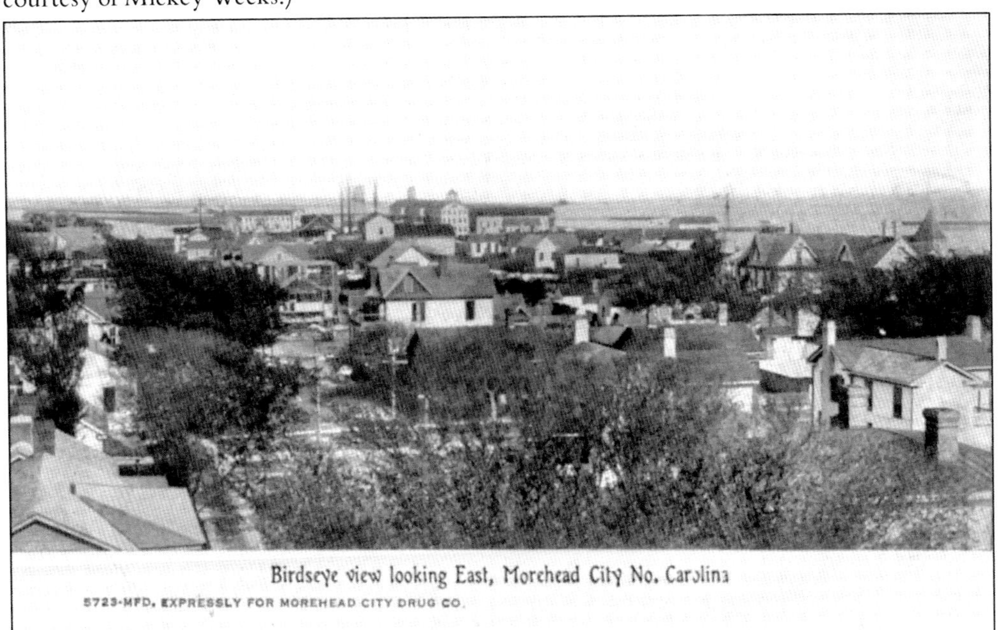

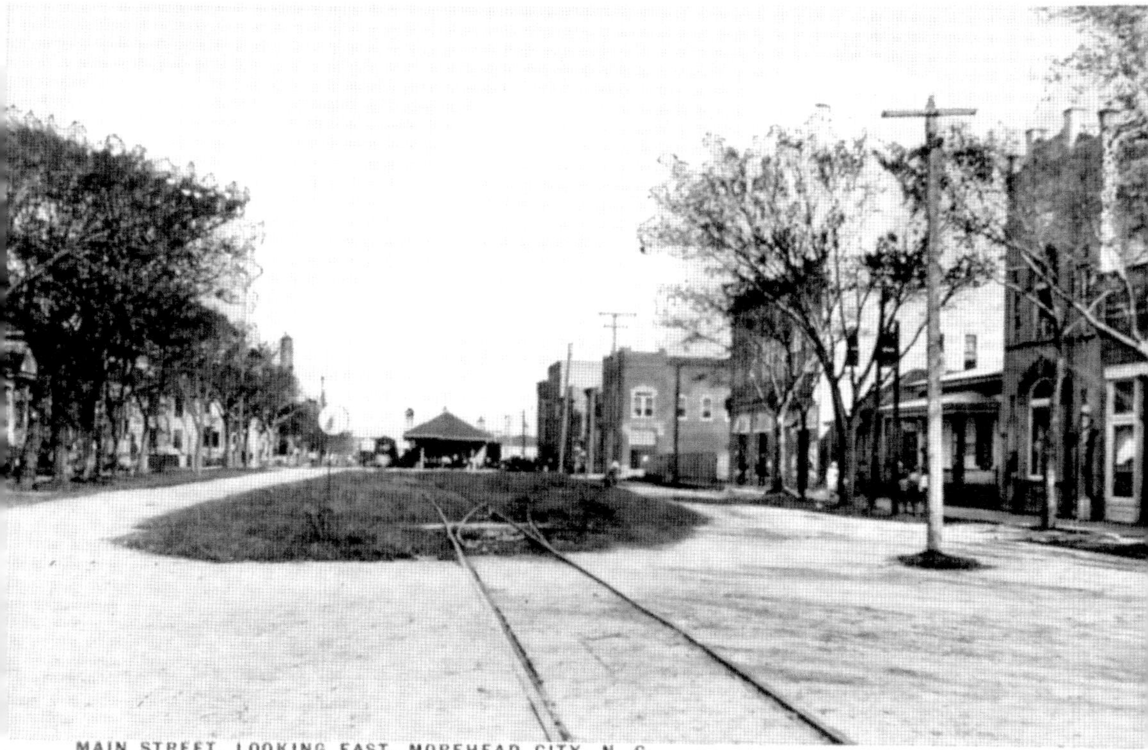

FIRST COASTAL RAILROAD RESORT. Through a bill passed by the North Carolina Legislature, a railroad line was built from Goldsboro to Morehead City. Morehead City, the eastern terminus for the railroad, had a 130-foot-wide thoroughfare leading through the center of town for the tracks and ended at Pier One. The first passenger train arrived in June 1858 at the depot near the freight wharf. At that time, the Atlantic Hotel was in Beaufort, and guests wanting to travel to the hotel were taken by sailboat to Beaufort. There were several flag stations in the area that provided shelter for passengers who waved the train down to get on. Several carloads of fish were shipped each week, and fish dealers rode the train daily to Goldsboro and back selling fish at stations and crossroads. The railroad was nicknamed "Old Mullet Line."

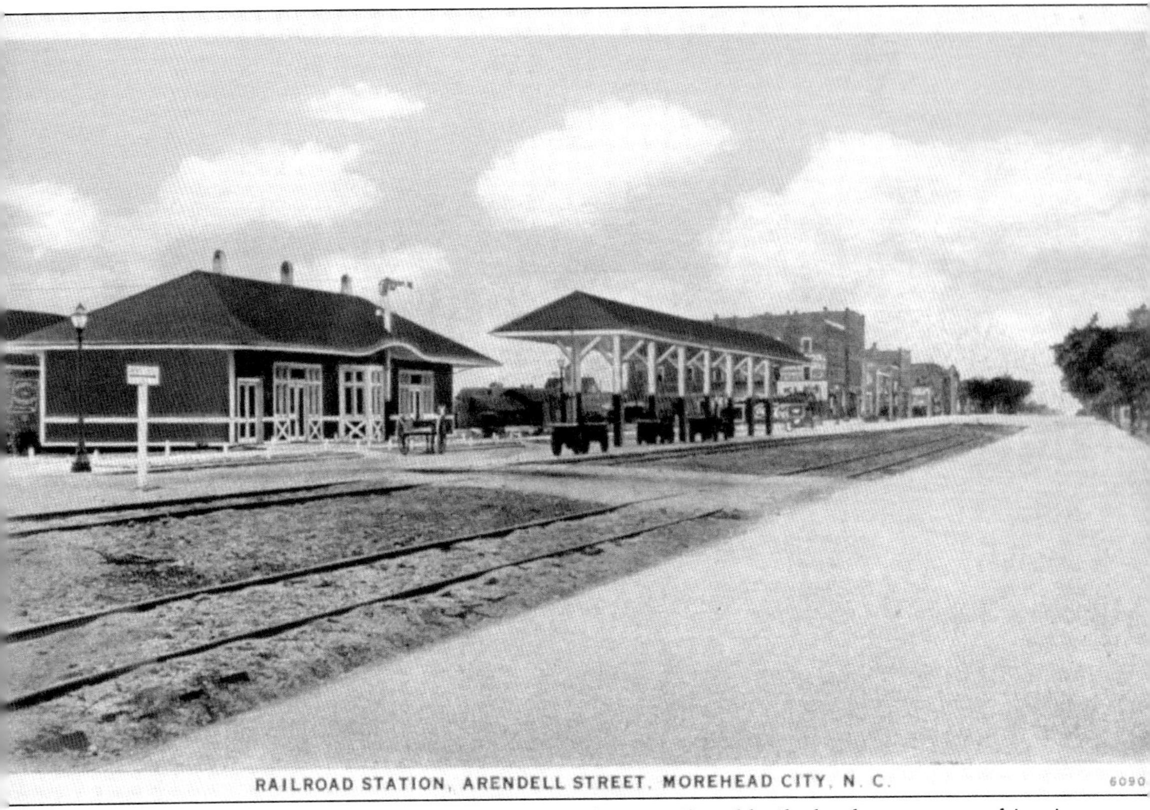

TRAIN DEPOT. In 1904, the Norfolk and Southern Railroad built the depot as a combination freight and passenger station in the middle of the street in the 900 block of Arendell Street in front of the Macon Hotel. The depot served as a center for commerce as well as a place to receive passengers. The railroad extended to Beaufort in 1906, and the depot was moved east to the 800 block. It was later moved, along with a new freight building, to the 700 block. In 1925, after Arendell Street was paved, the depot was divided into two sections and moved to the corner of Sixth Street on land created by the seawall. The depot's final move was in 2003 to the corner of Tenth Street. The last passenger train arrived in Morehead City in March 1950. This postcard shows the depot as it looked on the corner of Sixth and Arendell Streets. (Courtesy of Mickey Weeks.)

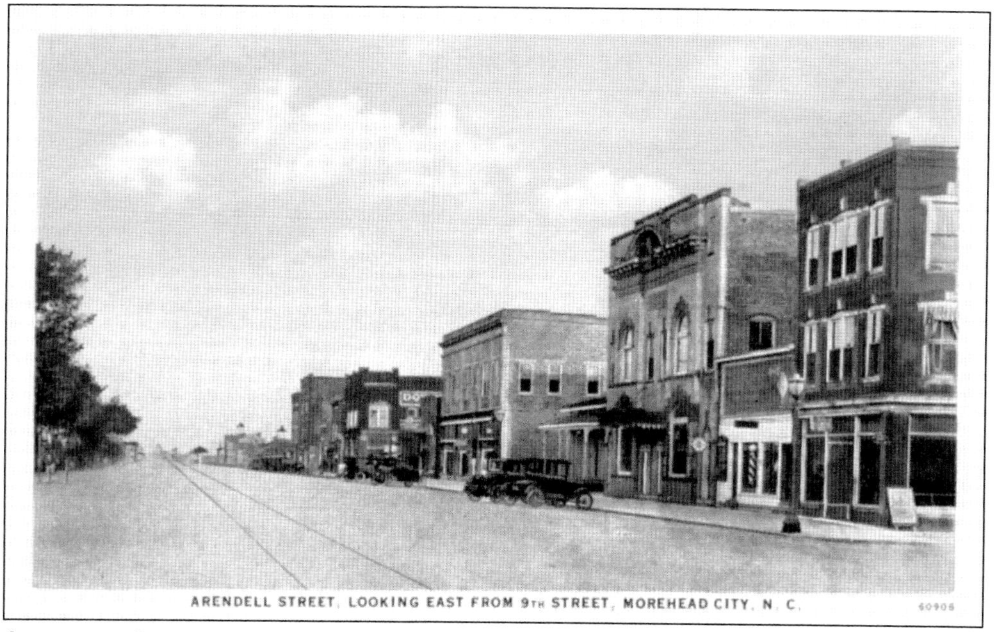

ARENDELL STREET LOOKING EAST. Wooden buildings built on the south side of Arendell Street between Eighth and Ninth Streets during the Civil War became the first business section of Morehead City. In 1908, a fire destroyed many of the buildings west of Eighth Street. L. L. Leary bought 75 feet of road frontage and built the Paragon Building. Ballance, Dill and Company moved into the west side and became Morehead City Drug. The Paragon Store was on the east side, and the second floor housed Morehead City Hospital Company. Dr. William Headen's office, fourth from the right, is pictured in the top postcard with cars in front; the Paragon Building is on the left and the Bank of Morehead City on the right. The bank doubled its size and had room for Western Union, the telephone company, a dentist, and a lawyer.

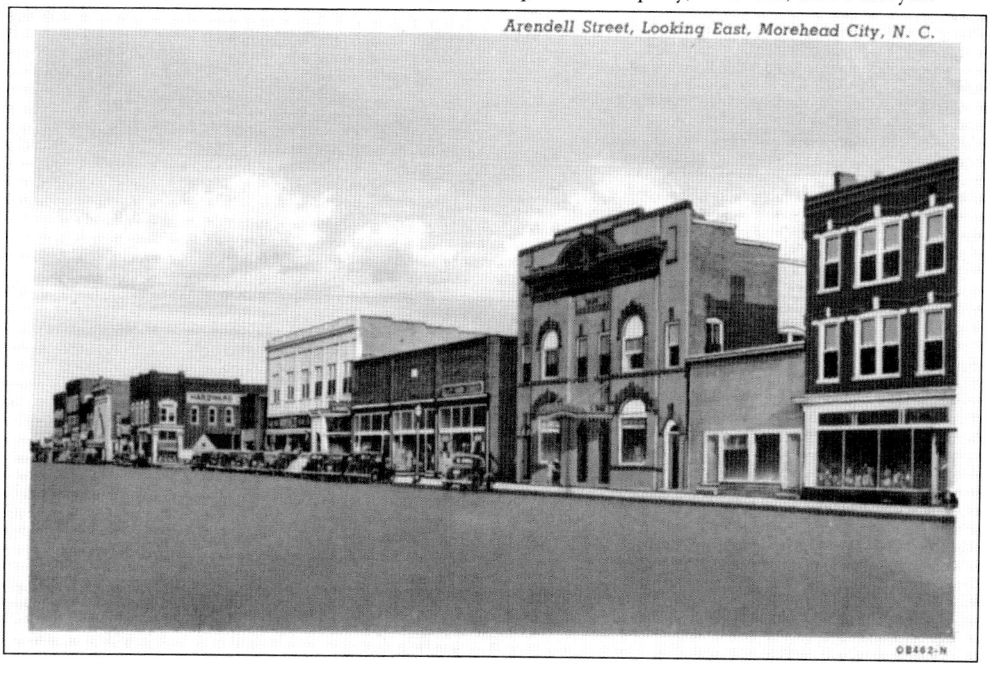

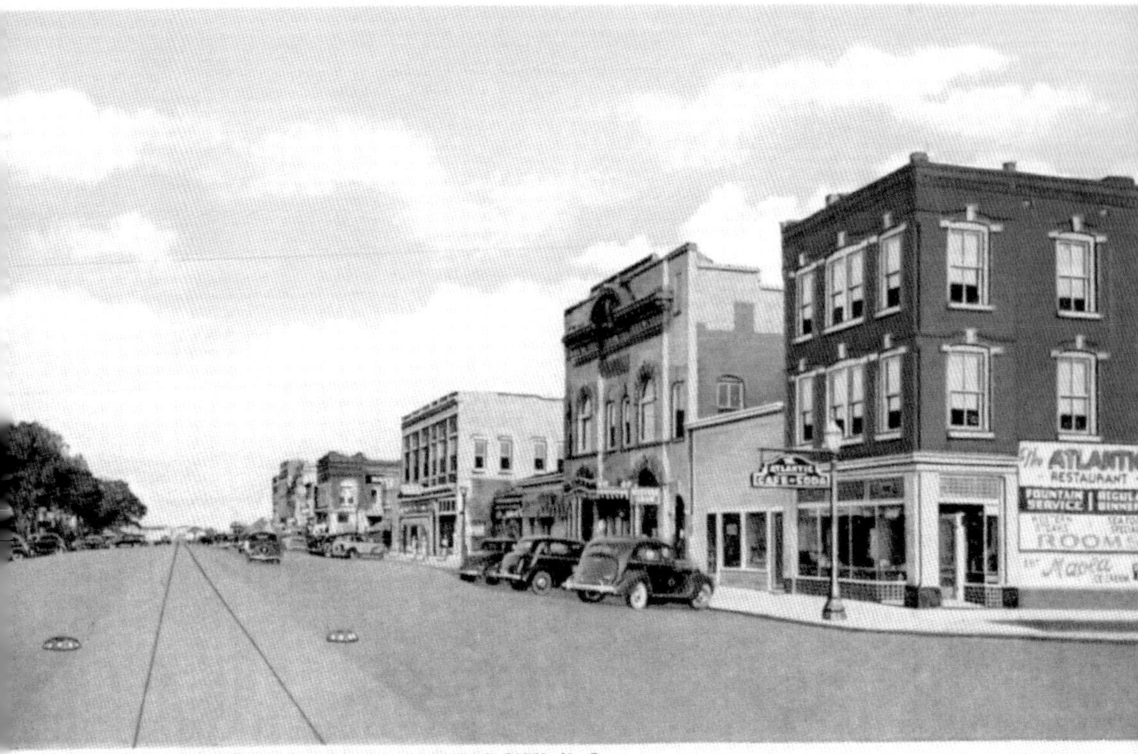

ARENDELL STREET, LOOKING EAST, MOREHEAD CITY, N. C. 6A268

NORTH SIDE OF ARENDELL STREET. On the northwest corner of Ninth Street between Arendell and Bridges Streets was the town commons. Among the oak trees, public gatherings were organized, children played, and sometimes small boats were built. For several summers, there was a merry-go-round. The First Methodist Church faced it on the west and the First Baptist Church on the north. The commons was broken up in 1883 when T. D. Webb built a general store on the corner. T. D. Webb Furniture was built on the east side of the general store in 1913. Also on the north side of Arendell Street were the homes of T. D. Webb, Norman Webb, Dr. Headen, Fred Royal (built for a hospital during the Civil War), and Charles S. Wallace. When the streets were paved in 1925, lighted domes, nicknamed "warts," were placed in the streets as dividers to show which side to drive on. These can be seen on either side of the railroad tracks.

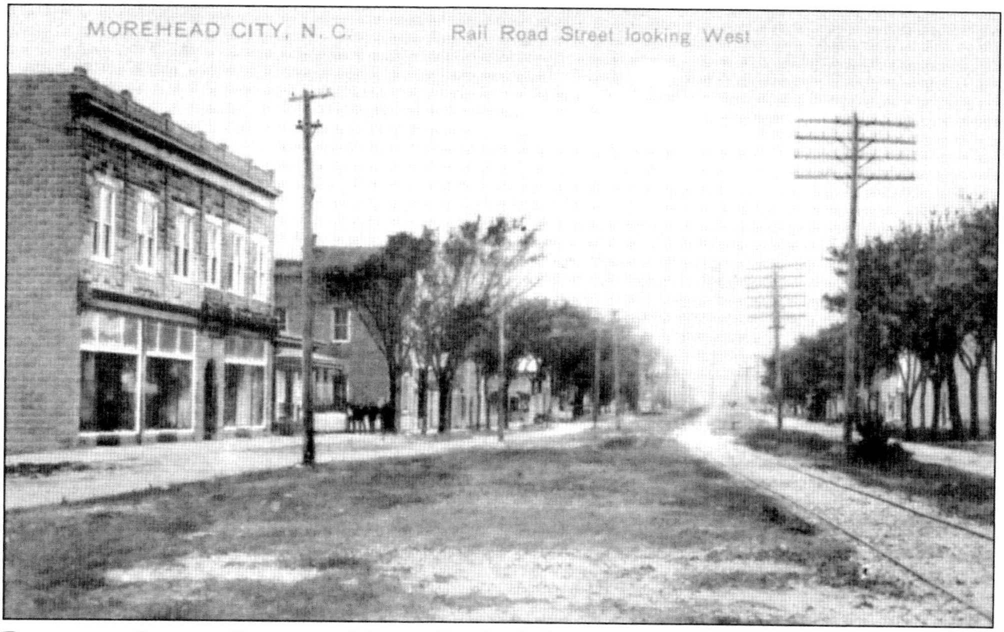

RAILROAD STREET LOOKING WEST. On the left are the Paragon Building, Dr. Headen's office, and the Bank of Carteret in the 800 block of Arendell Street. The railroad tracks ran the center of the street with a grassed median and a dirt street. In 1950, Arendell Street was widened to four lanes and became Highway 70, replacing Highway 10, which stretched from Tennessee to Morehead City and followed Bridges Street.

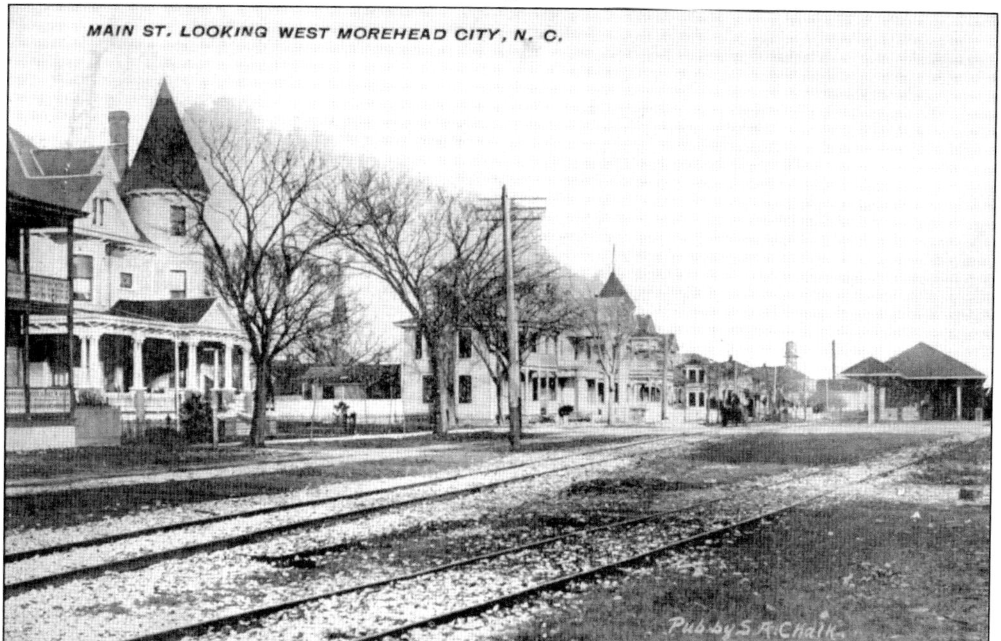

CHARLES S. WALLACE HOUSE. On the left of this 1912 postcard is the Charles S. Wallace house, located on the corner of Eighth and Arendell Streets. The three-story 15-room house was built in 1903 using lumber salvaged from a shipwreck. Morehead City's first sewer was run from this house. The property now is the site of Wachovia bank. (Courtesy of Mickey Weeks.)

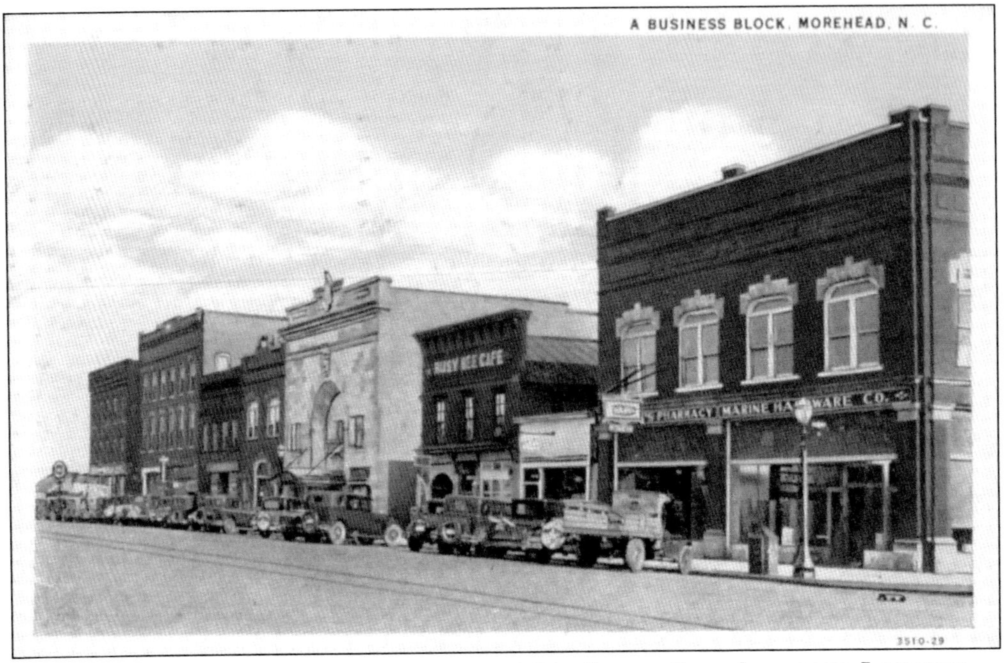

SOUTH SIDE ARENDELL LOOKING EAST FROM EIGHTH STREET. The postcard shows a glimpse of one block of the business district in 1933. From right to left was Marine Hardware later to become Cheek's, Hufham's Pharmacy, R. T. Willis Hardware, Busy Bee Café, Wade Theatre, Marine Bank, Pool Hall, Cherry Hotel, Freeman Brothers Wholesale, and Garner Gulf Station.

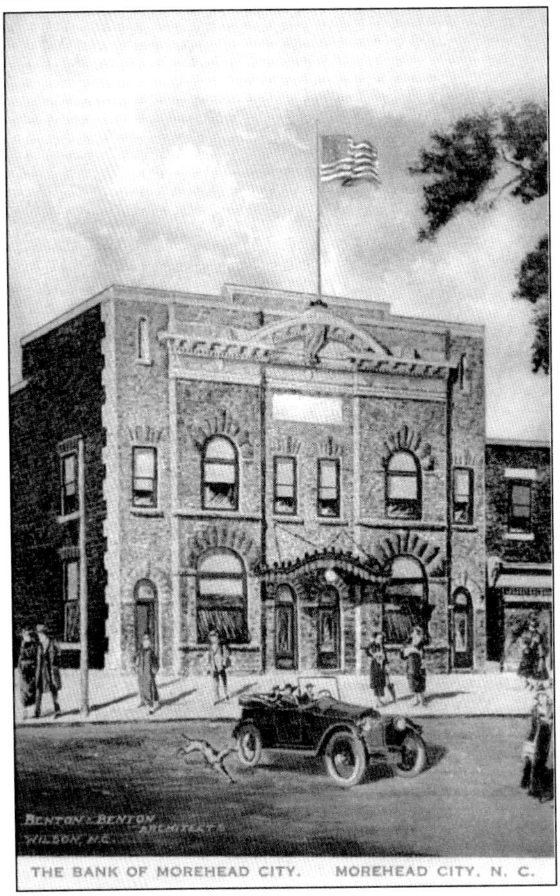

BANK OF MOREHEAD CITY. The Bank of Morehead City was the second bank to open in town. It opened in 1909, one year after the closing of the Bank of Carteret. This bank was located in the 800 block of south Arendell Street, and it remained in business until the early 1930s at the time of the Depression. The bank became the site of First Citizens Bank in 1934.

HOTEL FORT MACON. The first floor of the Hotel Fort Macon in the 700 block of Arendell was a furniture store before being converted into a hotel. At one time, the hotel was known as the Cherry Hotel. The hotel burned in the 1970s. Also shown is the Busy Bee Café on the left.

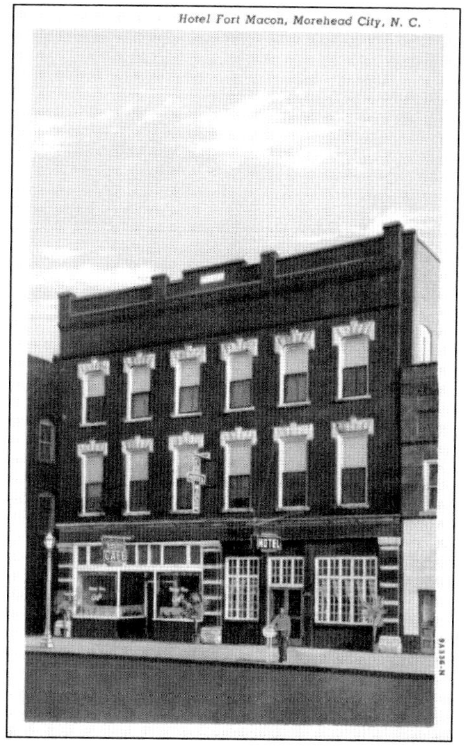

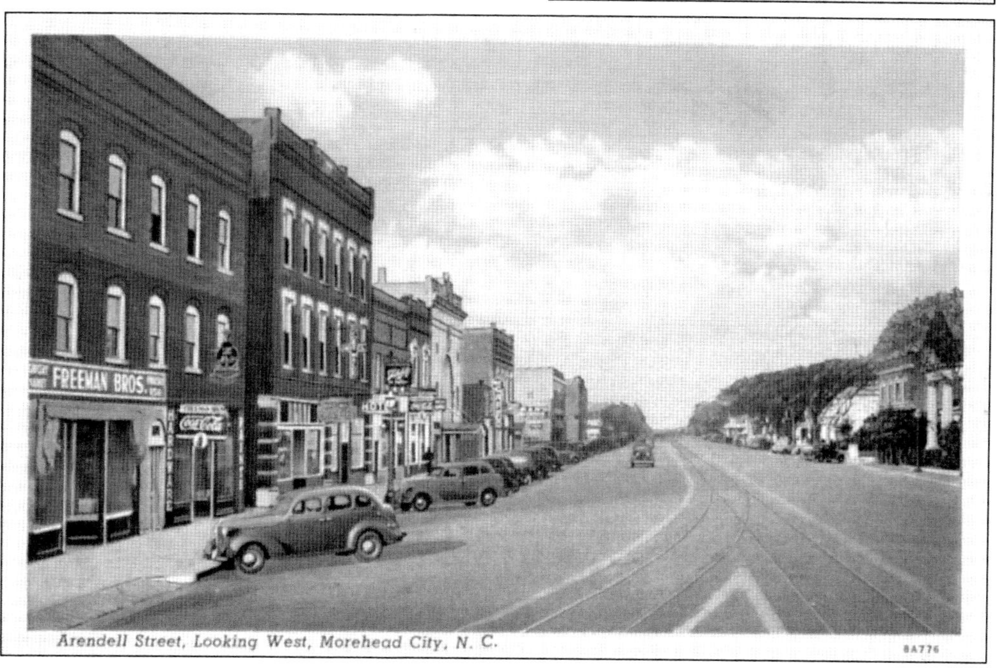

THE 700 BLOCK, NORTH SIDE ARENDELL STREET. The columns seen on the right of the postcard are on Dr. Ben Royal's house. The brick building is the Wade Building on the former site of George Dill Sr.'s house before its move to Bridges Street. The post office and Royal's Theatre were once in the Wade Building. The turreted roof in the distance is on the home of Charles S. Wallace.

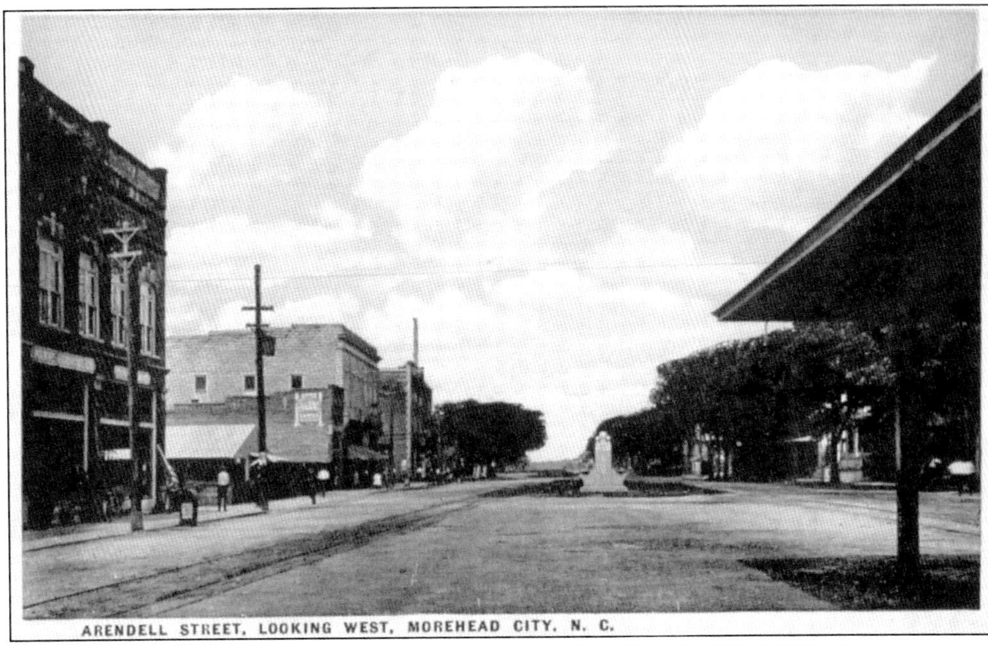

DAY-FULFORD MEMORIAL. The memorial was built in 1921 after World War I in memory of Leonard Day, who died in the Battle of France, and Irving Fulford, who was aboard the USS *Cyclops* when it mysteriously sank. It stood near the intersection of Eighth and Arendell Streets. The memorial was moved to a small plot near the junction of Evans and Jib Streets and later moved to the Municipal Building lawn.

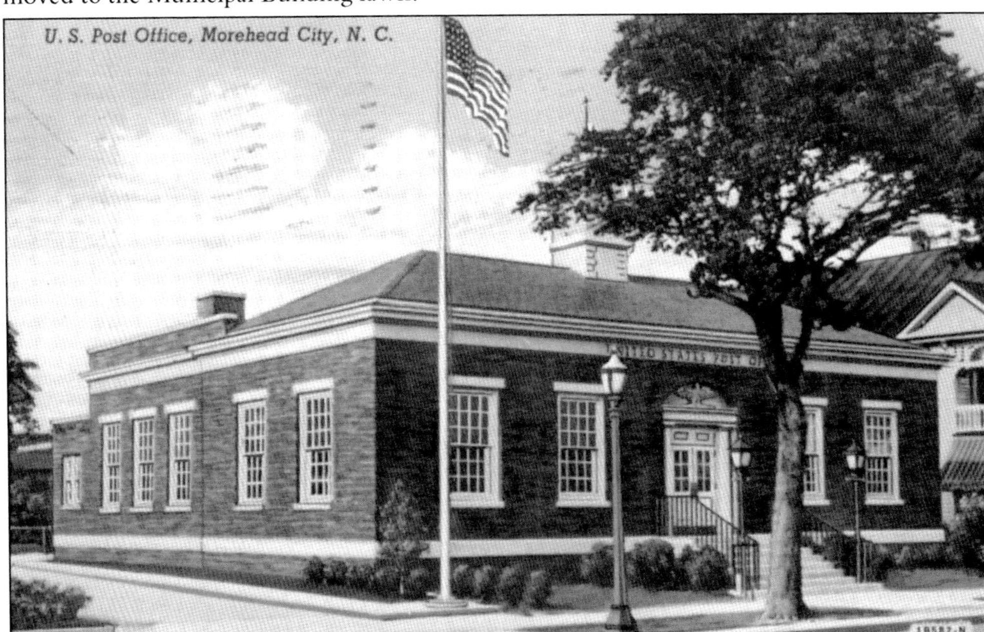

U.S. POST OFFICE. The post office was established in 1859 and operated in numerous locations around town until the Federal Building was completed in 1940 on Arendell Street. The post office was considered a symbol of progress. In 1977, the building became the administration offices for the Town of Morehead City after a new post office was built.

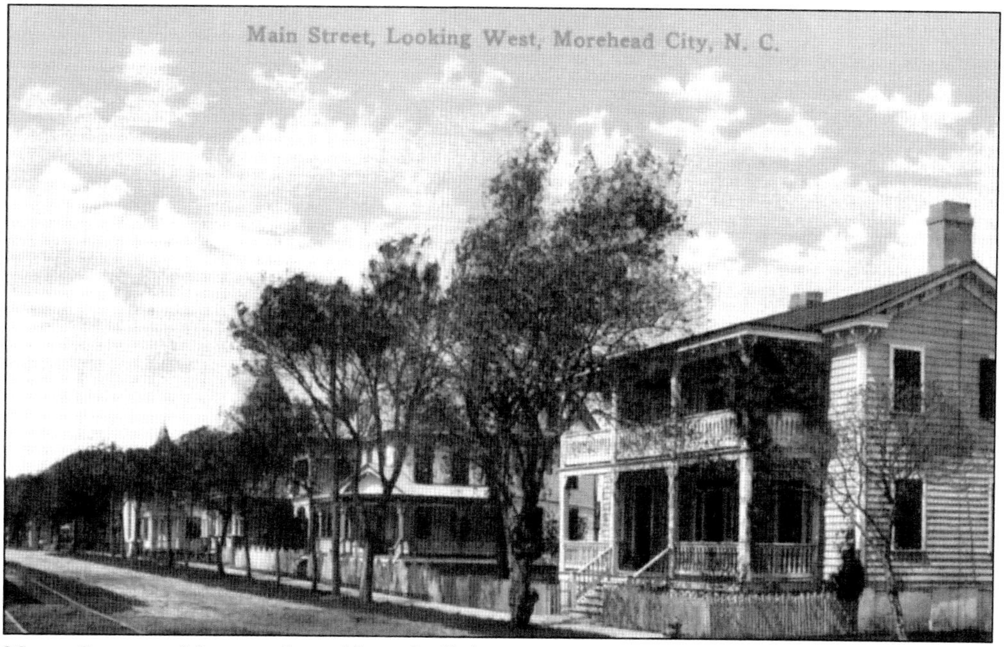

MAIN STREET. Many early residents built houses along the railroad tracks on Arendell and Bridges Streets close to the business activity of town. In the forefront of the postcard is the Dank Bell house, built before 1885 on the northwest corner of Seventh and Arendell Streets. It was moved to 703 Fisher Street in the 1950s, and the former site became Belk's Department Store.

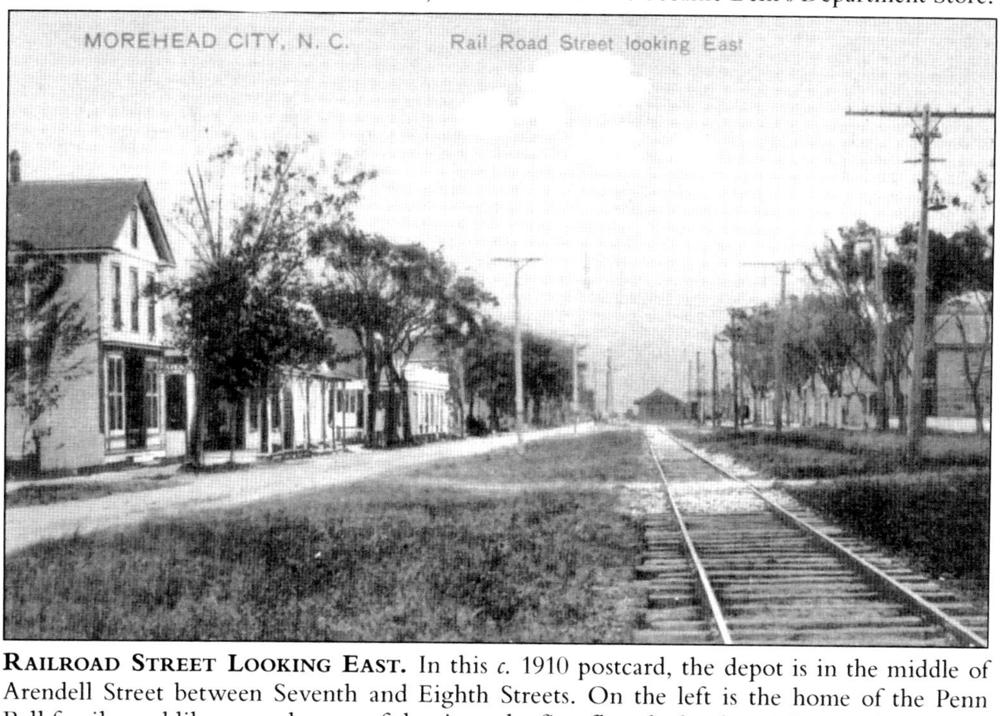

RAILROAD STREET LOOKING EAST. In this *c.* 1910 postcard, the depot is in the middle of Arendell Street between Seventh and Eighth Streets. On the left is the home of the Penn Bell family, and like many houses of the time, the first floor had a shop. This one housed the Paragon and sold millinery. Down the street where the columns are seen is the R. T. Willis General Store.

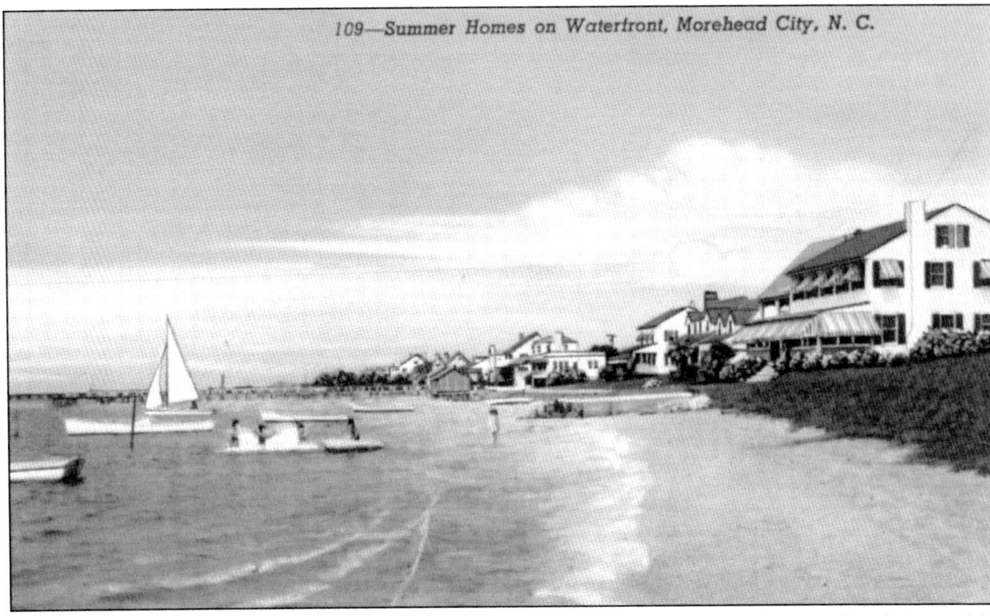

SUMMER HOMES. In 1899, Mrs. F. W. Barnes of Wilson purchased the Teachers' Assembly Building, transforming it into the first privately owned cottage. Summer homes became more popular as automobiles replaced the train as the most common way to travel. People who had vacationed in Morehead City began to build cottages. Popular styles were the bungalow and two-story wood shingle Cape Cod. Porches were the most popular feature.

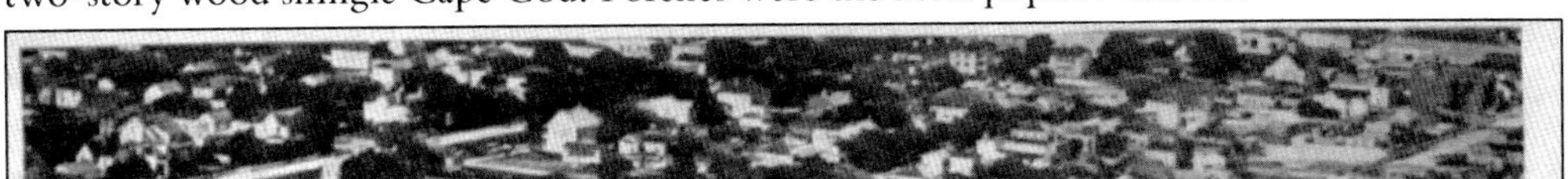

PROMISED LAND. The area between Tenth and Twelfth Streets from the railroad track to Bogue Sound is known as the Promised Land (foreground). The decline of the whaling industry and several destructive hurricanes early in the 20th century caused people to migrate from Core Banks and Shackleford Banks to Morehead City. Many brought their houses with them on boats.

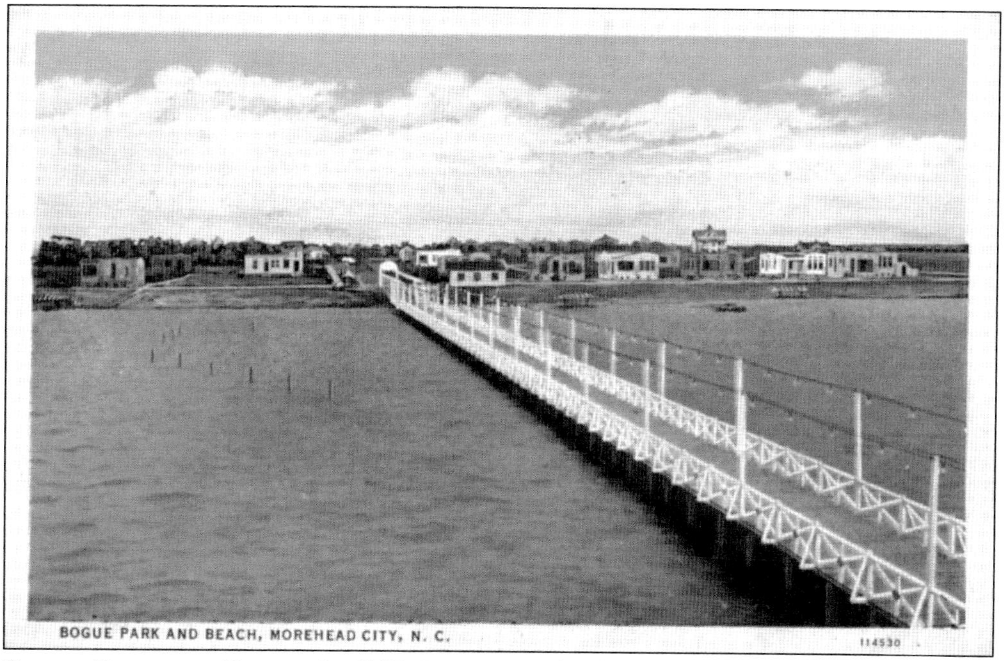

BOGUE PARK AND BEACH. In 1925, Larry West developed a new resort subdivision south of Arendell Street between Twentieth and Twenty-second Streets on the former site of the G. D. Canfield Saw Mill. Twenty-first Street led from Arendell Street to a 16-foot-wide pier extending into the sound. Bogue Park Pier, the longest in town, became known as the "White Pier." There was a sandy beach and lights for strolling and swimming at night. When a lot was purchased, a house plan was picked from a selection of Spanish-style plans, and West built the house. The houses had stucco walls, terra-cotta tile roofs, and patios. Blocks for the houses were made on-site. West sold the development after 20 houses had been built.

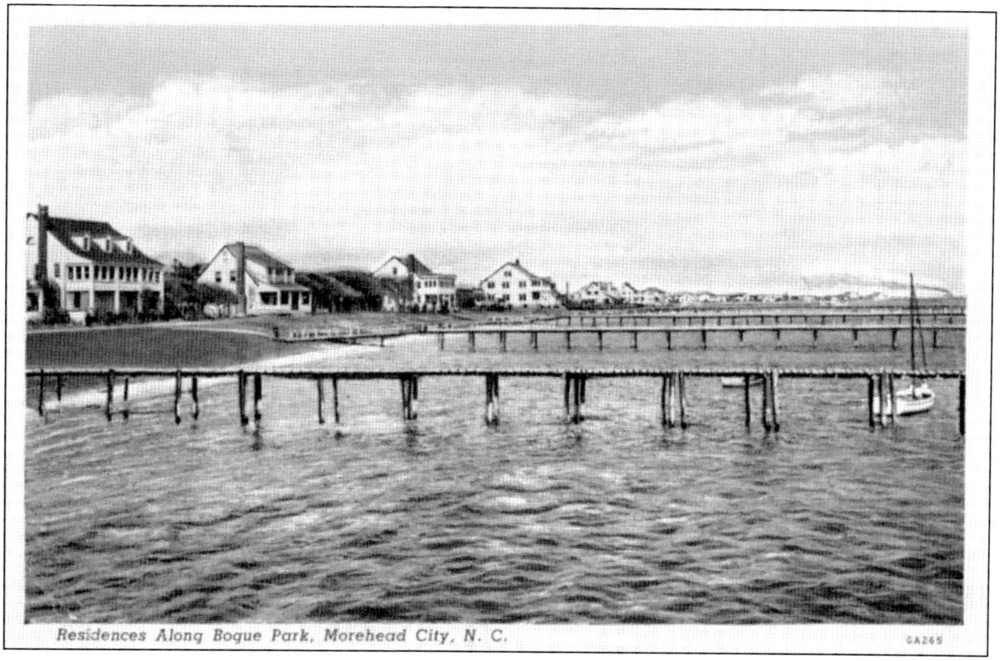

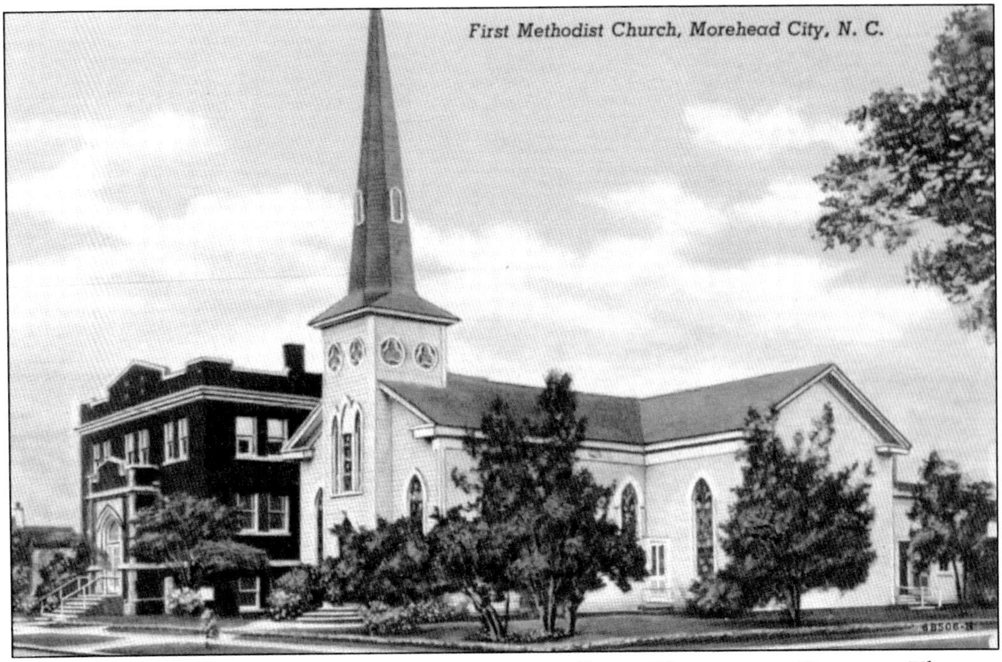

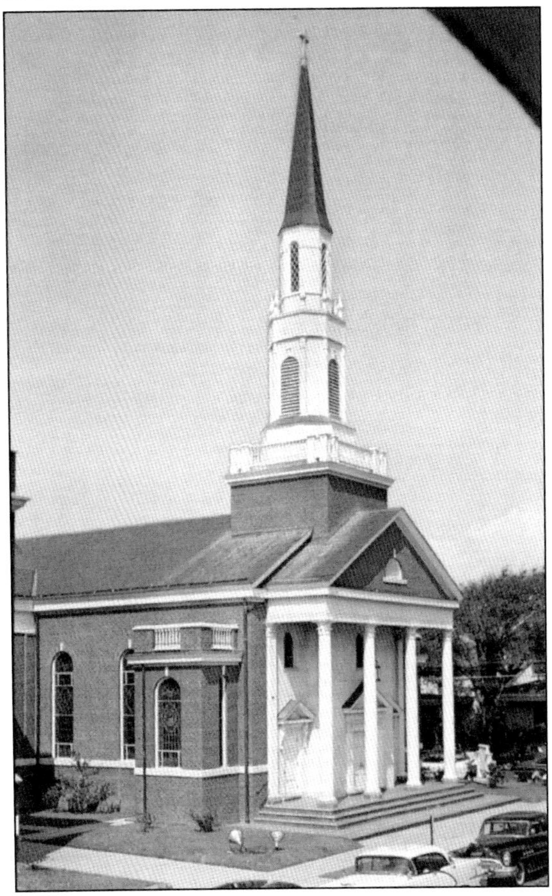

First Methodist Church. The Methodist Society was the first Christian organization to start a permanent church. In 1879, a wood frame church was built on the corner of Ninth and Bridges Streets using money given by the government in retribution for burning a church during the Civil War. It was built on land donated to the church by the Shepard Point Land Company. The church also operated a school on the corner of Tenth and Bridges Streets called the Harry North School from 1899 to 1903. In 1925, the Education Building (top postcard) on the left of the church was dedicated. The present brick church (bottom postcard) replaced the wood one in 1952.

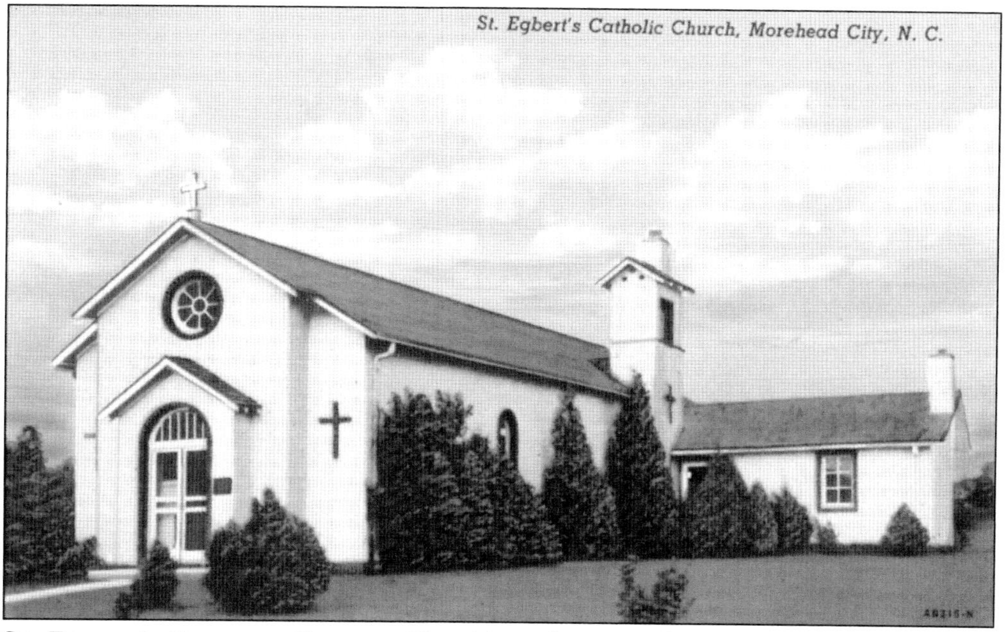

ST. EGBERT'S CATHOLIC CHURCH. The vision of a priest who traveled throughout Eastern North Carolina by chapel railcar gave the Catholic parish a permanent home. While visiting Beaufort in his "Steel Apostle" in 1928, Father Egbert Albert secured the land for a church. He died shortly thereafter. A church built in Morehead by his parents was dedicated to Father Egbert in April 1929.

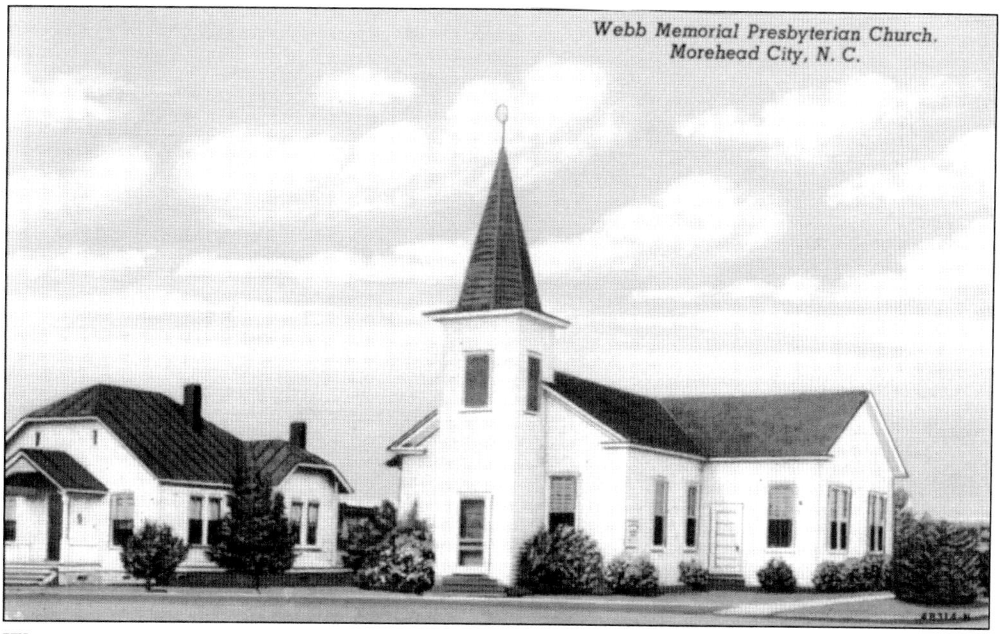

WEBB MEMORIAL PRESBYTERIAN CHURCH. The First Presbyterian Church was organized in 1929 with 41 members. The church's name was changed to George Webb Memorial Church in 1931 and back again to the First Presbyterian Church in 1954. The church became known as the "Little White Church on the Corner." The fellowship hall and education building were completed in 1959 and a new sanctuary built in 1983.

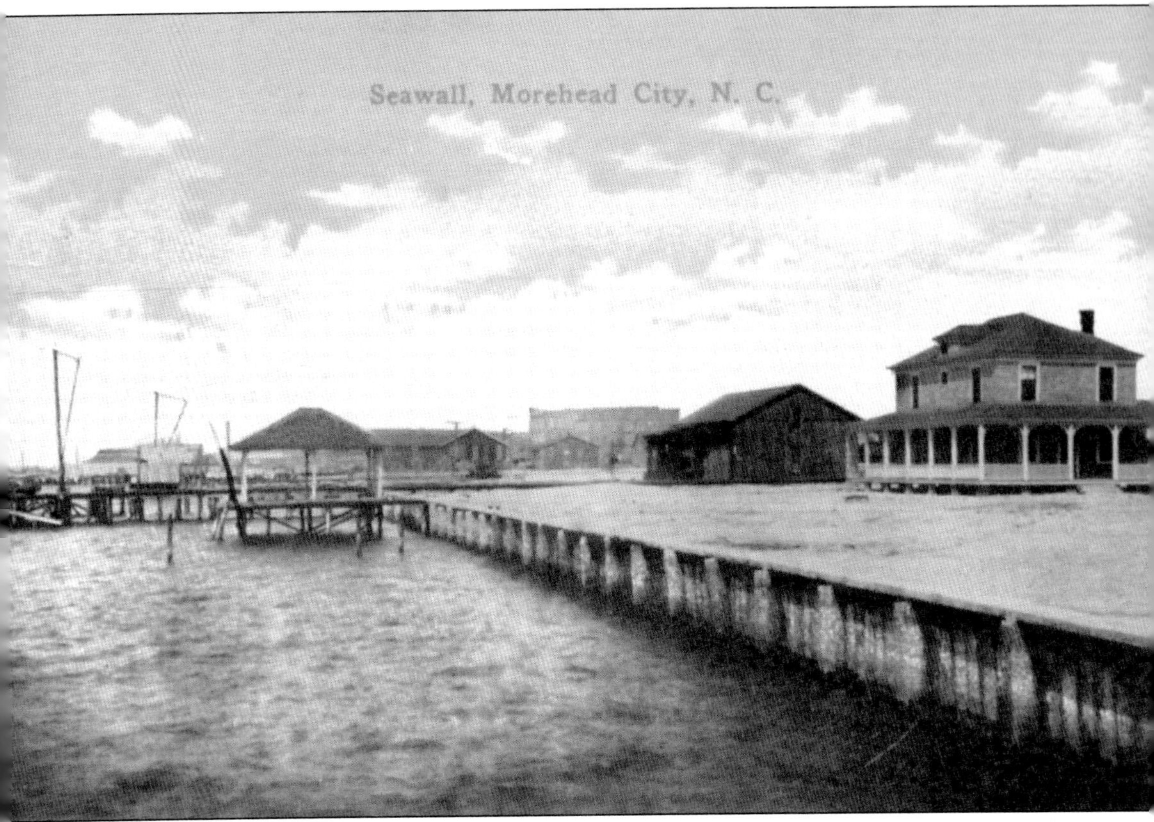

SEAWALL. Before the seawall was completed in 1913, the railroad tracks bordered the shoreline on the south between Fourth and Seventh Streets. A wooden boardwalk extending along the marsh allowed fish houses to be built in this section. Long piers stretched out from the fish houses into the sound to reach water deep enough to dock boats. The Norfolk and Southern Railroad had the 2,400-foot concrete seawall constructed from behind the Atlantic Hotel to the corner of Ninth Street. Marshland was filled in behind it to create new land. Many fish houses were built on the water side of Evans Street. A covered commercial dock stood at the end of Fifth Street from which produce was shipped. A daily ferry also left the dock for Beaufort. Walter Scott Parker built a summer home (right) on the corner of Fifth and Evans Street. The construction of the seawall made the waterfront what it is today.

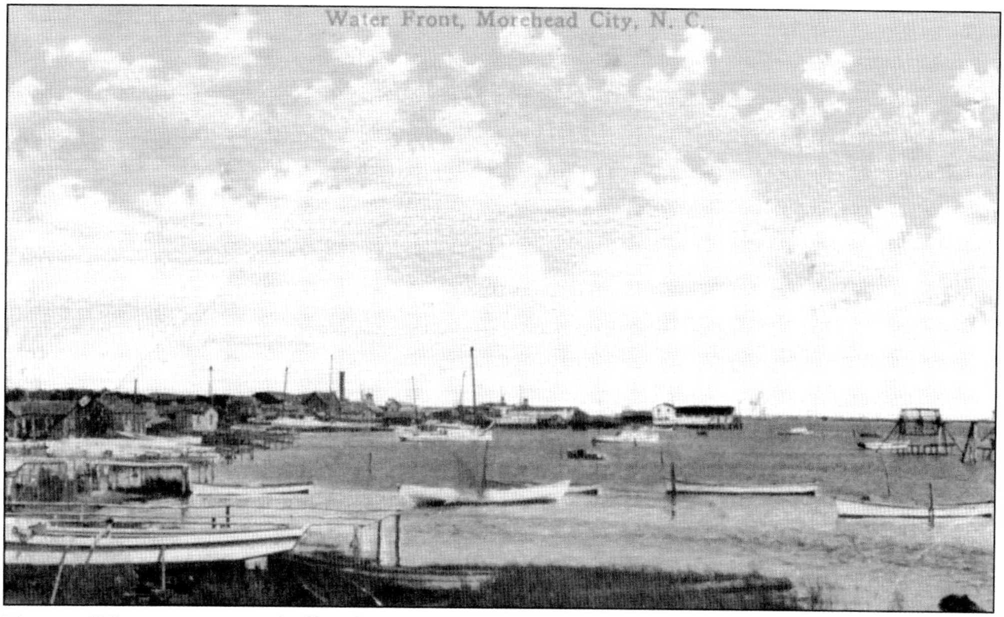

EARLY WATERFRONT. Skiffs, sharpies, and other sailing vessels were common along the waterfront in the early 1900s. It was a working waterfront home to small fish houses and other sea-related businesses. A Coca-Cola bottling plant opened in 1919 and was in operation until it burned in 1932. Brick was not used in the construction of buildings on the waterfront back then, and none of those early wooden buildings survive today.

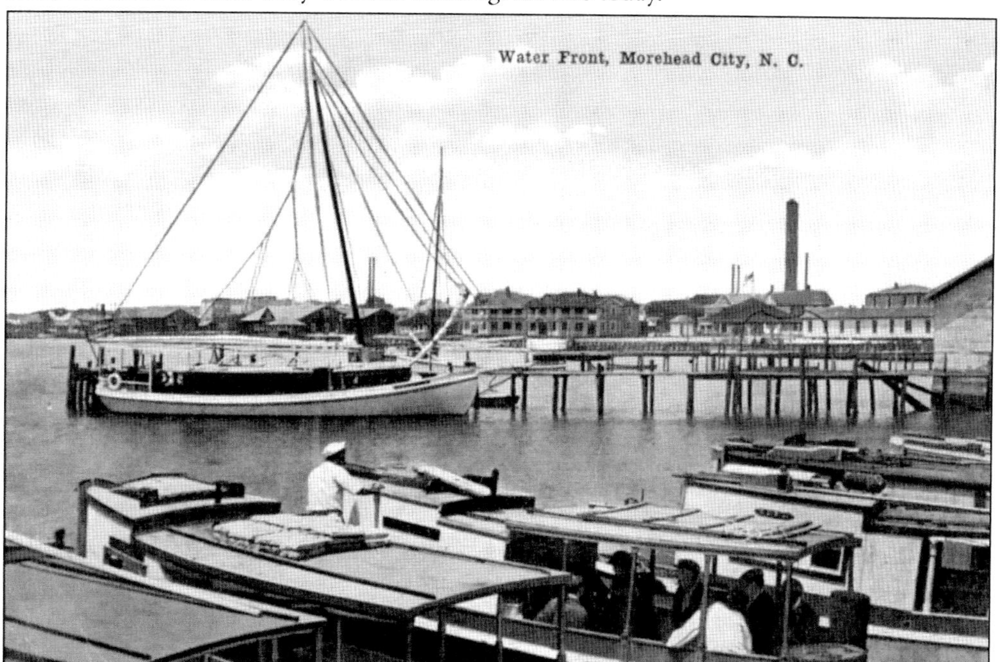

WATER FRONT. The boats in the foreground at the Atlantic Hotel docks have guests ready for a day trip to Money Island across the sound. The long, one-story, 52-room white building (right) known as Cottage Row was built to house single men who came to fish. Behind it is the Standpipe, near Fifth and Arendell Streets. It was the town water supply from 1910 until 1979.

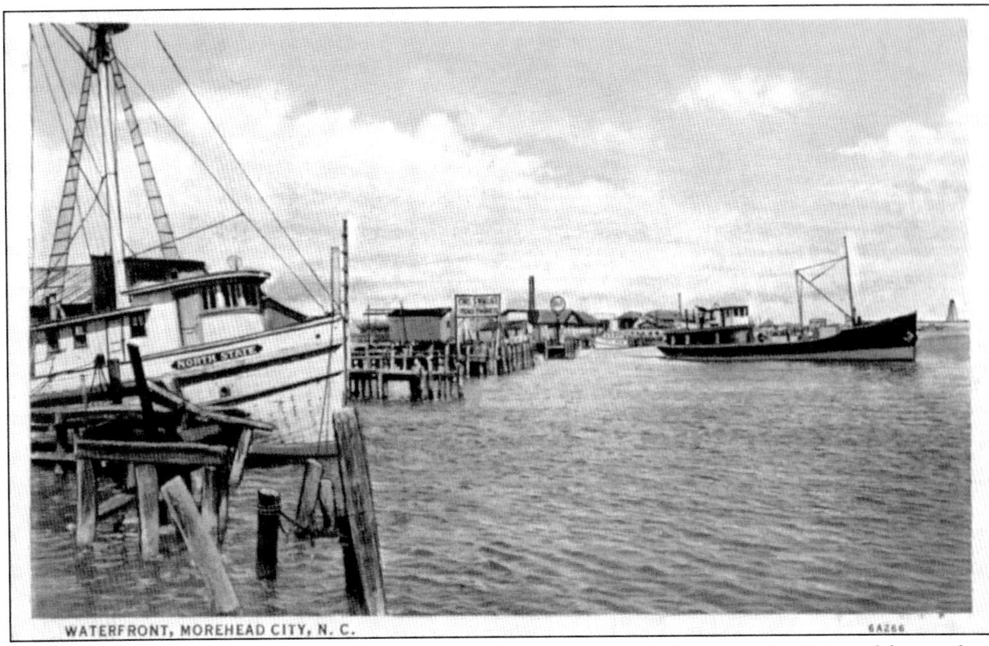

WATERFRONT. The Morehead City Seafood Company was built around 1914 and located on Evans Street across from the water. It is visible in the center of this 1930s-era postcard just beyond the Texaco and Gulf docks owned by Charles S. Wallace and P. H. Greer, respectively. Wallace purchased Morehead City Seafood and the neighboring ice plant in 1918. A menhaden boat sits at dock in the foreground.

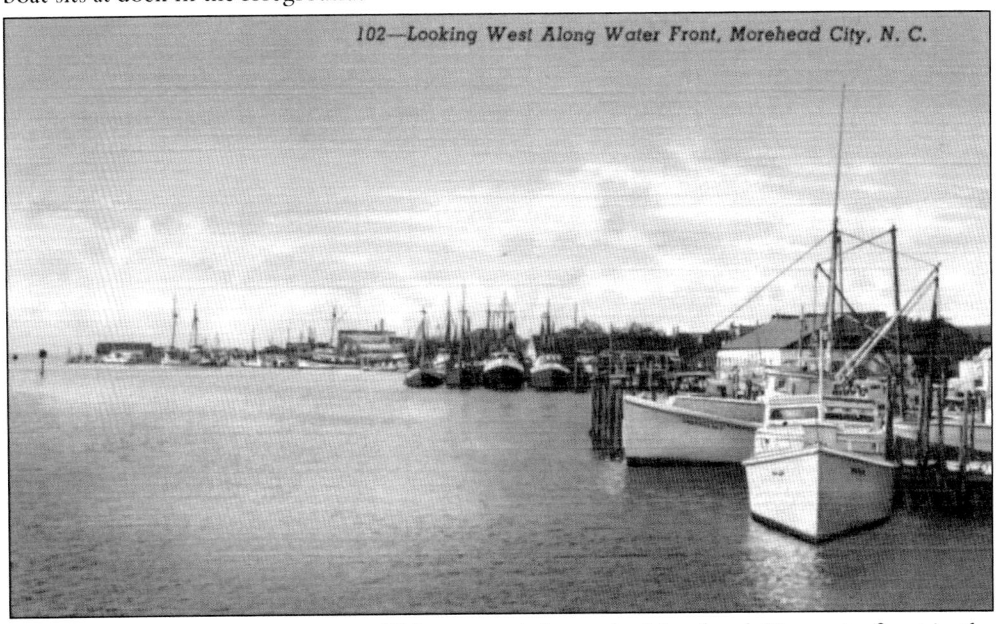

MOREHEAD CITY WATERFRONT. This postcard shows the Morehead City waterfront in the 1950s. On the right you can see the Sanitary Restaurant and Puck O'Neal's Fish House. In the center, the early Morehead City Hospital and the Paragon Building are visible. On the point at the far left stands Gordon Willis's Fish House, which began as an oyster shucking and packing house in the early 1900s.

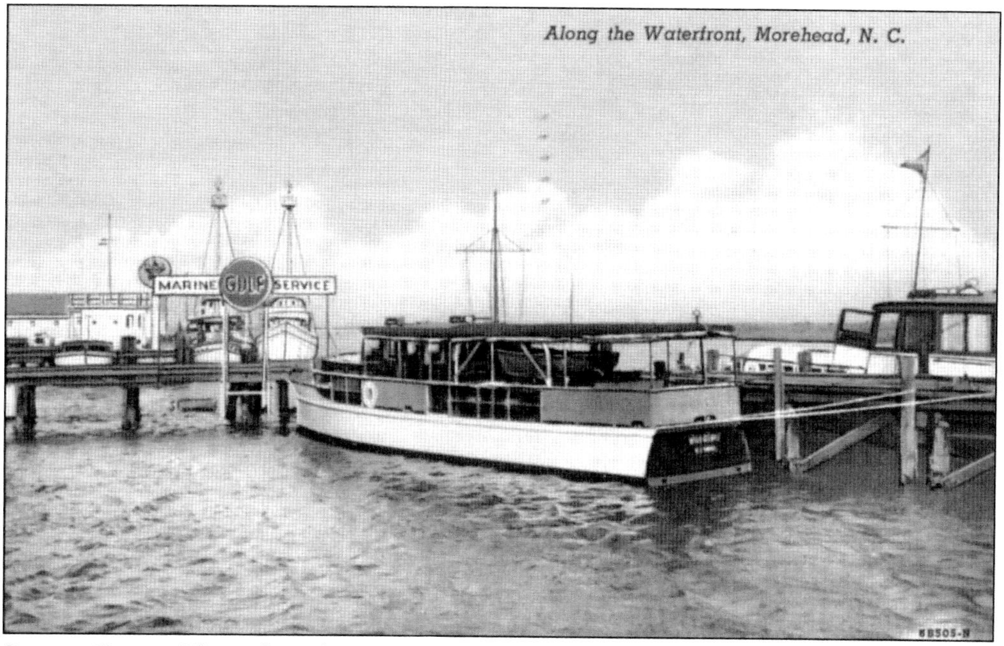

STORM FLAGS. Throughout history, Carteret County has been susceptible to storms. After the Storm of 1933, an early-warning system was devised. Tall metal towers were erected in Morehead City near Tommy Russell's boatyard on Shepard Street and in Beaufort. Flags were flown from the towers indicating weather conditions. A kerosene lamp lit them at night. The towers were discontinued around 1960 because of television and radio weather reporting.

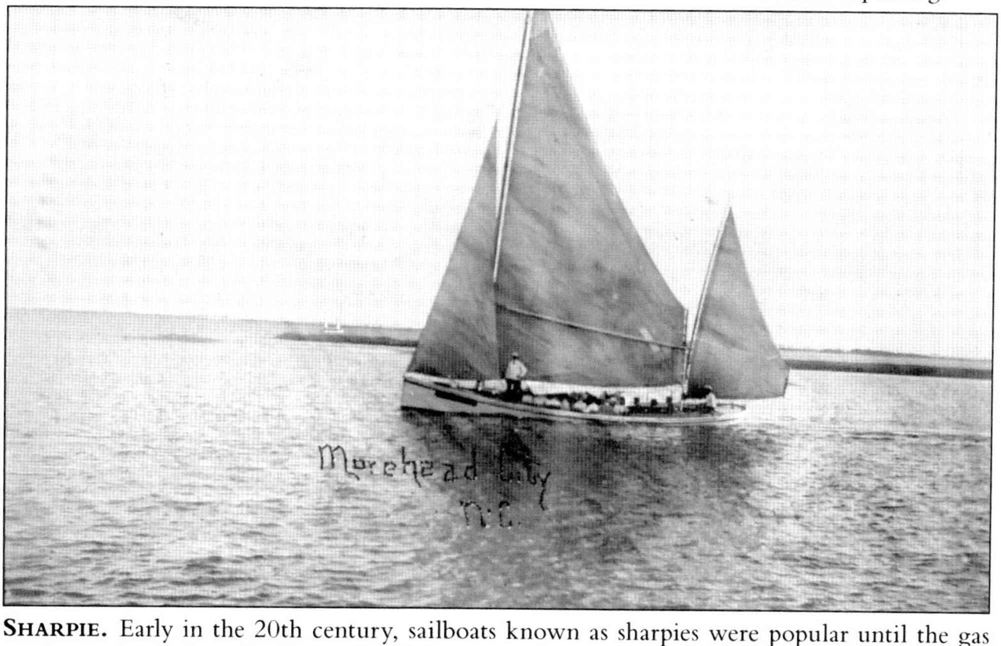

SHARPIE. Early in the 20th century, sailboats known as sharpies were popular until the gas engine replaced the sail. Also called Fair Haven sharpies after the Connecticut town where they originated, sharpies were long, flat-bottomed boats with a centerboard and one or two masts carrying sails. Many smaller sharpies catered to Atlantic Hotel patrons waiting at the dock for a sailing or fishing party. (Courtesy of Mickey Weeks.)

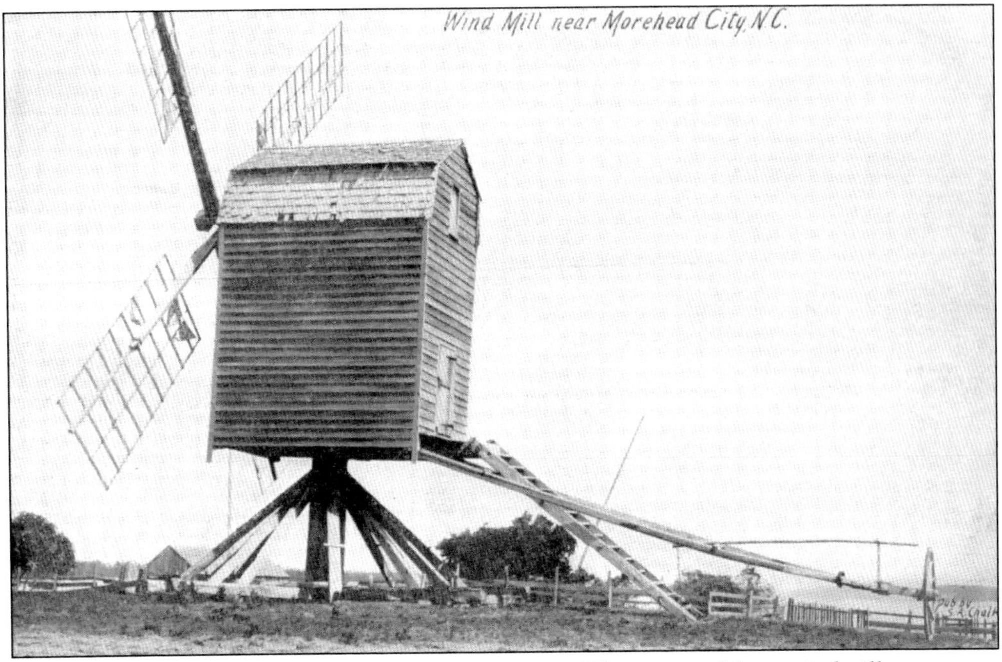

WINDMILL. Many windmills were present in the town of Morehead City during its early years. The vanes turned in the wind to generate power to grind corn or to draw water. Windmills could be seen along the shoreline, and there was one near Shepard's Point that ground grain to make flour. (Courtesy of Mickey Weeks.)

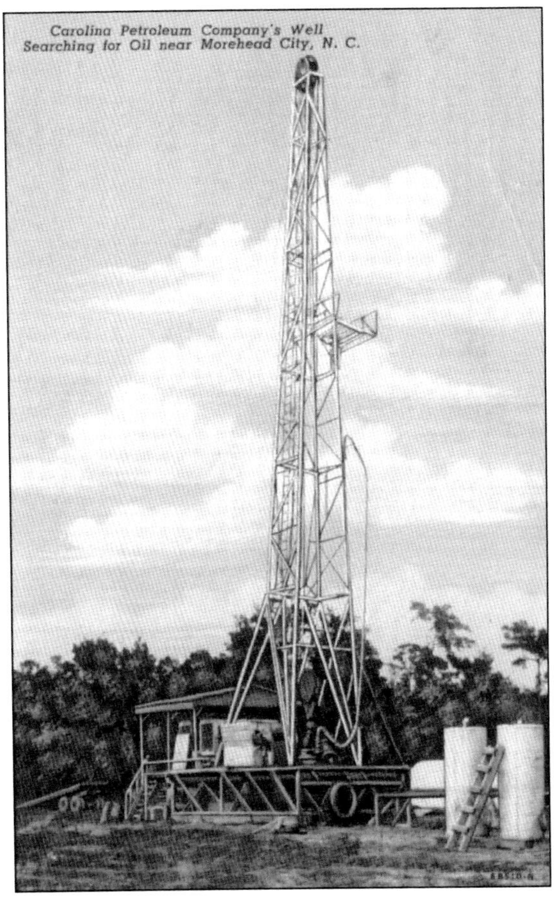

OIL DRILLING. The Carolina Petroleum Company set up temporary headquarters in Morehead City in 1946 while searching for oil in Carteret County. The company conducted extensive exploration in the Merrimon area where they drilled five wildcat wells. Though the presence of oil was indicated by some of them, it was not of sufficient quantity to warrant commercial drilling.

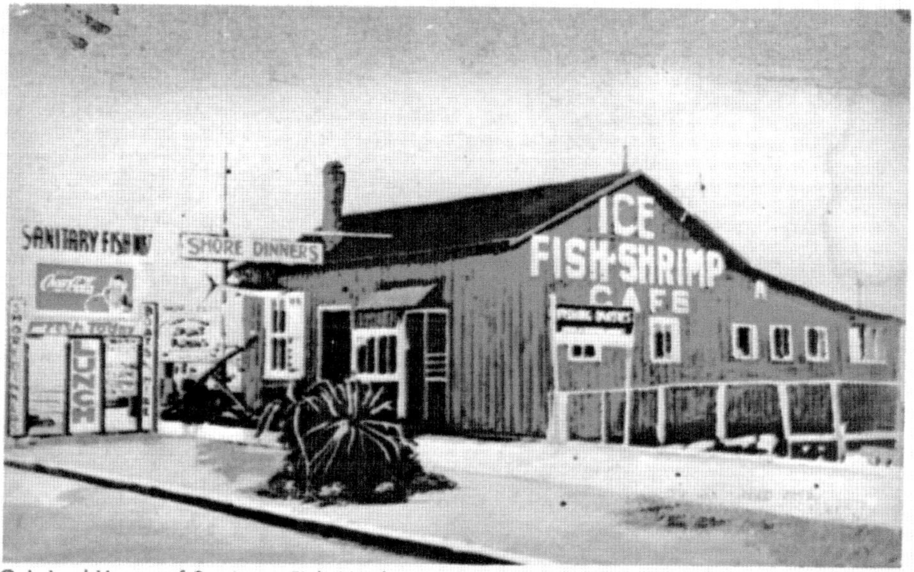

Original Home of Sanitary Fish Market and Restaurant, Morehead City, N. C. — 1938

Sanitary Fish Market and Restaurant. The first seafood restaurant on Morehead City's waterfront was established in 1938. "Captains" Tony Seamon and Ted Garner rented a small building from Charles S. Wallace for $5.50 a week with the understanding that no beer would be sold, no drinking would take place, and the place would be kept clean and neat. Thus they named it the Sanitary Fish Market. A two-burner kerosene stove and 12 stools were soon added, and the freshest catch has been served there ever since. The fish market slogan was "They slept in the ocean last night." The original building became the home of Dee Gee's Gift Shop when the new Sanitary Restaurant was built in 1949. The restaurant has been enlarged several times and now has seating for 600 people.

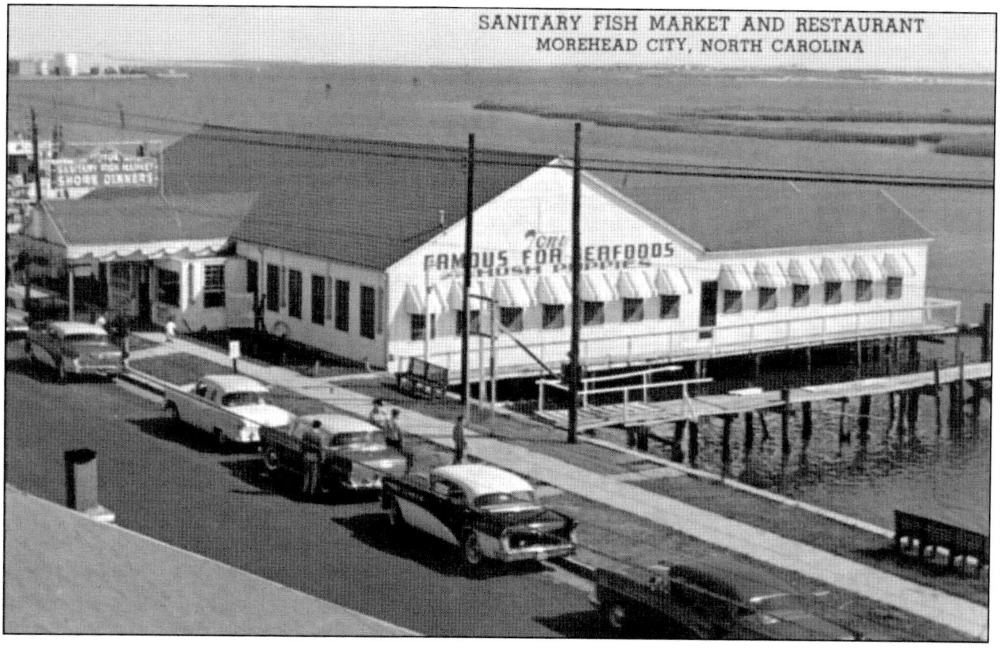

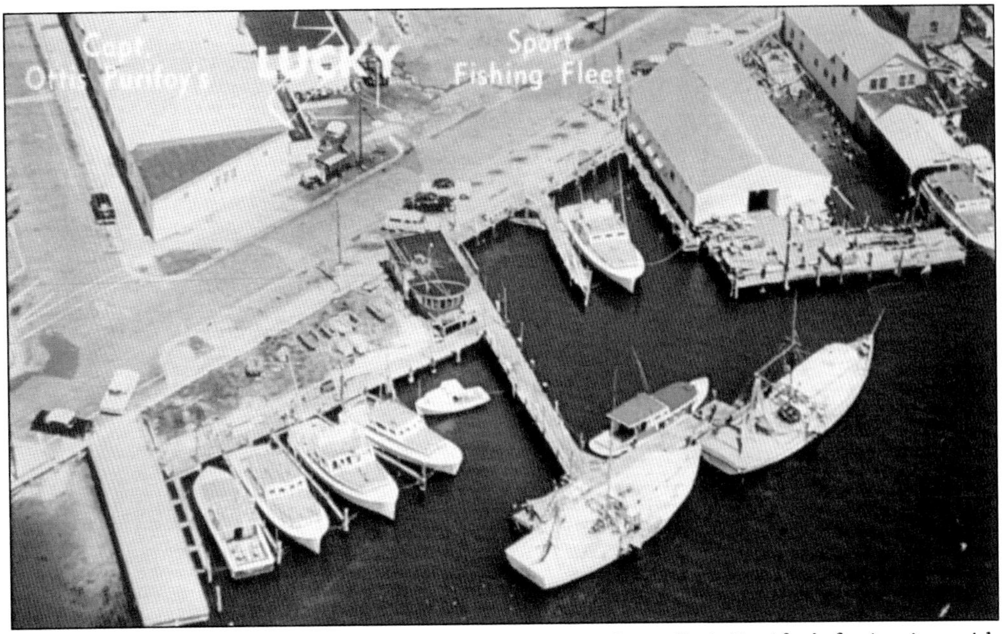

Ottis' Fish Market and Lucky 7 Fishing Fleet. Capt. Ottis Purifoy's fascination with boats and fishing began when he was a boy spending time on the waterfront. He helped pioneer sportfishing, and his Lucky 7 Fishing Fleet became well-known along the Atlantic Seaboard. Boats were chartered to tourists for deep-sea fishing. His fish market was remembered for the mermaid pictures painted on the walls.

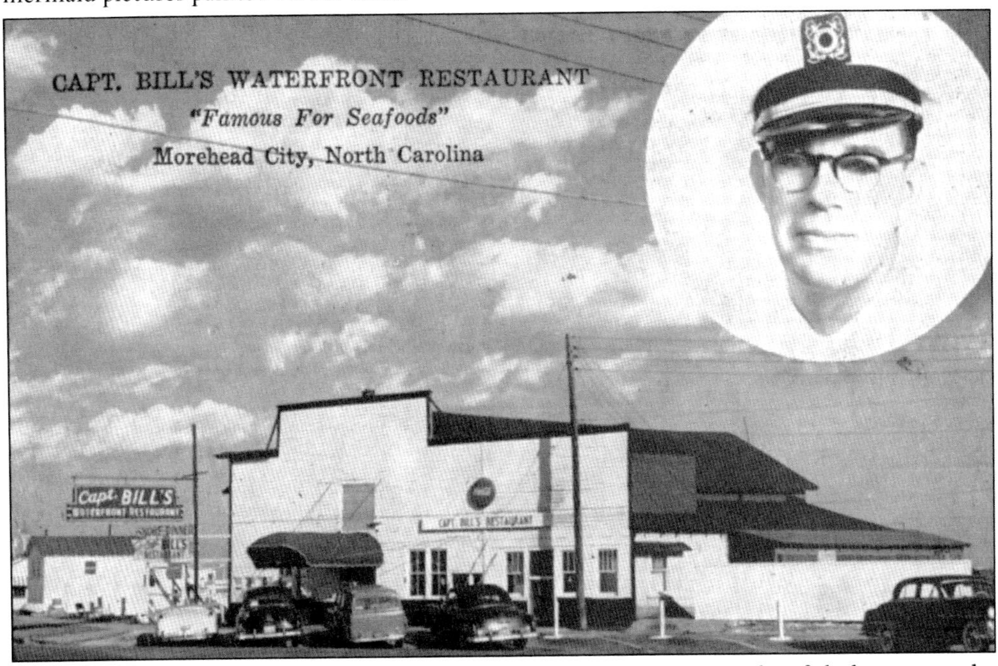

Capt. Bill's Restaurant. Capt. Bill (Headen) Ballou renovated a fish house on the waterfront and made it into an officers club during the war. He had formerly operated a restaurant on Arendell Street. Near the end of the war in 1945, he converted it into Capt. Bill's Restaurant, and it became the second most famous restaurant on the waterfront.

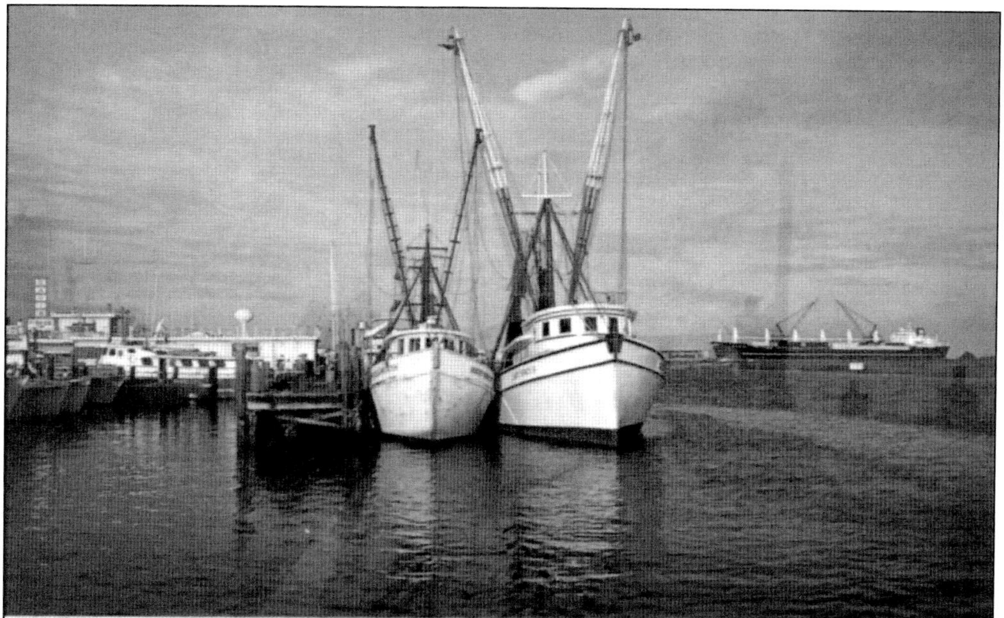

Shrimpboats bring in the catch of the day — *Morehead City, N. C.*

SHRIMP BOATS. Shrimp boats like these docked in front of Davis Fish Company are prevalent along the waterfronts of the county. It is hard to imagine that before the 1940s, shrimp were not actively fished. In fact, they were thrown back as trash when they were caught. With the advent of the trawler in the 1920s, shrimp began to be caught in large numbers and an important industry was born.

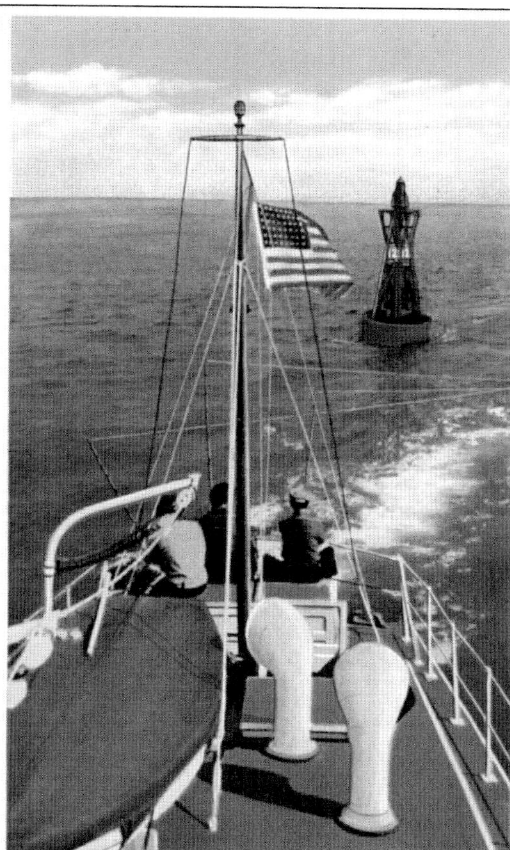

Fishing in the Gulf Stream, near Morehead City, N. C. 9A904

FISHING IN THE GULF STREAM. Morehead City is famous for its deep-sea fishing, and along the waterfront, there are many charter boats for hire. Sportsmen from across the country come to fish in the Gulf Stream and try their skills against the many large game fish found in the Atlantic Ocean.

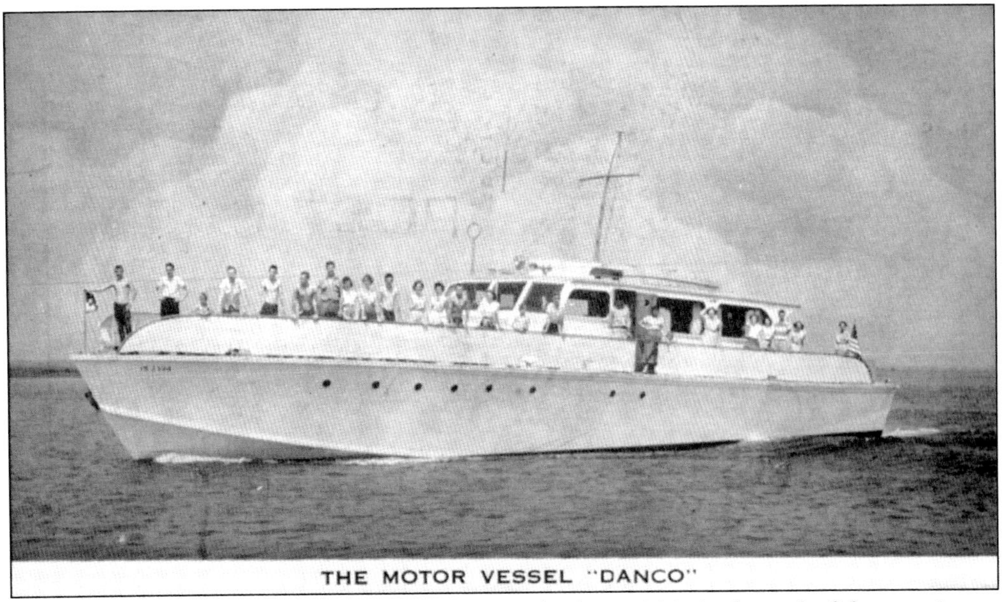

DANCO. The *Danco* was a World War II PT boat built in 1945. At the end of the war, it was purchased by a Shelby businessman and converted into a head boat. On the first run in 1953, it carried 20 passengers with a fare of $6 for adults and $3 for those less than 12 years old. The first captain of the party boat was Teen Piner.

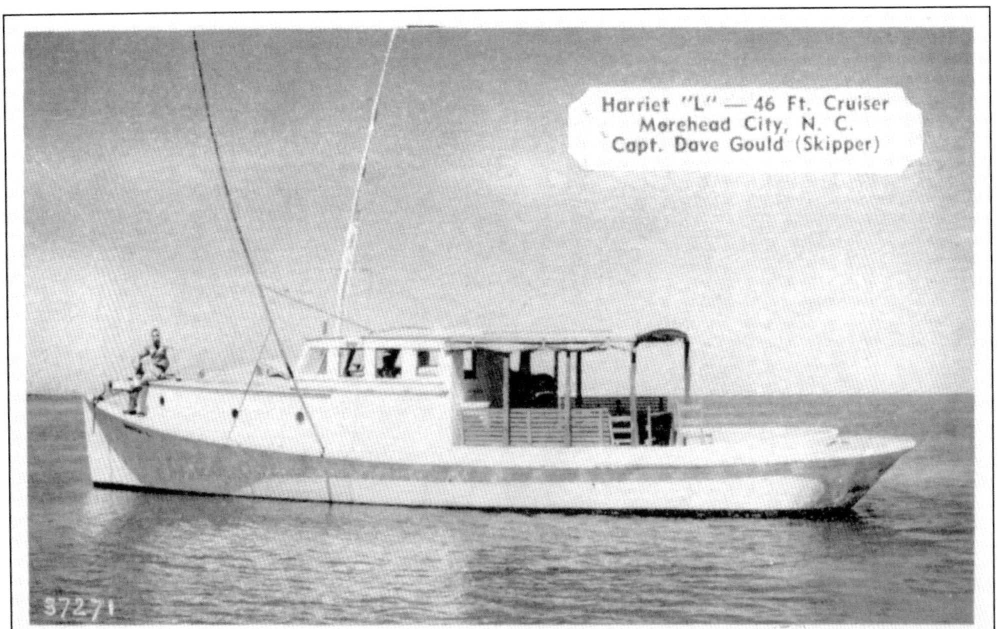

HARRIET **"L."** Among the many party boats on the waterfront was the 46-foot charter boat *Harriet "L"* captained by Dave Gould. The postcard states, "We are in business for your pleasure." Services offered were Gulf Stream fishing, inshore fishing, ship-to-shore radio, and moonlight sails. (Courtesy of Mickey Weeks.)

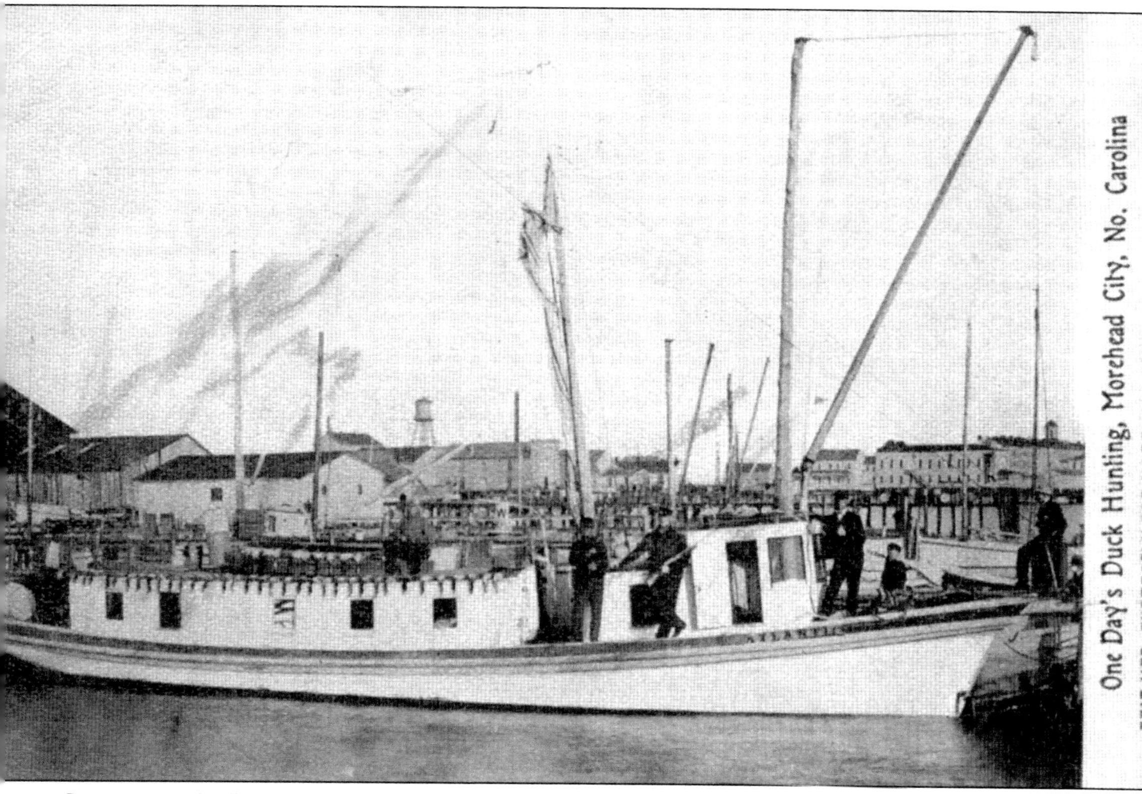

SPORTSMAN'S PARADISE. With the construction of large resort hotels such as the Atlantic Hotel in the late 1800s, Northern sportsman began to become aware of the excellent hunting and fishing in Carteret County. The large numbers of migratory waterfowl in particular attracted hunters to the area. Local brochures began advertising Beaufort and Morehead City as a sportsman's playground, stating no finer hunting could be found anywhere. Down East became a gateway to the hunting grounds, and hunting lodges began to dot the area. Duck blinds were a common site in Core Sound. Local guides would take hunting parties to such places as Portsmouth Lodge, Hog Island Hunting Club, Davis Ridge Hunting Lodge, and the Harbor Island Club. Built on small islands, these clubs were perfect launching points for guided hunts. Waterfowl were so plentiful in the early 1900s that 100 or more could be taken in a single day's hunt. However, by the mid-1950s, hunting began to wane with the decline in waterfowl populations because of over-hunting. (Courtesy of Mickey Weeks.)

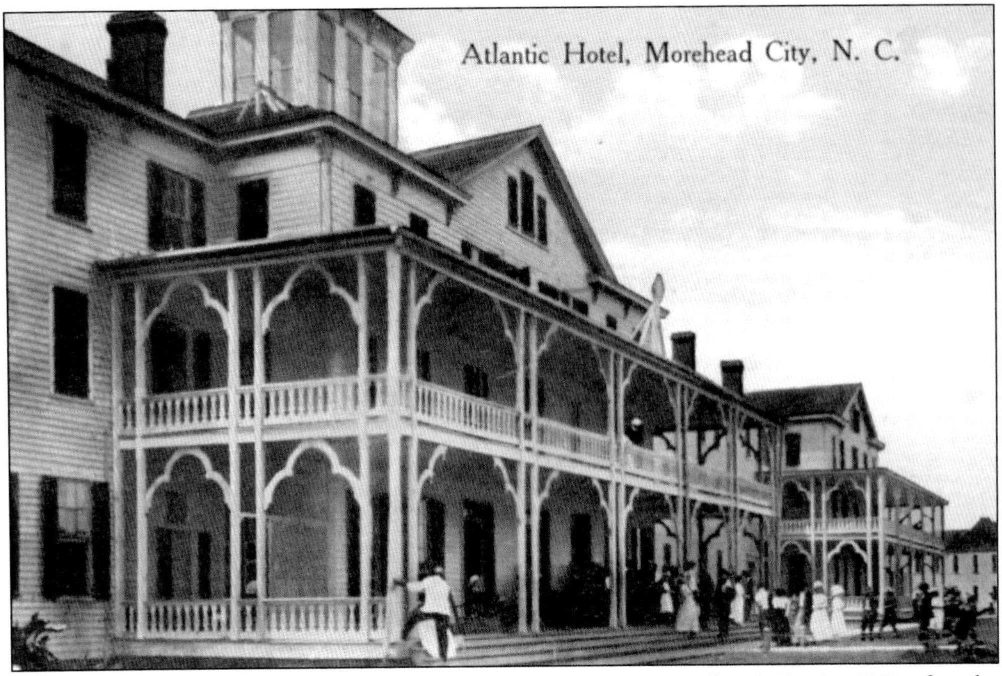

NEW ATLANTIC HOTEL. The Atlantic Hotel was rebuilt in Morehead City in 1883 after the original hotel in Beaufort was destroyed by the 1879 hurricane. Few resorts along the Atlantic Seaboard could match the elegance and luxury of the "Summer Capital of the State." The hotel was erected near the end of the railroad line and had a covered platform with a boardwalk to the entrance for the arriving guests. The political and societal elite from all over the South were treated to some of the greatest social events ever held in the state. The three-story wooden hotel had double porches across the front, two wings extending from the rear toward the sound, and piers with bathhouses for men and women.

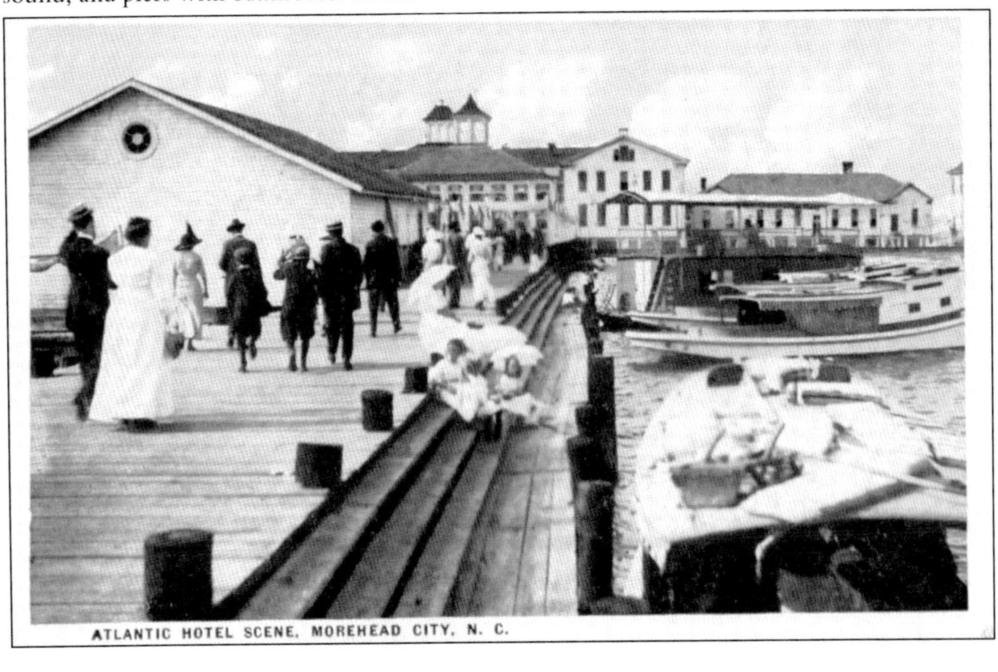

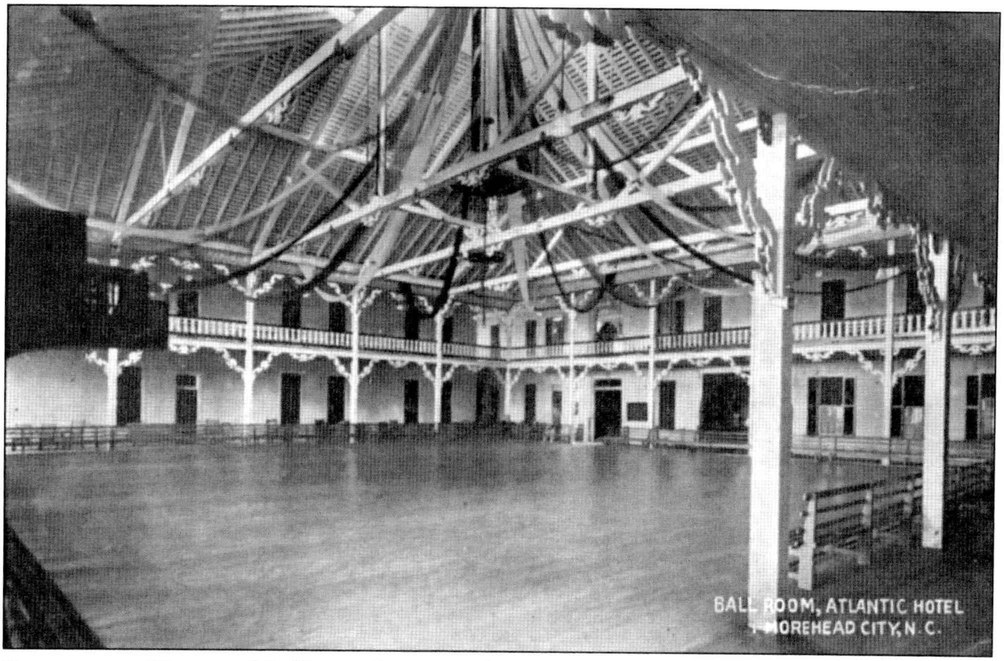

BALLROOM. The grand ballroom between the two wings was brilliantly lit by a revolving crystal ball light fixture with electricity from the hotel's own electric light plant. The best orchestras were hired by the hotel to play for the cotillions and fancy dress balls. Balconies, which seated observers, were often filled. Camp Glenn soldiers were entertained at a regiment ball at the end of each two-week summer session in 1912.

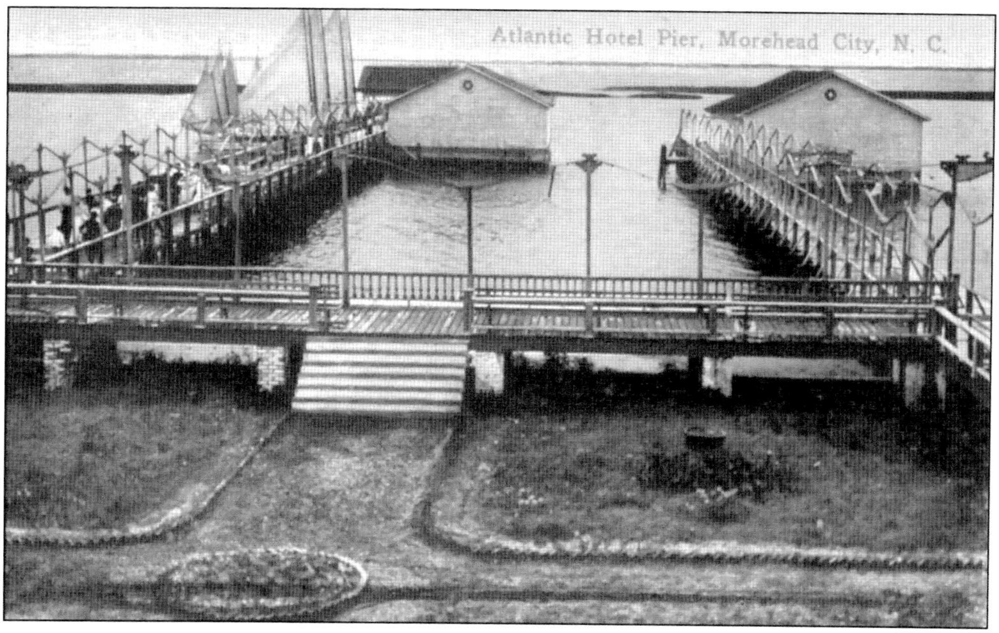

ATLANTIC HOTEL PIERS. Long 16-foot-wide piers extended out over the sound. Hotel-owned sharpies as well as other boats for hire carried guests to Bogue Banks for surf bathing. Capt. Teen Piner with his sharpie, *Mamie C. Daniels*, became the favorite boatman at the hotel. Dressing rooms and beach pavilions were provided on the banks for the comfort of the guests.

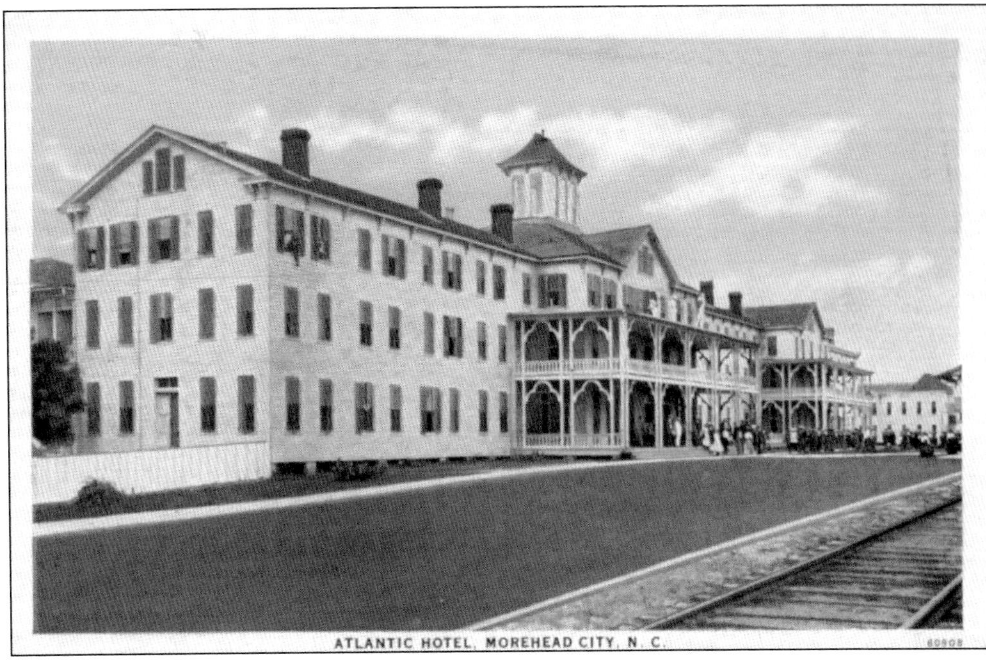

ATLANTIC HOTEL. A cupola on top of the hotel housed a large conservatory where guests could enjoy a view. The cupola also had a light that could be seen several miles out at sea. There were 233 rooms, and the dining room could seat 300. The hotel offered electric lights; an enormous ballroom; writing, reading, and smoking rooms; a telegraph; and a long-distance telephone office. The season for the hotel was from July through Labor Day. The top postcard shows the proximity of the railroad tracks to the hotel, and to the right of the hotel is the North Carolina Teachers' Assembly Building. In 1933, a fire destroyed the hotel.

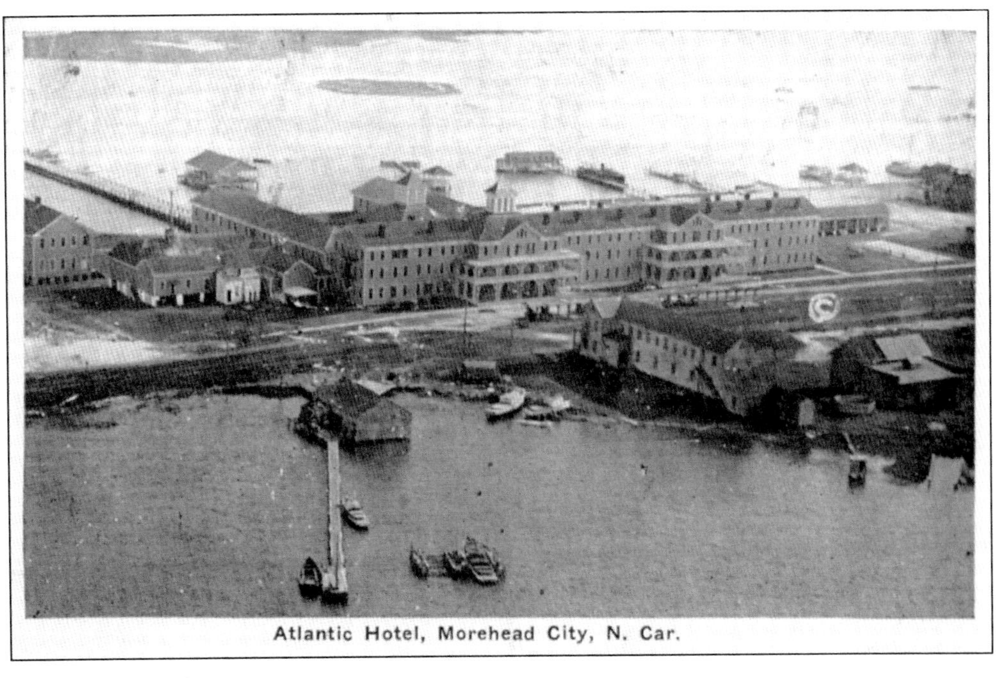

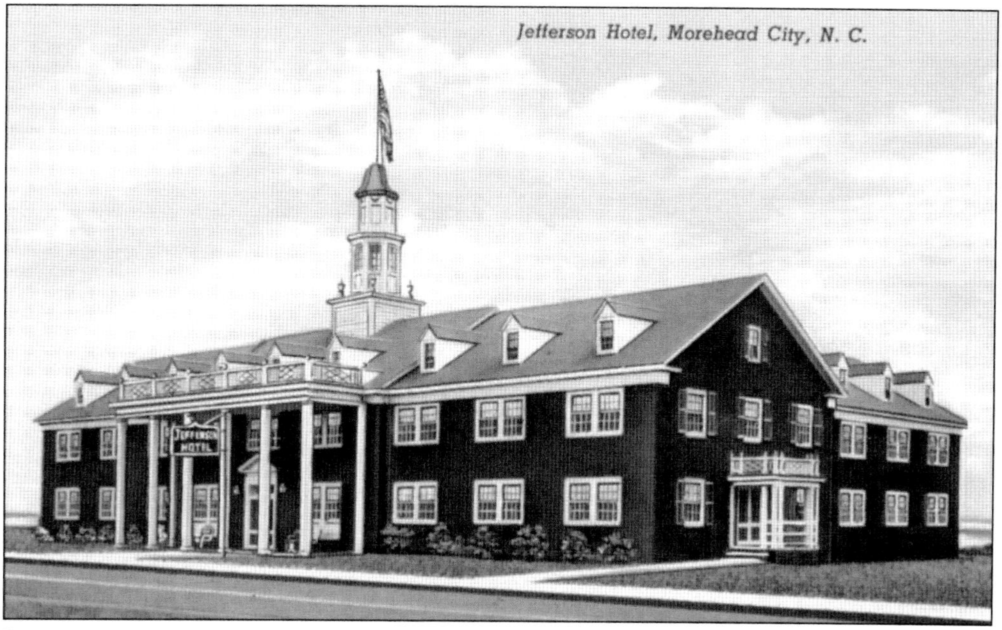

JEFFERSON HOTEL. Just west of the former Atlantic Hotel stood the Jefferson Hotel. Before the hotel was built in the 1940s, a carnival would set up a Ferris wheel and merry-go-round on the corner. The North Carolina Teachers' Assembly, built in 1888, stood close to this area and housed the association's meetings until 1892 and then operated as a school for three years. It was later torn down in 1934.

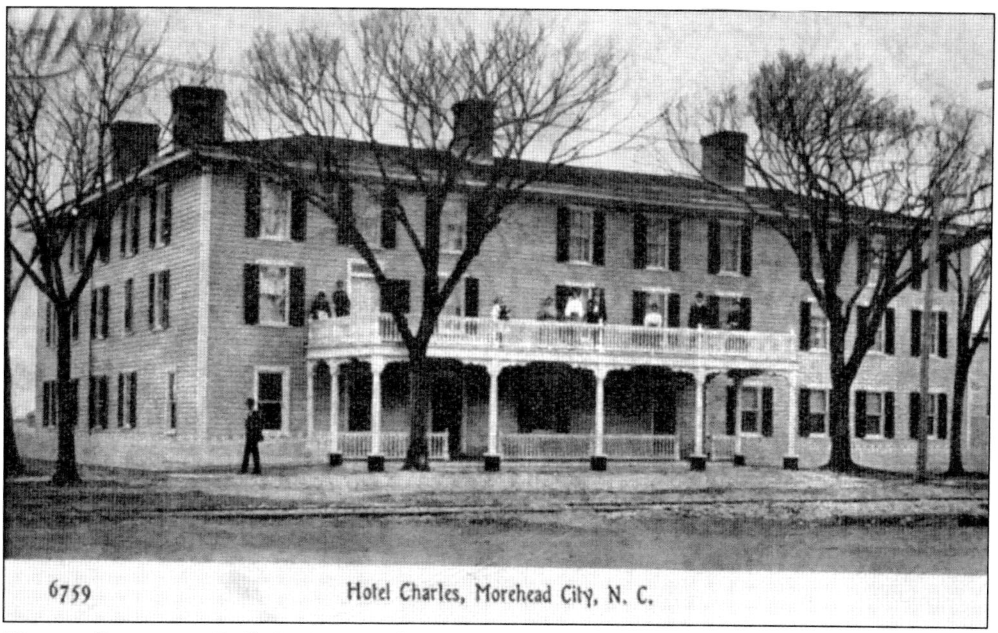

HOTEL CHARLES. Built in 1860 and originally know as the Macon House, the three-story hotel was the first hotel in Morehead City. It stood on the corner of Ninth and Arendell Streets and served as a Union hospital and officers' quarters during the Civil War. Gen. U. S. Grant and Gen. William Tecumseh Sherman were guests of the hotel. It became the Hotel Charles in 1907 when purchased by Charles S. Wallace.

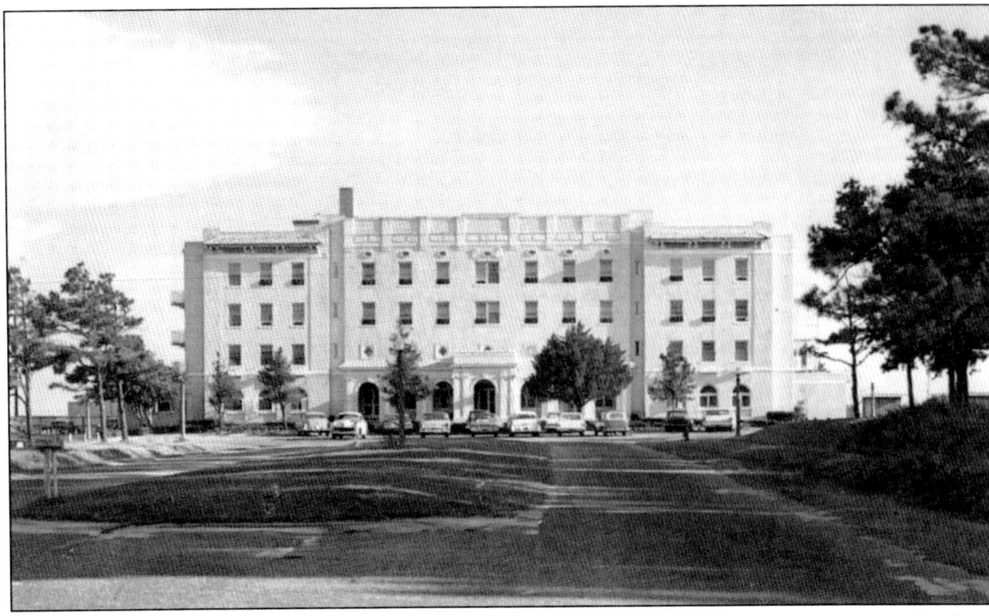

MOREHEAD VILLA HOTEL. The four-story luxury hotel west of Morehead City was built on a bluff overlooking Bogue Sound and the Intracoastal Waterway. It took nearly 100 days and $300,000 to complete and opened in 1926. The hotel had an impressive two-lane road with a grassed median leading to the front entrance. "Cool comfortable rooms with baths" were advertised in 1937 at $1.50 to $3 a night.

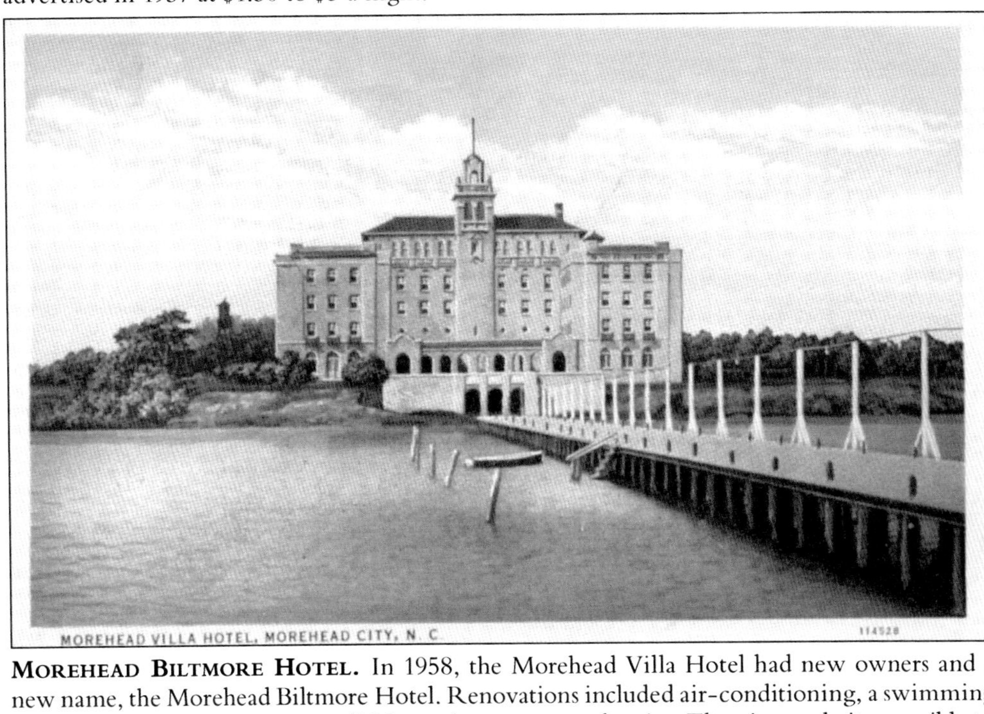

MOREHEAD BILTMORE HOTEL. In 1958, the Morehead Villa Hotel had new owners and a new name, the Morehead Biltmore Hotel. Renovations included air-conditioning, a swimming pool, putting green, Ping Pong, fishing, a boat ramp, and a pier. The pier made it accessible to yachting guests. The hotel was destroyed by a fire in 1969. The site is now the location of the Bluffs townhouses.

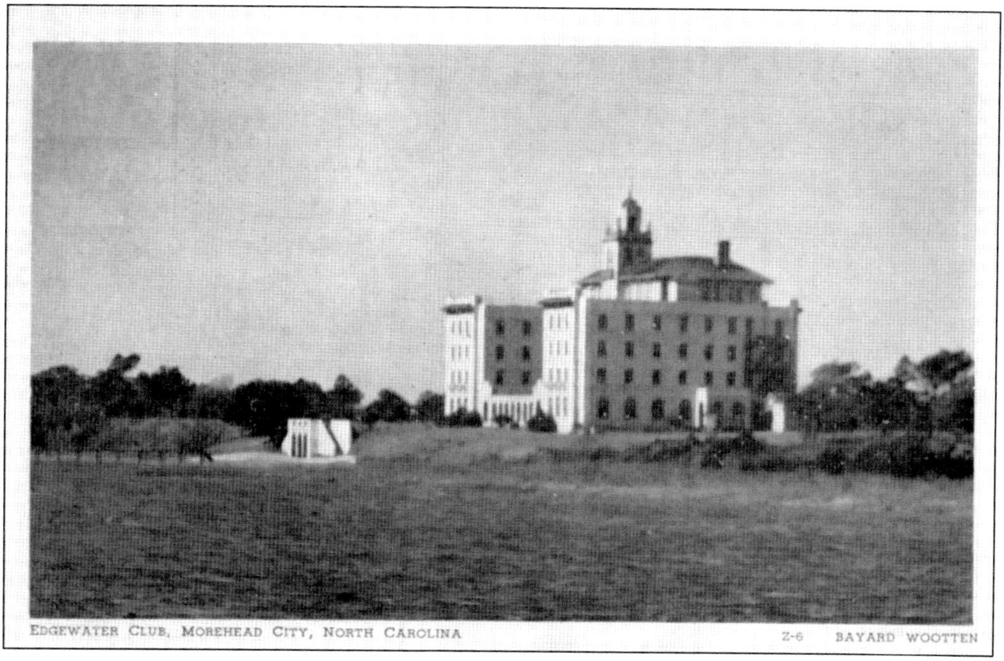

EDGEWATER CLUB. The Edgewater Club was previously known as the Villa Hotel and later as the Morehead Biltmore Hotel. It was on a bluff overlooking Bogue Sound west of Morehead. The back of the postcard advertises, "Open to non-members June to September, on Intracoastal Waterway and near beautiful Atlantic Beach." Also noted are the Edgewater Club's schooners *Buccaneer* and *Flying Dolphin*. (Courtesy of Mickey Weeks.)

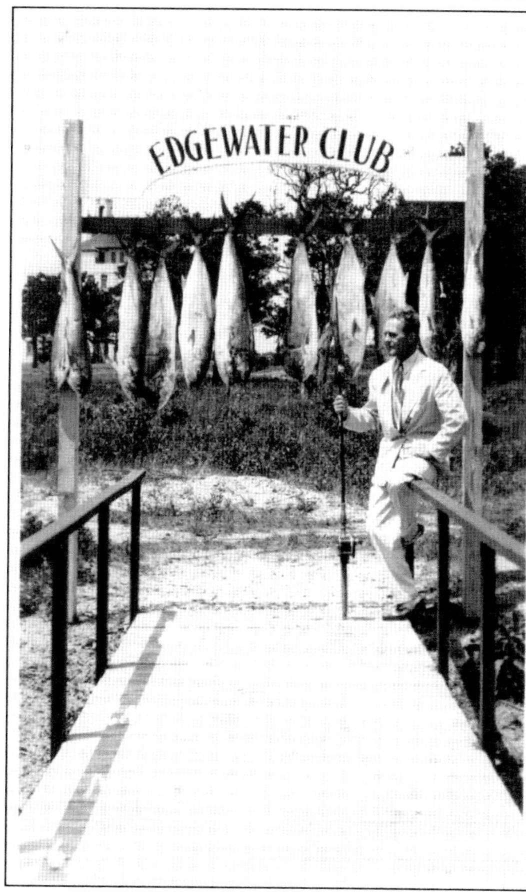

EDGEWATER CLUB FISHING. The Edgewater Club, built on a high natural bluff, had a wide view and accessibility to Bogue Sound. This postcard mailed in 1935 advertised, "Largest Amberjack 28 lbs., largest Dolphin 22 lbs., Gulf Stream fishing is now especially attractive. We will be pleased to assist in effecting arrangements for your trip to the Stream." (Courtesy of Mickey Weeks.)

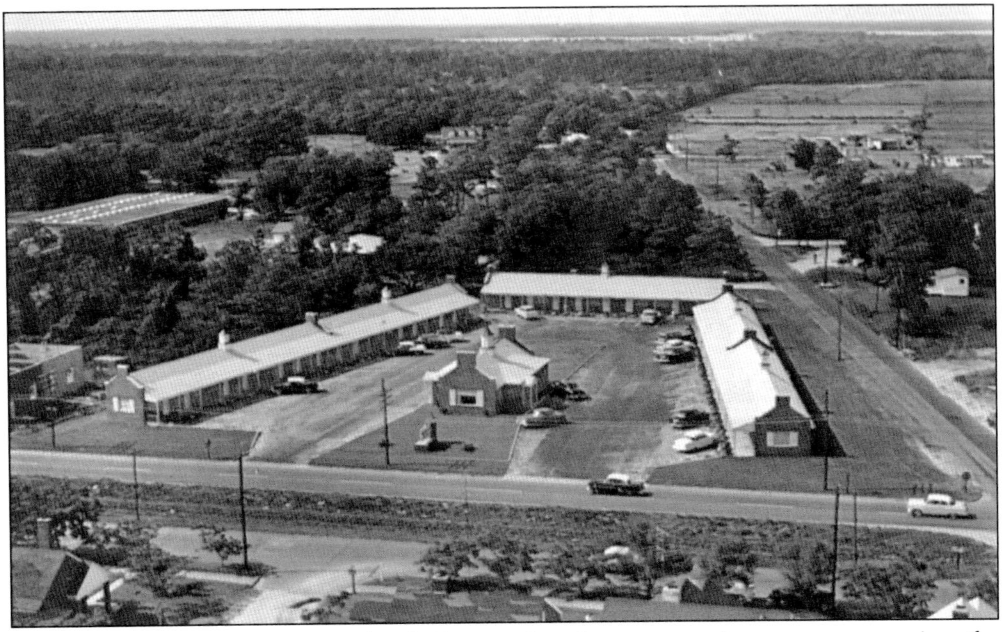

Bud Dixon's Motel. As Morehead City continued to grow and attract more tourists, the need for accommodations increased. Motor hotels, or motels, were built and provided direct access to lodging with guests being able to drive right up to their rooms. Bud Dixon's Motel was opened in 1955 by Bud Dixon, who was elected mayor in 1969. It is the oldest in town and is now named Morehead Motor Inn.

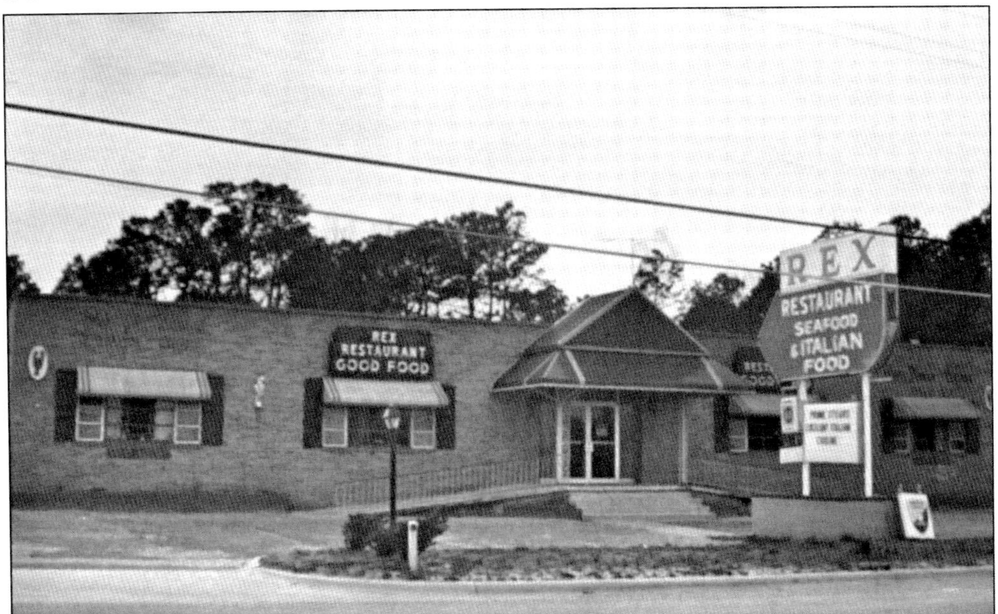

Rex Restaurant. The Rex Restaurants located in Morehead City and Atlantic Beach were owned and operated by the Marino family, who moved from Jacksonville in 1948. The restaurants specialized in Italian food. The Morehead City building, a new, white asbestos-shingle building, was destroyed by a fire in the 1950s. The brick restaurant shown in the postcard replaced it and remained in business until 1997.

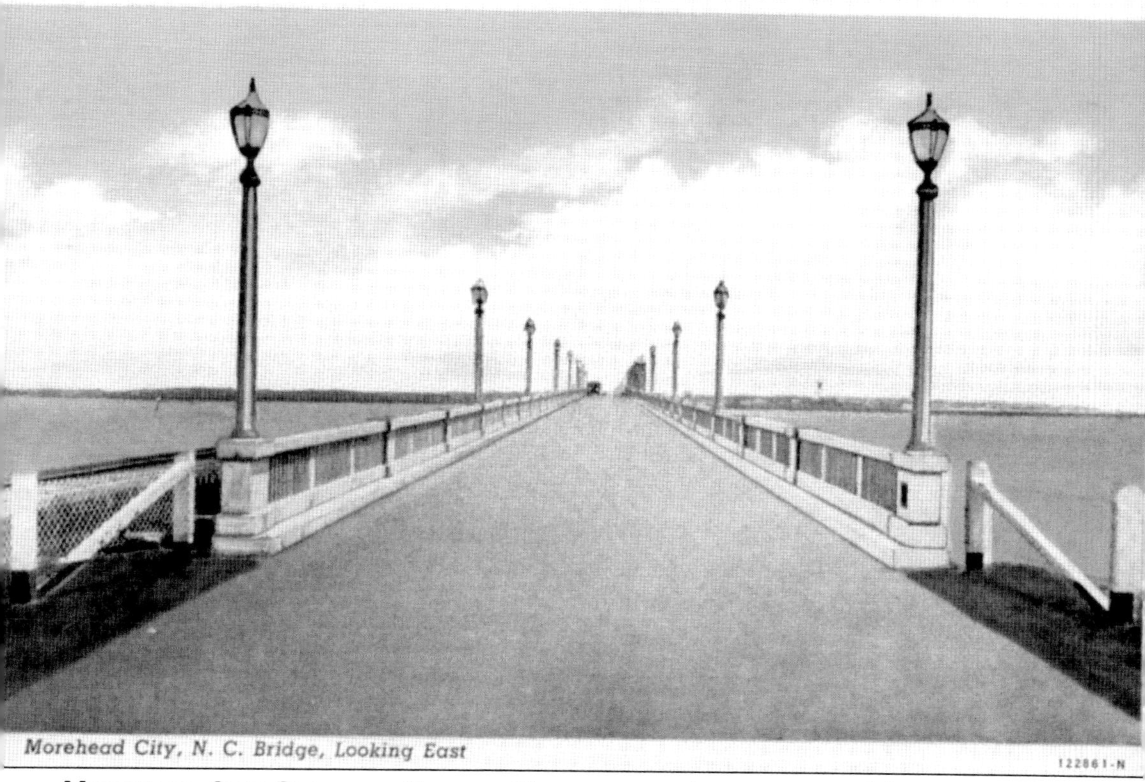

MOREHEAD CITY–BEAUFORT BRIDGE. The western and eastern parts of the county were connected when the two-year bridge project was completed in November 1927. The causeway and bridge were the state's most expensive bridge projects and cost $750,000. The 285 concrete pilings were made at the shipyard plant at Pier One. Fill between the bridges was made by a hydraulic dredge. The two bascule bridges were operated by electricity and opened in the middle. There were sidewalks for pedestrians and steel railings. One hundred and twelve illuminating standards lit the bridges. The bridge was 2.218 miles long from the Atlantic Hotel in Morehead City to Ann Street in Beaufort. An article in the *Beaufort News* stated, "Now that the bridge is a realization and not a dream, full advantage should be taken to use it as an important accessory in the up building of friendship between the two neighboring towns and to bring the rest of Carteret County nearer to the outside world."

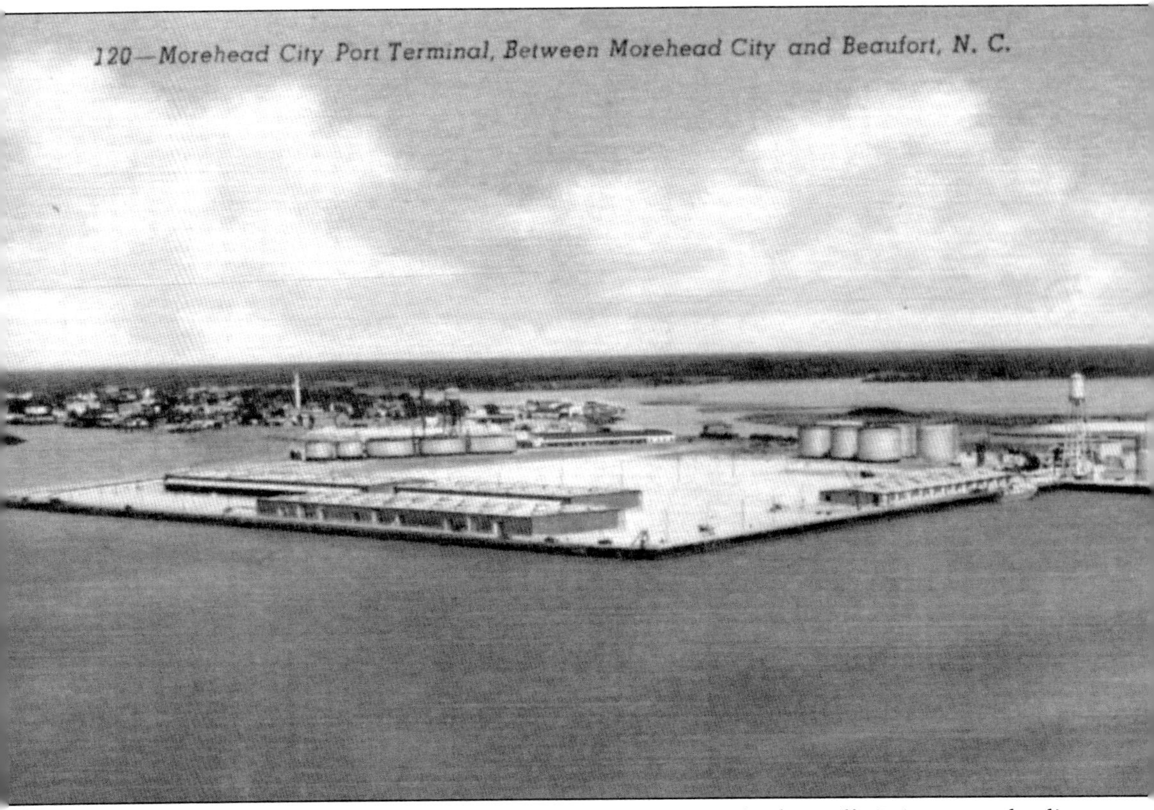

PORT TERMINAL. Long before Morehead City was created, Shepard's Point was a landing and loading point for boats. In 1857, lots were offered for sale and construction started on Pier One. Railroad tracks led to the wharf and warehouse, making loading and unloading directly from railroad cars possible. The Civil War put a stop to shipments from the port when it was taken over by Federal troops. The Northern and Southern Railroad leased the pier from 1904 to 1907 and stopped shipments, rerouting them to Norfolk. The pier was left to rot. The Point was used during World War I as a shipyard for the government. During the Depression, the Public Works Administration financed the construction of the Morehead City Port Terminal. The terminal was completed and the first ship docked in 1936. The first foreign cargo also arrived that year. The port was leased by the navy in World War II. In 1949, the port was acquired by the State Ports Authority.

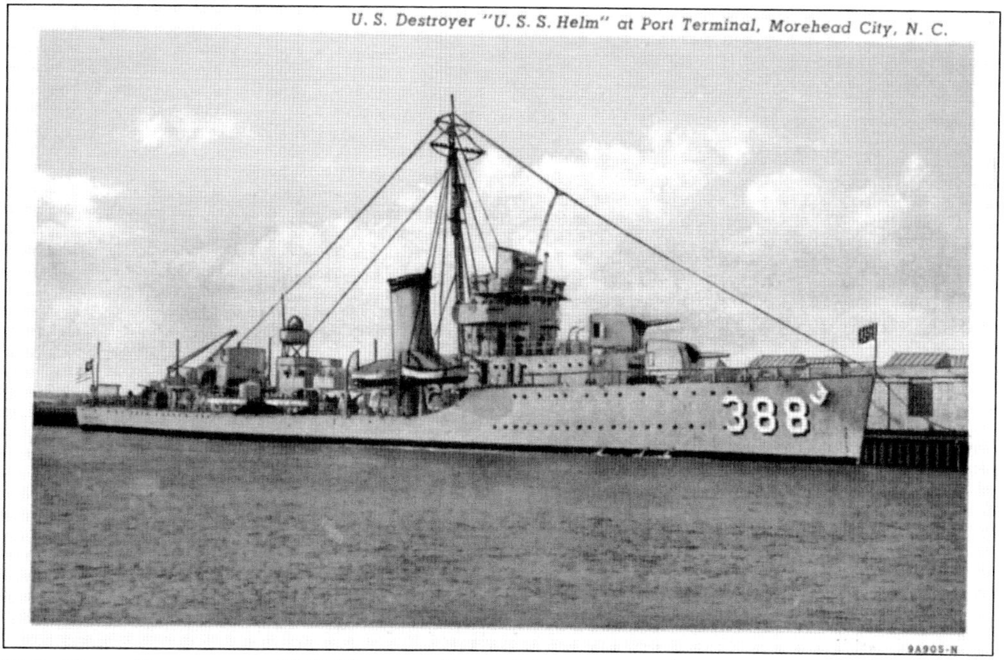

U.S. NAVY DESTROYER USS *HELM* AT PORT TERMINAL. The Morehead City Port, one of two deepwater ports in North Carolina, has been a frequent stop for U.S. Coast Guard cutters and U.S. Naval warships. It serves as the port of embarkation for the marines stationed at Camp Lejeune and Cherry Point Marine Air Station.

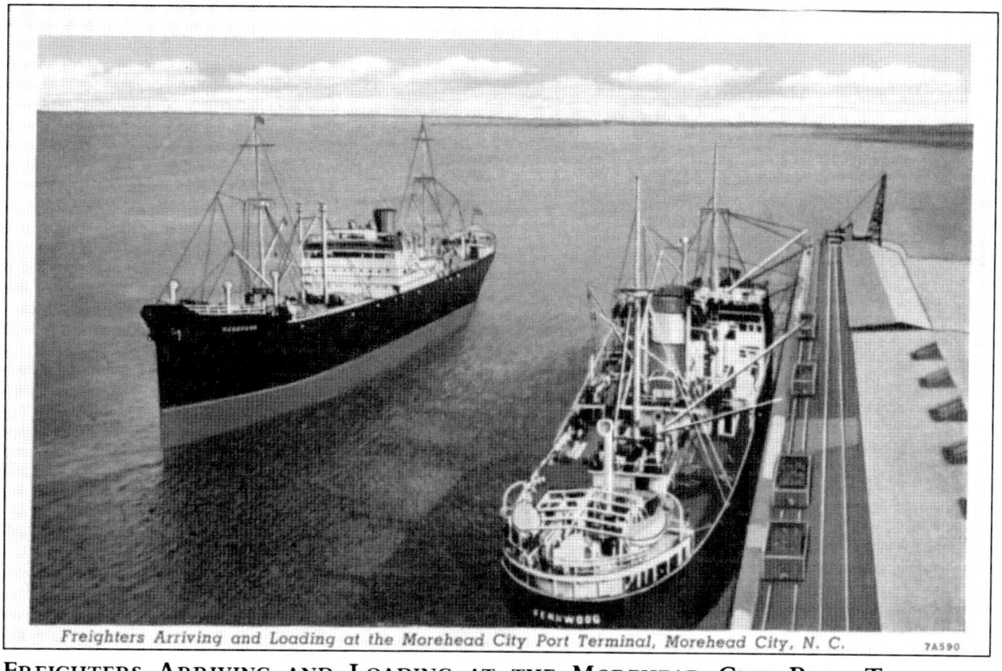

FREIGHTERS ARRIVING AND LOADING AT THE MOREHEAD CITY PORT TERMINAL. The first cargo leaving from the port was scrap iron and steel loaded on the SS *Fernwood* headed for Japan in 1937. The *Fernwood* is shown next to the pier in the postcard. The port can accommodate several ships at the same time and is valuable for both export and import.

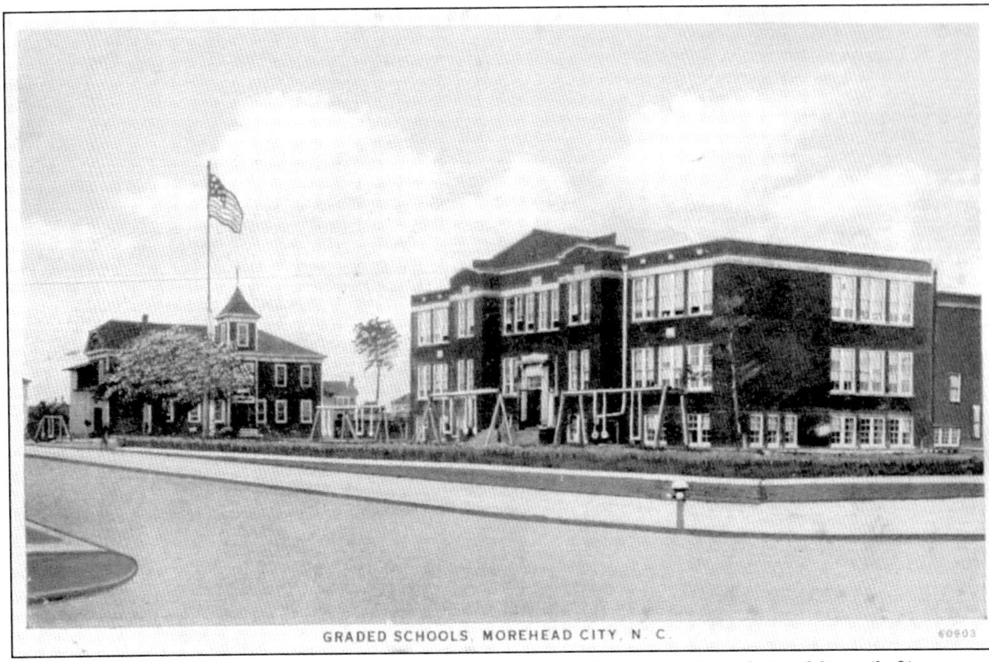

GRADED SCHOOL. In 1909, the Atlantic Institute and the Harry North Building (left) opened as Morehead City Graded School (right), the first free school in town. Diplomas were given for the first time for completion of the ninth grade. A new brick school opened in 1921 on the site, and the 11th grade was added in that school year. In 1928, it was destroyed by fire, but records were saved and only one day of school was lost. Commencement was held in the City Theater. In 1930, the new Charles S. Wallace School opened. The 12th grade was added for the 1945 school year. Over the years, the school saw the addition of a gym, cafeteria, and library. The class of 1964 was the last to graduate from this school. (Above, courtesy of Mickey Weeks.)

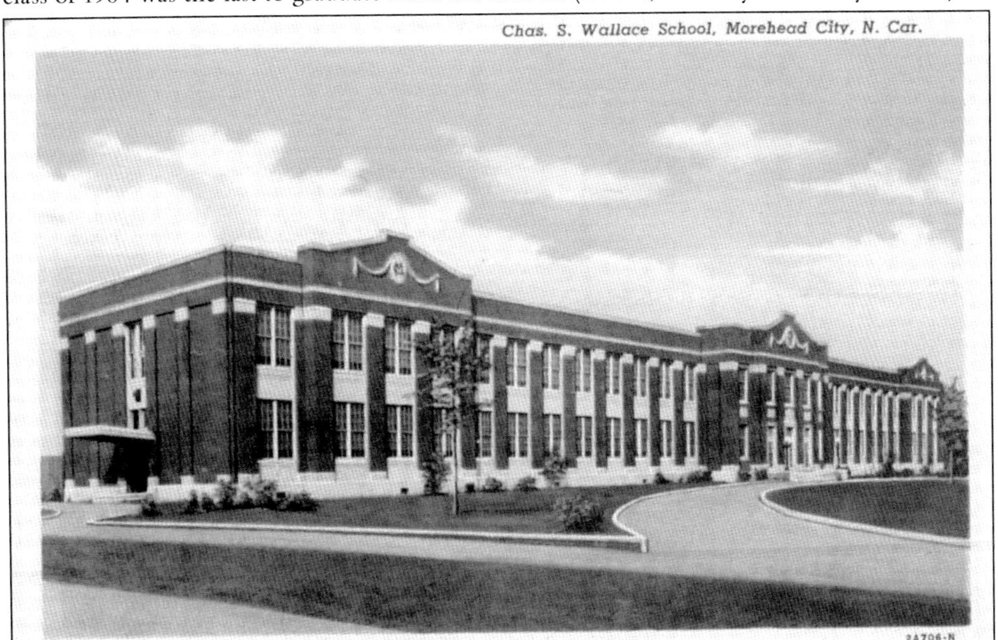

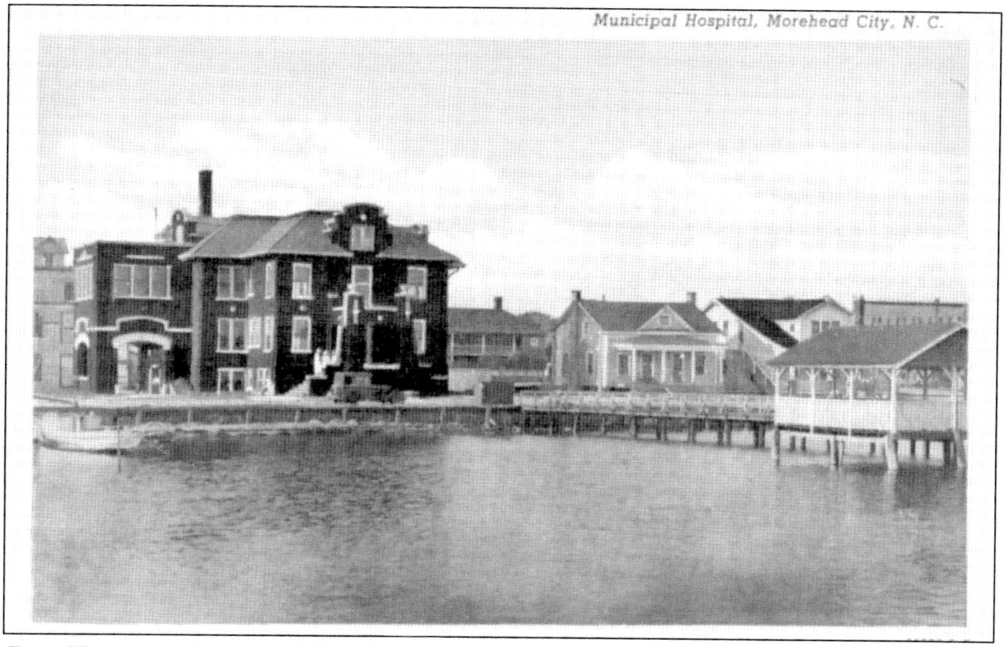

CITY HOSPITAL. Morehead City Hospital Company opened in 1912 through the efforts of Dr. Ben Royal shortly after he completed his education. The original seven-bed hospital on the second floor of the Paragon Building increased to 14 beds. Royal obtained financing to build a new hospital on the corner of Ninth and Shepard Streets. The 28-bed hospital was considered by many to be too large for the community. Edith Broadway, known for her devotion to duty, served as head nurse for both hospitals until her retirement in 1936. A nurse's training school operated by the hospital in the 1920s graduated 10 nurses from the program. Instructors were Royal, Dr. Headen, Dr. K. P. B. Bonner, and Broadway. In 1957, Royal was named Morehead City's Citizen-of-the-Century.

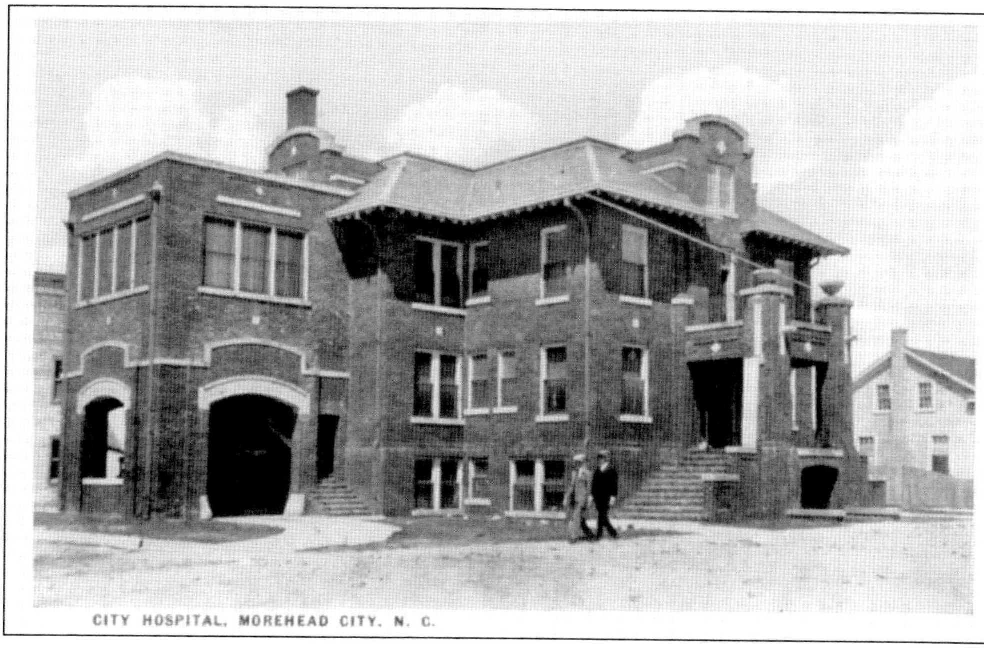

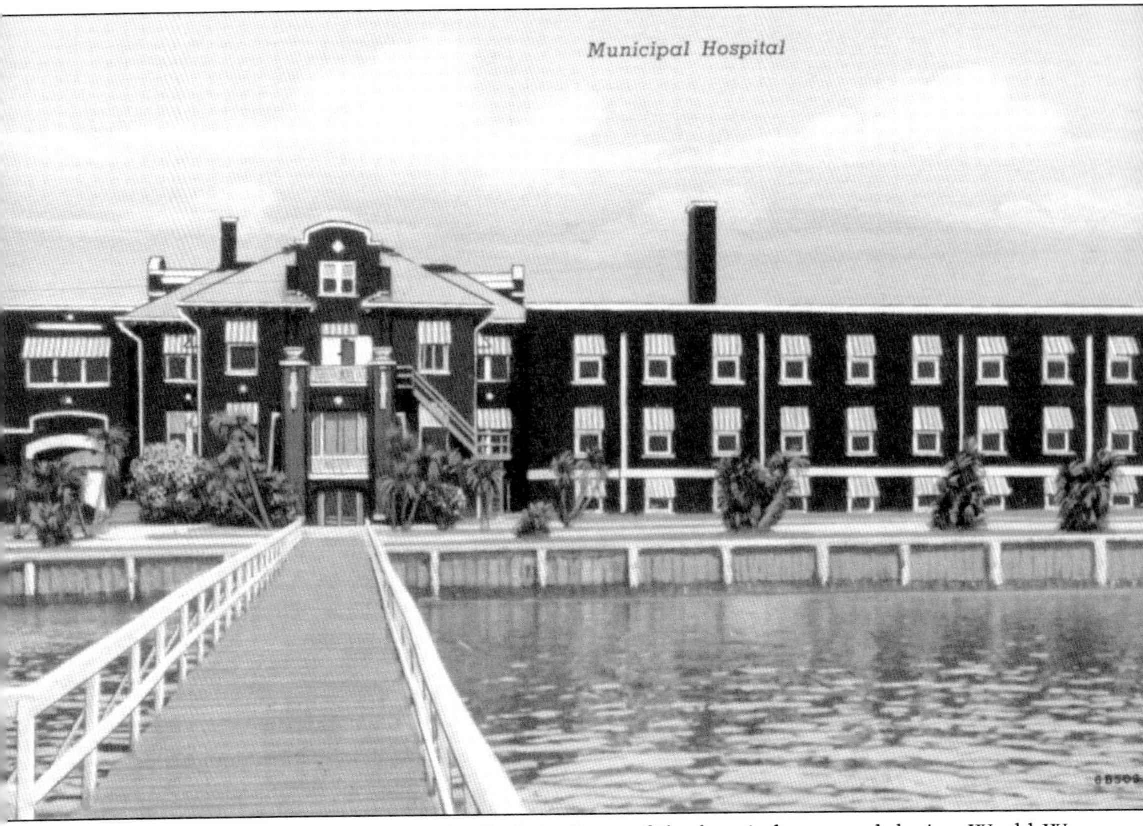

MOREHEAD CITY HOSPITAL. The dock in front of the hospital was used during World War II in the Battle of the Atlantic to bring survivors in from vessels sunk offshore. Sometimes as many as three boatloads were brought in a day. Crowded conditions prompted the government to build a 32-bed annex, which was never used for the war because submarine warfare soon ended. In 1943, the Coast Guard took over use of the annex for its sick bay. Staffed by a graduate nurse and enlisted men, it was used for about 18 months. During this time, the community was called on to contribute items for a recreation room for the servicemen to use while they convalesced. After the Coast Guard left, the annex was converted into a maternity ward and saw the birth of about 800 babies. An east wing added in 1946 and a large renovation and expansion in 1956 brought the hospital to 75 beds.

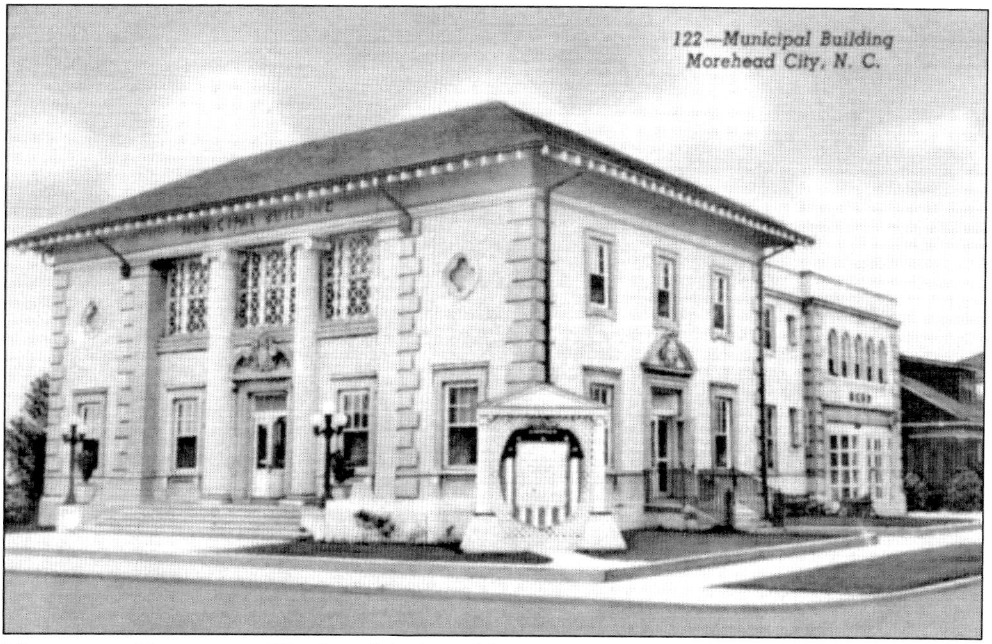

MUNICIPAL BUILDING. The Municipal Building was built in 1926 at south Eighth Street on land that was created when the seawall was built. It served as offices for the town and police department. The Day-Fulford Memorial is on the southeast corner, and the Veterans Monument is seen on the northeast corner of the building.

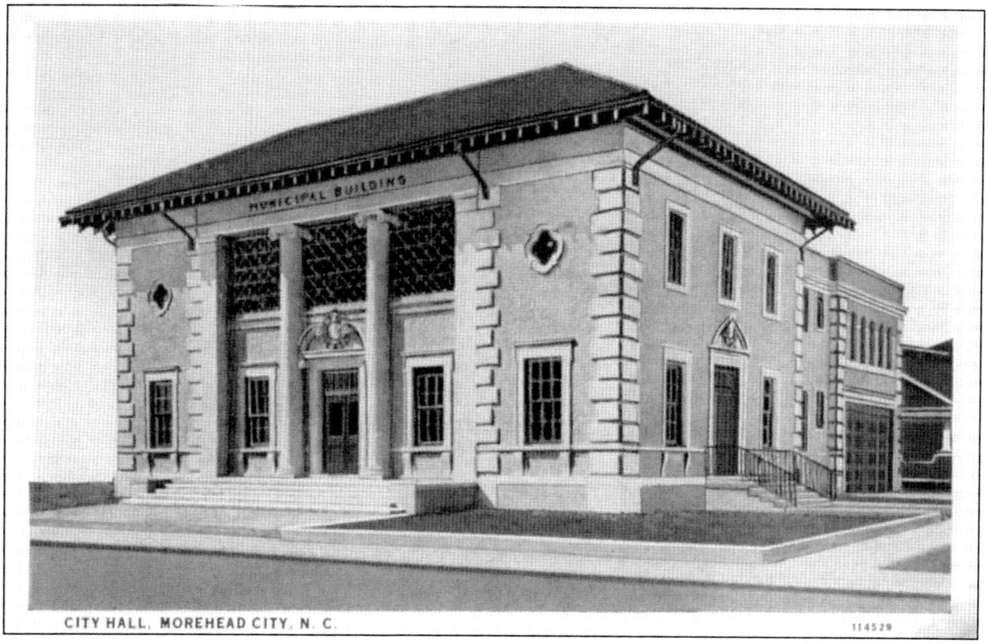

FIRE STATION. Before the water system was installed in 1910, most of the town buildings were wood and vulnerable to fires. The town progressed from a bucket brigade to a volunteer fire department with an alarm system and a motor-driven fire truck by 1926. The fire station, part of the Municipal Building with doors opening on the west side, is seen on the right of the postcard.

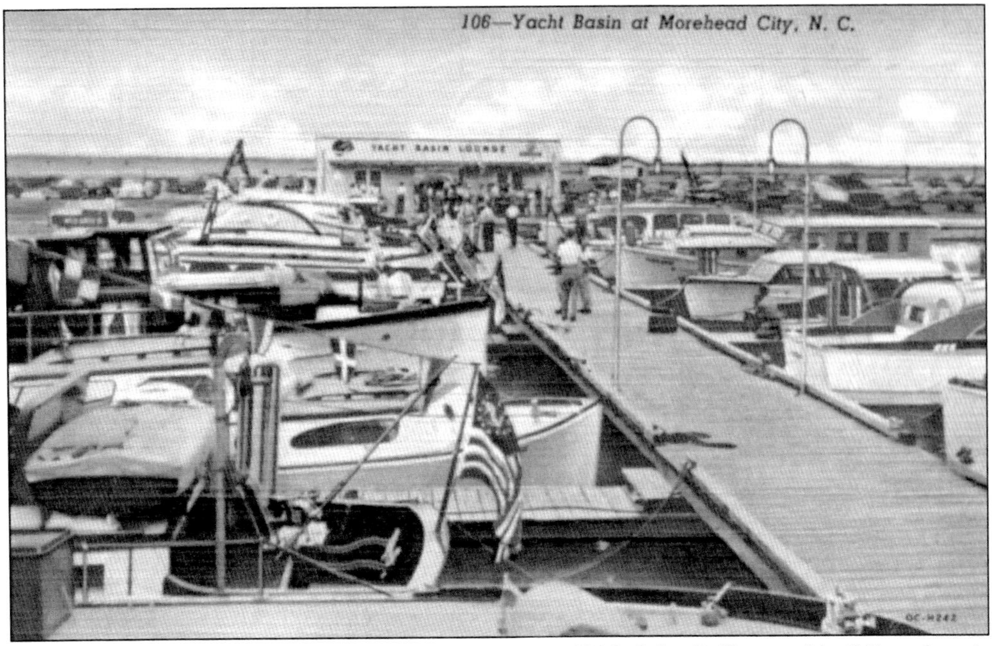

BELL-WALLACE SHIPYARD AND YACHT BASIN. In 1909, John Bell started building sharpie boats on Evans Street and then moved to the end of Bridges and Fisher Streets. The John F. Bell Company was formed with C. Manley Wade as partner. The yard also built fishing boats. The first boat built by government contract was the *Neuse*. Wade ended his partnership, and his interests were taken over by Charles S. Wallace, forming the Bell-Wallace Boat Plant. In 1946, Charles North Bennett bought the shipyard and built the Yacht Basin east of the plant. The Yacht Basin, which had a pier, lounge, and storage room, was a popular stop for boats traveling north and south. The plant and basin were sold in 1950 to Morehead Shipbuilding Company, which built Hatteras Trawlers before going bankrupt. (Below, courtesy of Mickey Weeks.)

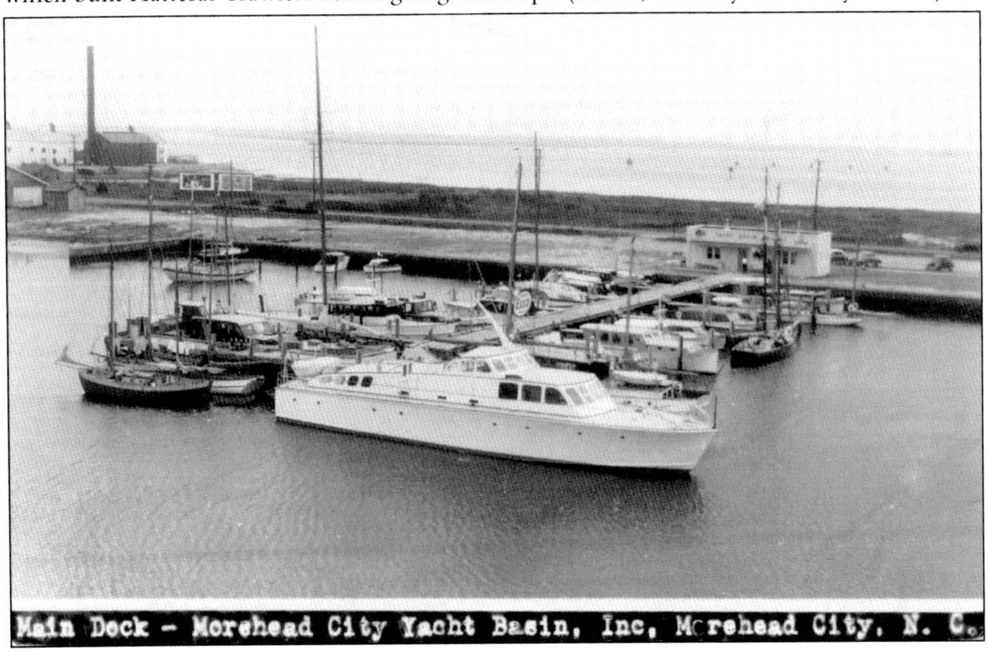

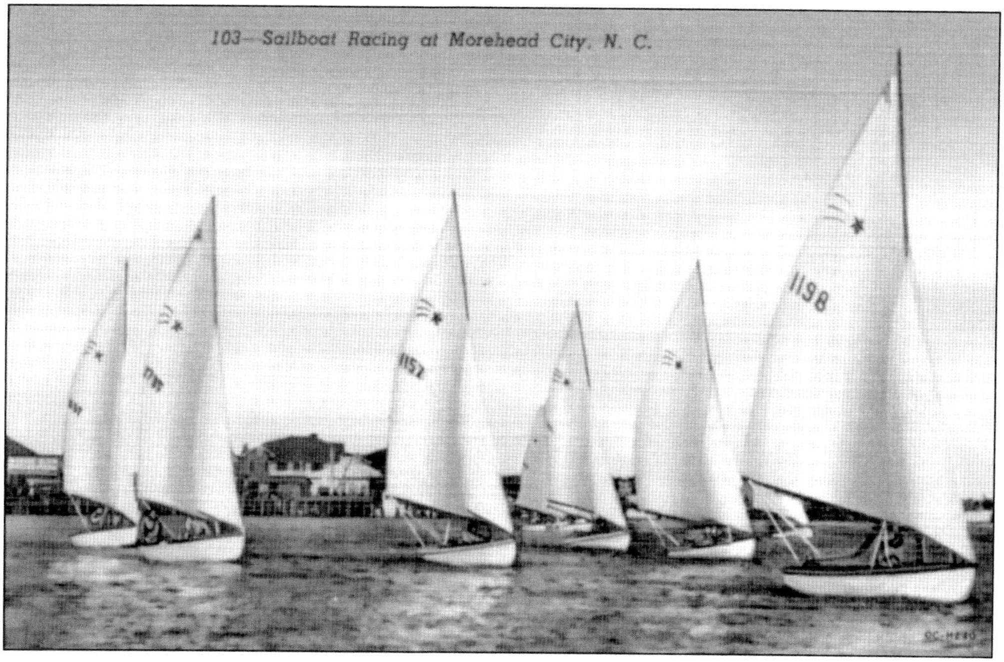

SAILBOAT RACING. Sailboat racing was a popular sport from the early days of Morehead City. In the late 1800s, sharpie races were of particular interest. The course began and ended at the Atlantic Hotel. After the race, the hotel threw a party honoring the winning crew. By the time of the First World War, interest began to wane. In an effort to revitalize sailing in the area, the Morehead City Boating Club was founded in 1934 and reorganized in 1962 to form the Morehead City Yacht Club, Inc. The early 1950s ushered in the motorboat era, which quickly eclipsed the popularity of the sailboat.

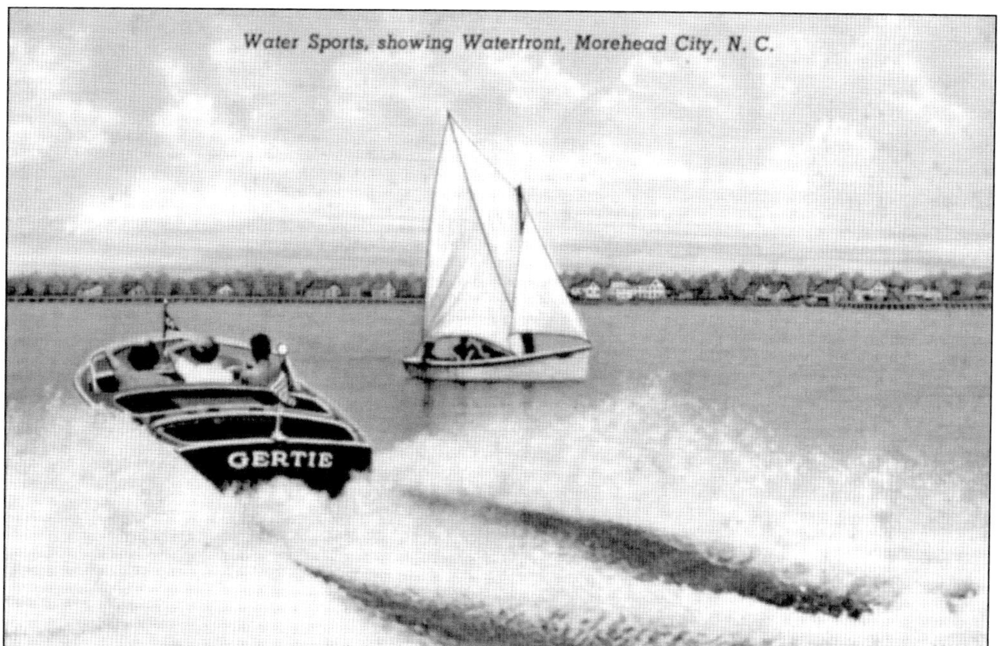

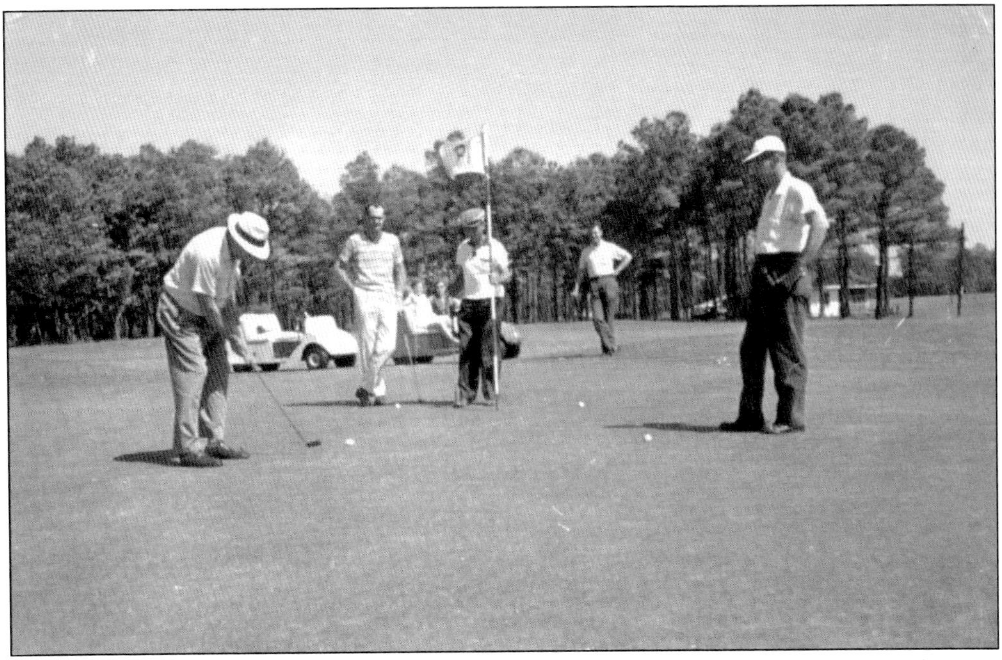

MOREHEAD CITY GOLF AND COUNTRY CLUB. The golf course was built on what became Country Club Road and was located between Crab Point Road and the junction of Highways 24 and 70 on an unpaved road. At the time, the land was mostly farmland and woods. The 18-hole flat-terrain golf course opened in 1953 with Dr. John Morris as president of the club.

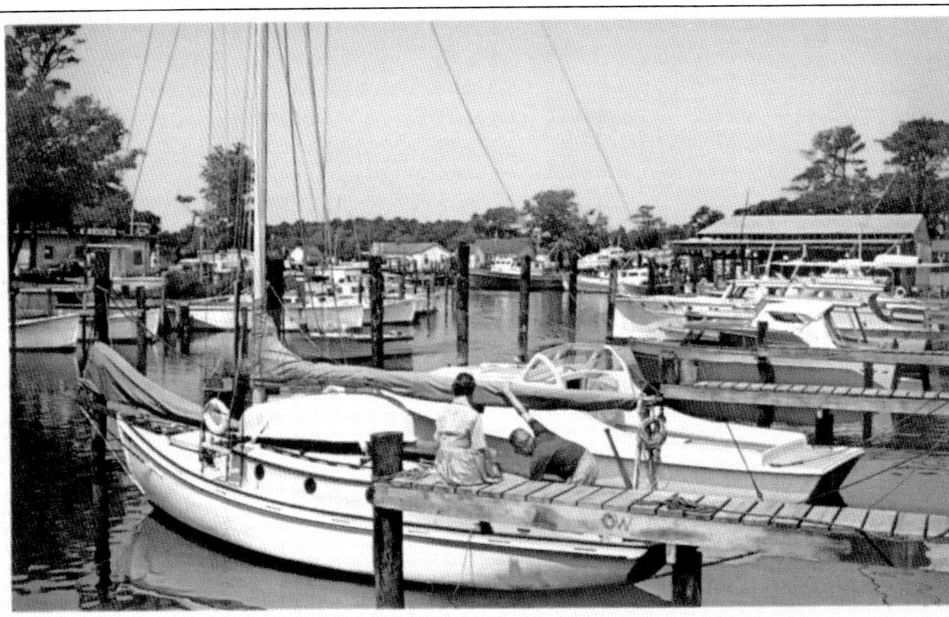

A Boat Basin on Bogue Sound Near Morehead City, North Carolina

BOAT BASINS. Over the years, personal yachts and pleasure boats have become more common, and the need for boat basins and marinas has increased. The basins provide an area sheltered from wind and stormy seas for boats to be docked. Many of the marinas now offer fuel, dry storage, and showers.

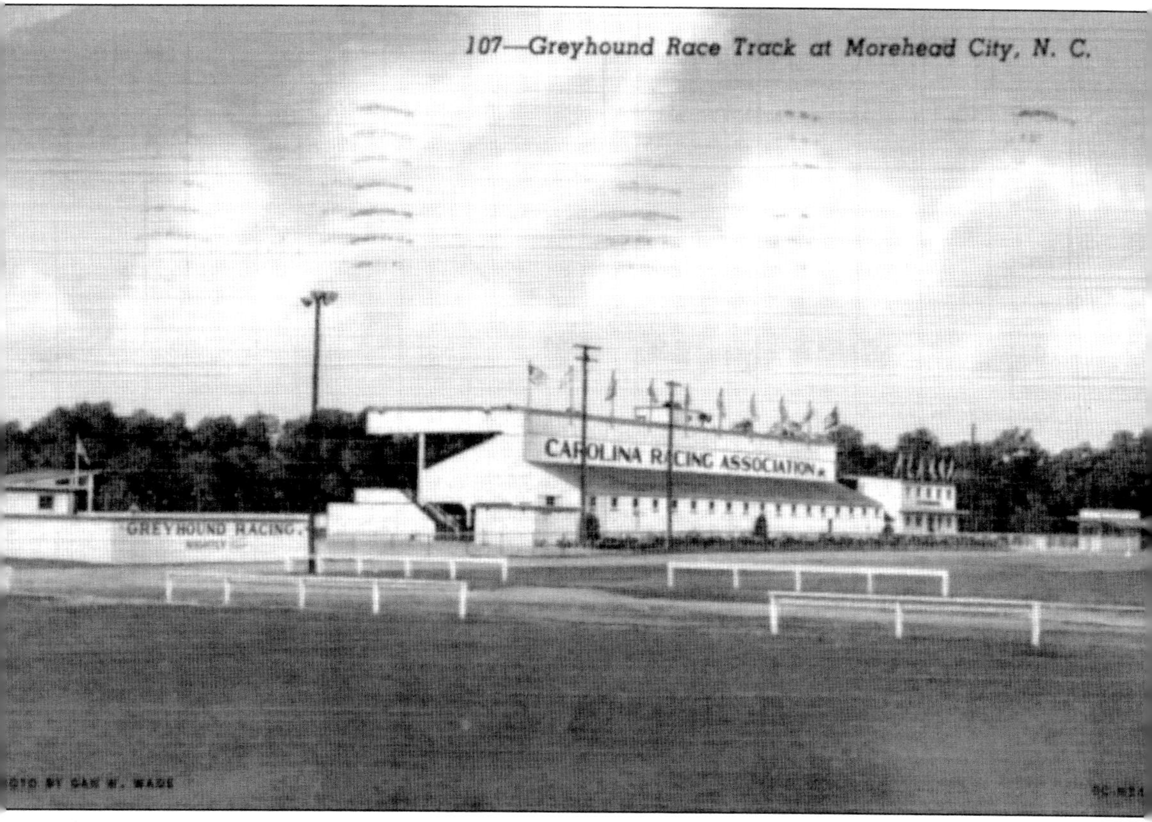

GREYHOUND RACETRACK. In June 1948, the Carolina Racing Association opened the racetrack. At the time, the Morehead City and Moyock, North Carolina, tracks were the only dog tracks between Florida and New England. The track offered a grandstand with a capacity of 3,000 and free parking on the premises for 1,500 cars. A racing school was offered free to the public in preparation of the grand opening. Bets could be placed at 21 windows prior to the race. The dogs were kept at a kennel away from the track and were brought to the track at 6:00 p.m. on the night of the race. The race began when a mechanical rabbit was released. The greyhounds wore numbered satin banners, and the number of the winning dog was displayed on an electronic scoreboard. Races were held each night Monday through Saturday, rain or shine. In 1953, the North Carolina State Supreme Court ruled that dog tracks were illegal and the track was closed. The Miss North Carolina Beauty Pageant was held at this location in 1953.

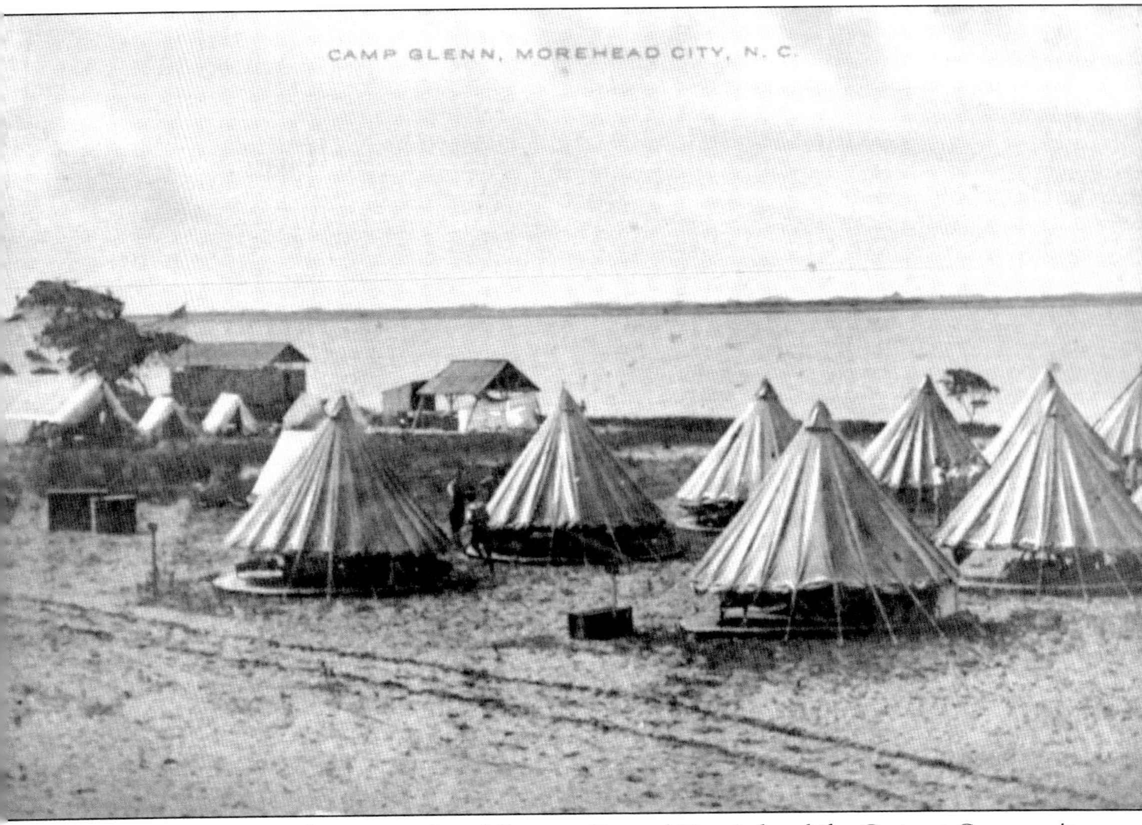

CAMP GLENN. At the present site of Carteret General Hospital and the Carteret Community College, Camp Glenn evolved from a State Guard encampment in 1906 to a navy base in 1916–1917. The guardsmen met there each summer, and many of them brought their families to stay at the Atlantic Hotel. In the early 1920s, it became the first U.S. Coast Guard Air Station in the world. Seaplanes were moored in Bogue Sound in front of the camp and were reached by boat. Pilots not only hunted enemy submarines but also looked for distressed vessels, spotted schools of fish, and looked for bootleggers smuggling liquor. Pilots took pigeons in small cages with them, and if they spotted something, messages were sent by carrier pigeon to Camp Glenn and then passed on to boat captains. During World War II, Camp Glenn again became a Navy Area Section Base and had PT boats docked there.

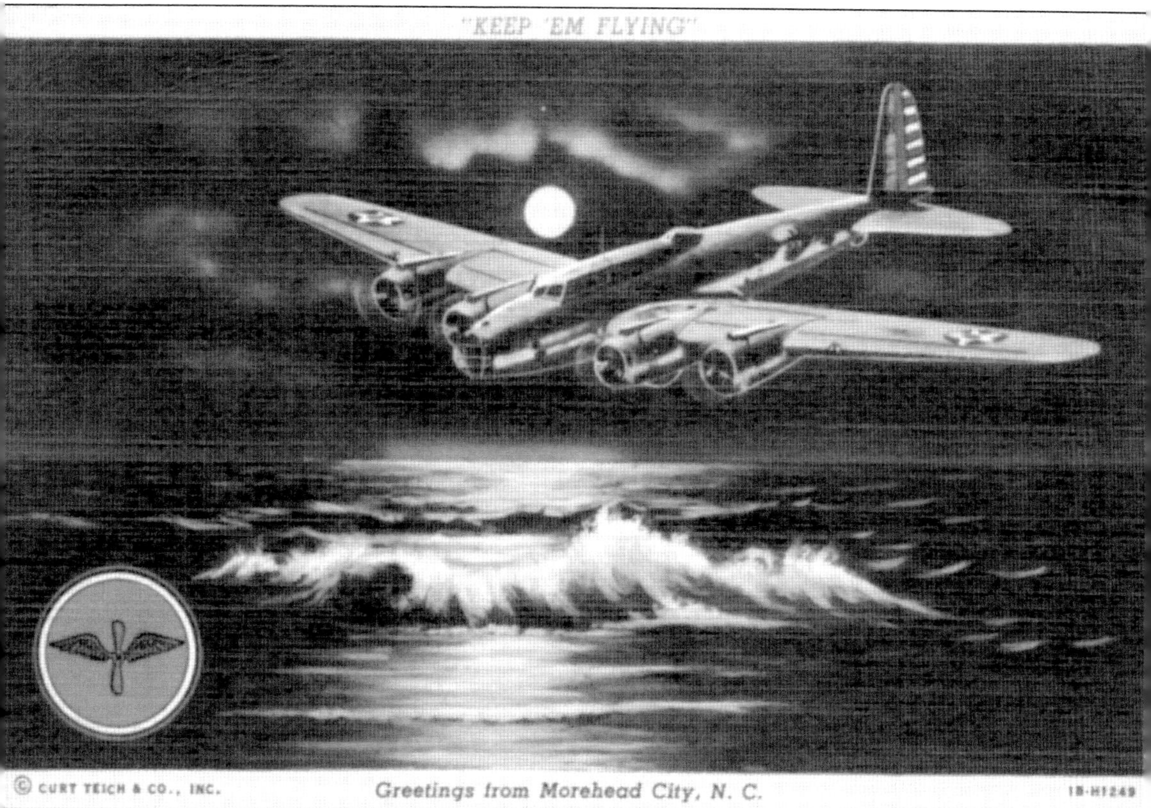

WARTIME. World War II came closer to Carteret County than most residents realized. German U-boats off the coast presented a real danger. On March 11, 1942, the *Caribsea* became the first casualty when she was torpedoed at Cape Lookout. Seven survivors were rescued by the *Norlindo*, which was sunk a month later. A steel submarine net was placed at Cape Lookout to provide ships a safe harbor at night. Artillery guns at Fort Macon protected Beaufort Inlet. Other precautions were taken by the citizenry. Residents hung blackout shades over windows, limited night driving, and turned out streetlights. Air wardens were appointed to alert the towns of air attack. Female spotters worked in towers to identify enemy planes. Rationing food and gasoline became a way of life. Invasion was also a worry. Foxholes and sandbags were placed along the waterfronts, and sentries were stationed at the foot of each bridge. When the war finally ended, the Morehead City fire chief raced up and down Arendell Street in a fire truck with full lights and sirens announcing the wonderful news.

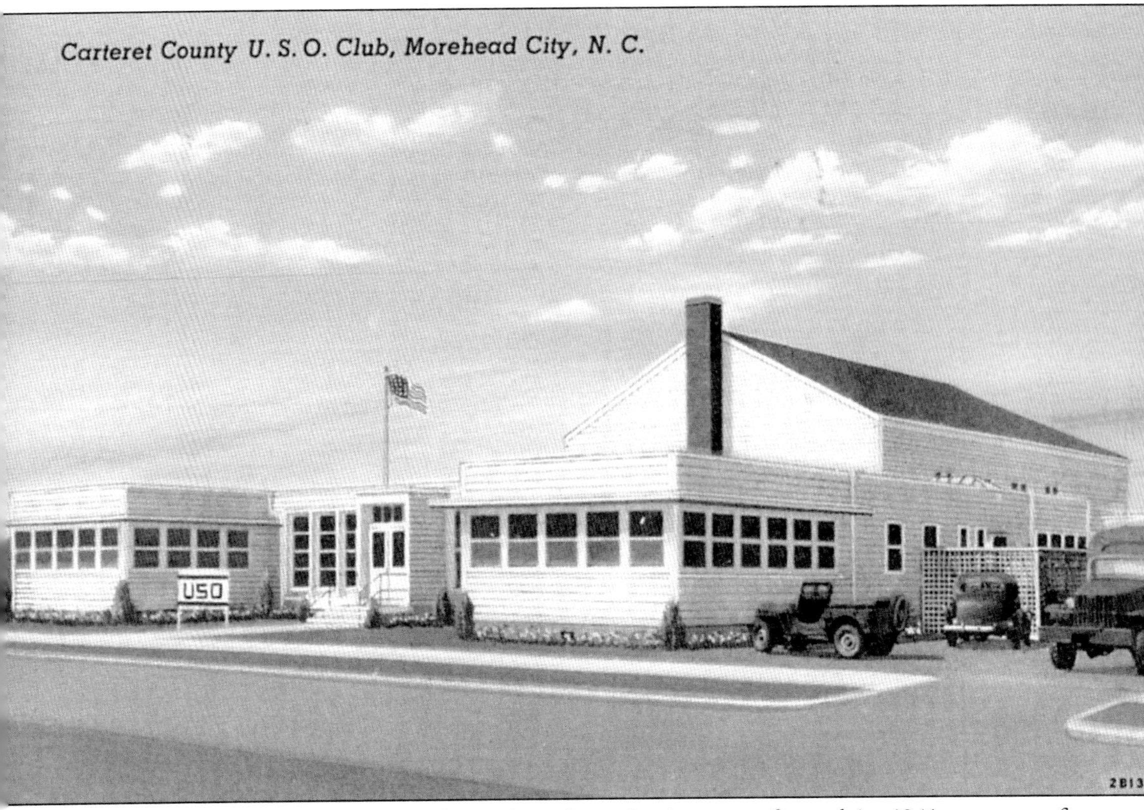

USO CLUB. The USO, United Services Organization, was formed in 1941 as a way for communities to participate in the war effort. USO centers were established to become the GIs' "Home Away from Home." By 1944, there were more than 3,000 USO clubs. Early in World War II, the government paid $1 for property in the 1500 block of Shepard Street for the use of servicemen in the area. The property was repurchased by the town for $3,500 when the government ordered that all USO buildings that would not continue in use as USO clubs had to be sold by January 31, 1948. Local teenagers helped raise the money to purchase the property. Until it was destroyed by fire in 1975, it served as a recreation center and teenagers' club.

Three

Atlantic Beach

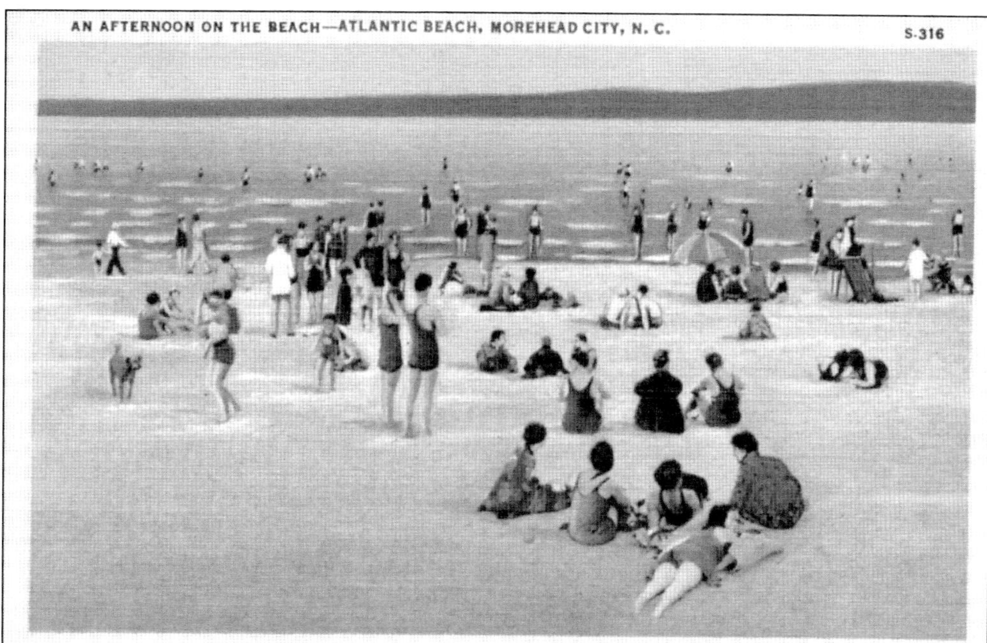

The Beach. Bogue Banks had its start with a fort on the eastern end and small fishing villages along the beach. From this small beginning came the beach resort of Atlantic Beach, which became a major tourist attraction. It is known as a great place for fishing, boating, and water sports and for its beautiful beach. The postcard posted in 1940 shows an everyday scene on the beach.

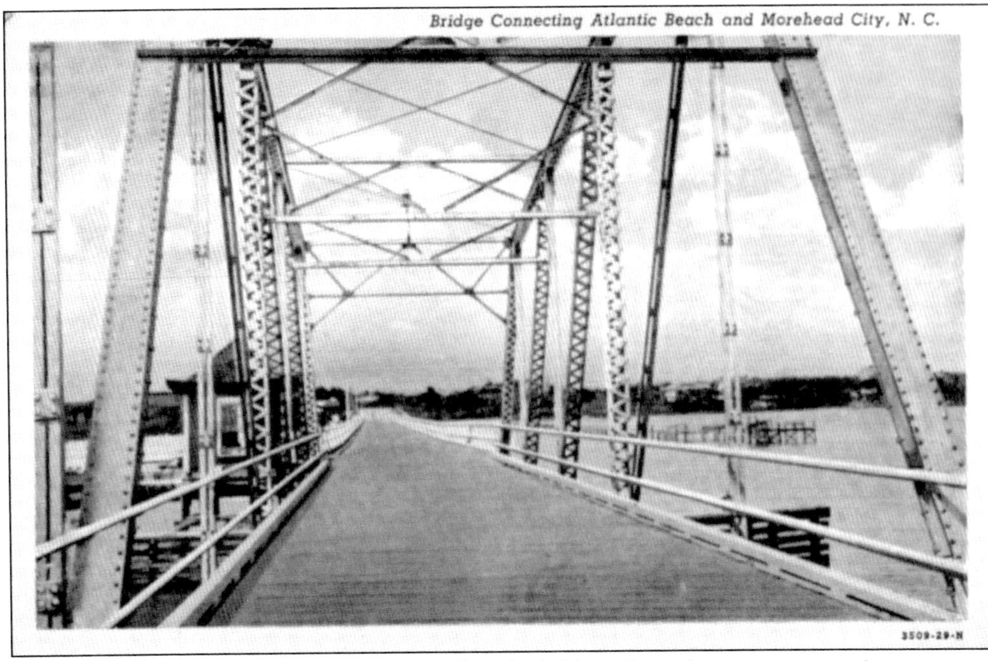

FIRST BRIDGE TO ATLANTIC BEACH. Before the bridge, the only way to get to the ocean was by boat. A wood-planked turnstile bridge was built at Twenty-eighth Street in 1928. It had a tollbooth with a pagoda-style roof. Tolls were 25¢ per car plus 15¢ per passenger. The toll was dropped in 1936 when the state bought the bridge.

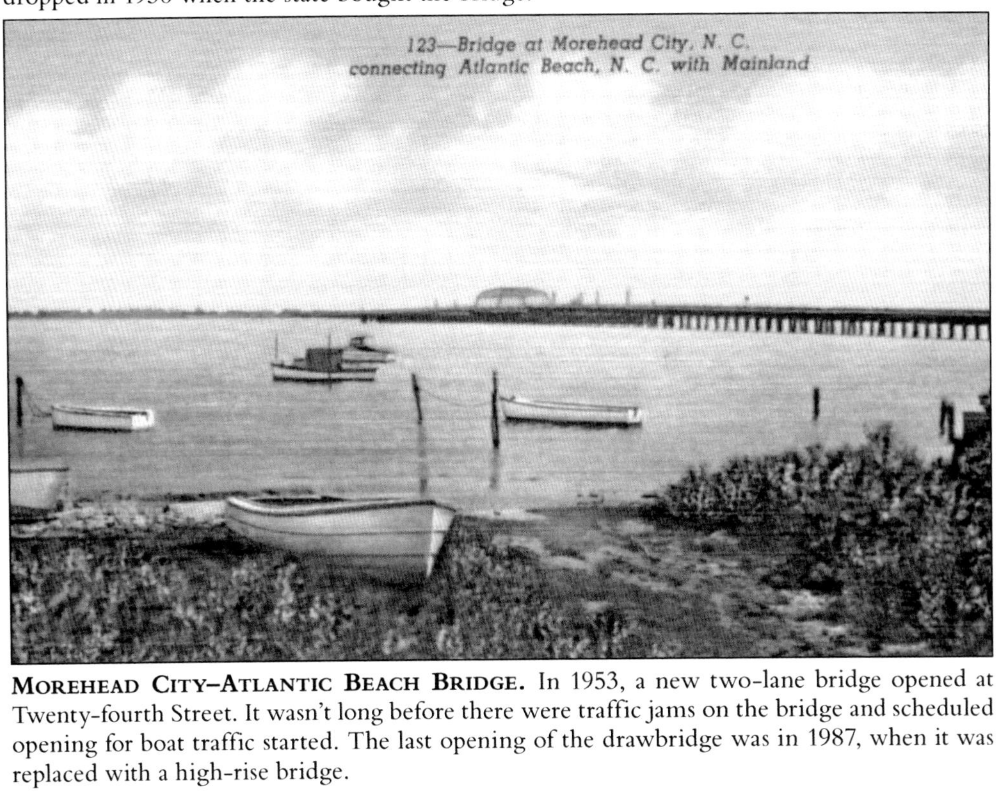

MOREHEAD CITY–ATLANTIC BEACH BRIDGE. In 1953, a new two-lane bridge opened at Twenty-fourth Street. It wasn't long before there were traffic jams on the bridge and scheduled opening for boat traffic started. The last opening of the drawbridge was in 1987, when it was replaced with a high-rise bridge.

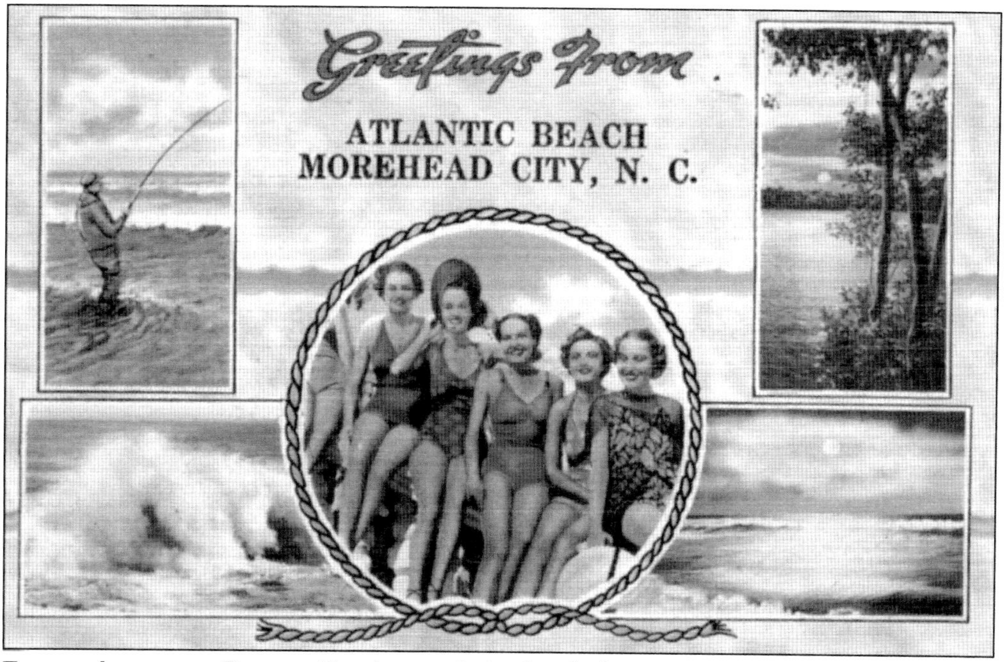

EARLY ATLANTIC BEACH. Tourists used the beach for years before Atlantic Beach was promoted as a separate entity. In the summer, sharpies rigged with white sails bound from the Atlantic Hotel were an ordinary sight as most carried tourists to the ocean beach. The fare was 15¢ to be taken to Money Beach for swimming. Money Beach, which had a small bathhouse, was thought to hide pirate treasure in its dunes. Even after Atlantic Beach was developed for tourism in 1928, most swimmers continued going to Money Beach to avoid paying the $1 swimming fee. Swimming on the waterfront of Morehead City was avoided except on incoming tides because of sewage emptying into the sound.

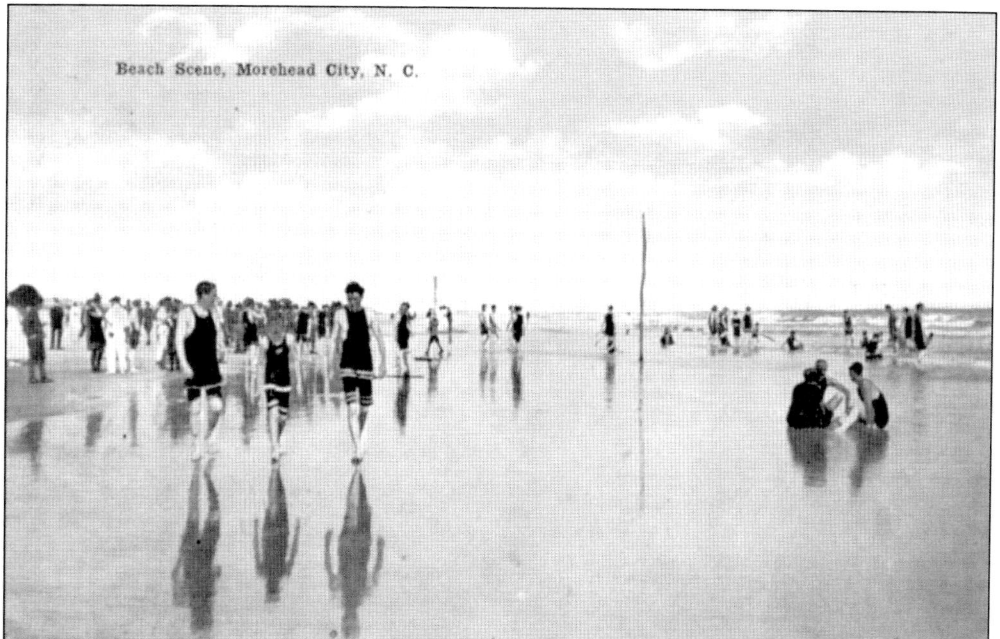

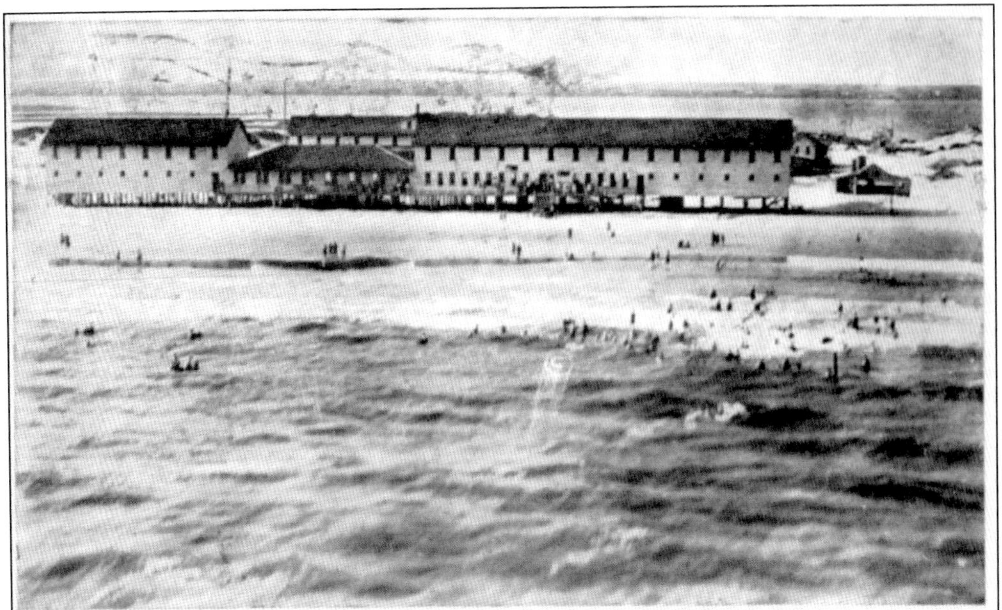

Atlantic View Beach Hotel, near Morehead City, N. Car.

ATLANTIC VIEW BEACH. J. J. Royal and Winfield Chadwick built a small pavilion, one-story bathhouse, and refreshment stand on Bogue Banks' ocean beach in 1887 and thus began the beach. Boats for hire took people to the sound side of the beach, where they walked across the sand and dunes to reach the ocean for surf bathing. When the partners split their interests, Royal moved west to Money Island and built a two-story pavilion and bathhouse. Oxcarts carried supplies for the refreshment stand over the sand dunes. In 1916, Vaughn Bedsworth bought 100 acres including the Royal property and named it Atlantic View Beach. Many improvements were made and a successful 100-room hotel was built. The hotel burned and the pavilion was torn down. (Courtesy of Mickey Weeks.)

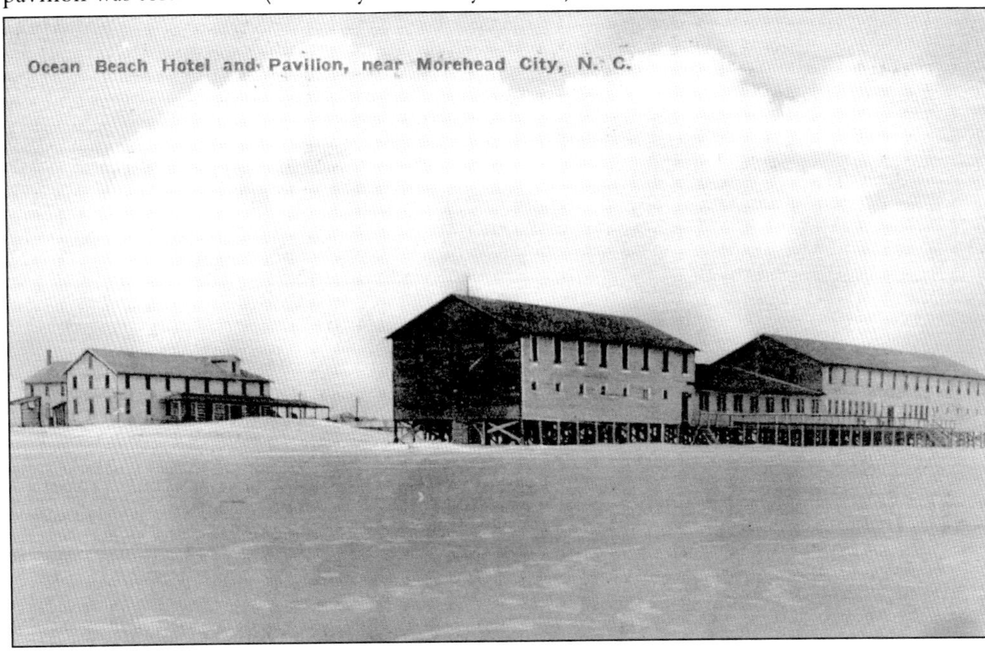

Ocean Beach Hotel and Pavilion, near Morehead City, N. C.

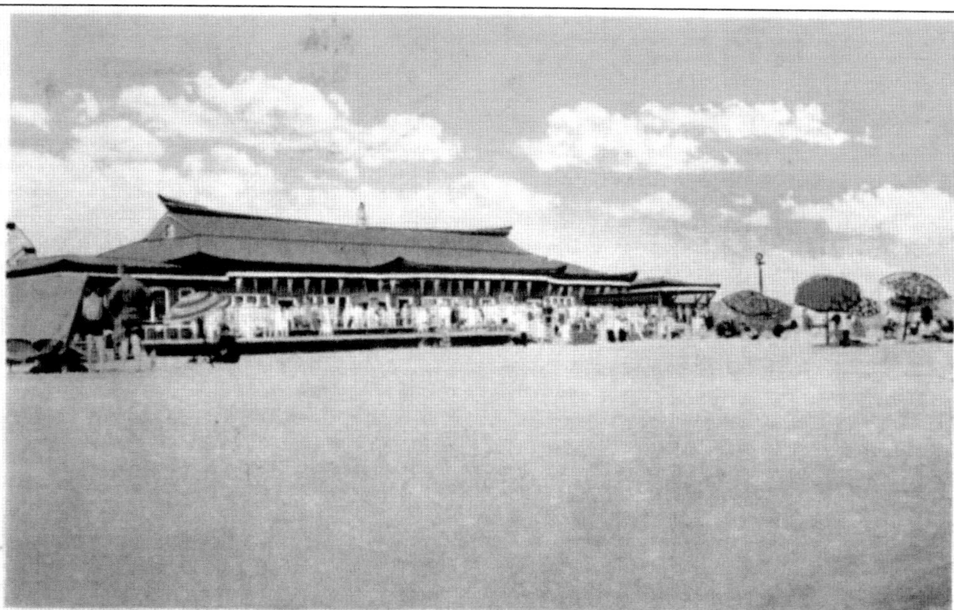

PAGODA ATLANTIC BEACH. BEAUFORT-MOREHEAD CITY, N. C.

PAGODA. The building of the toll bridge by the Atlantic Beach Company in 1928 helped to create the resort of Atlantic Beach. To promote the beach, they also built a dining hall, bathhouses, and the Pagoda. These were constructed in an Oriental style and had green roofs with bright-red exposed corners. The Pagoda was a large building where dances were held. Featured were such well-known orchestras as Paul Whiteman and Tommy Dorsey. After many buildings burned in 1929, the property was turned over to the State Trust Company and was later absorbed by the Manufacturers Trust Company. This company sent one of its associates to look over the property and as a result decided to rebuild the beach with a large casino, bathhouses, and the Atlantic Beach Hotel. (Above, courtesy Mickey Weeks.)

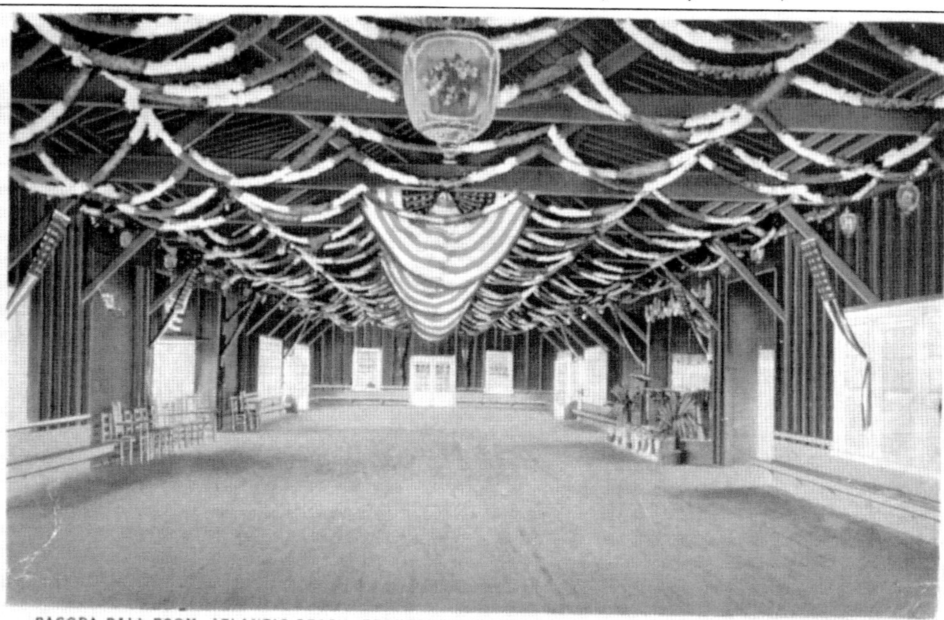

PAGODA BALL ROOM. ATLANTIC BEACH. BEAUFORT-MOREHEAD CITY, N. C.

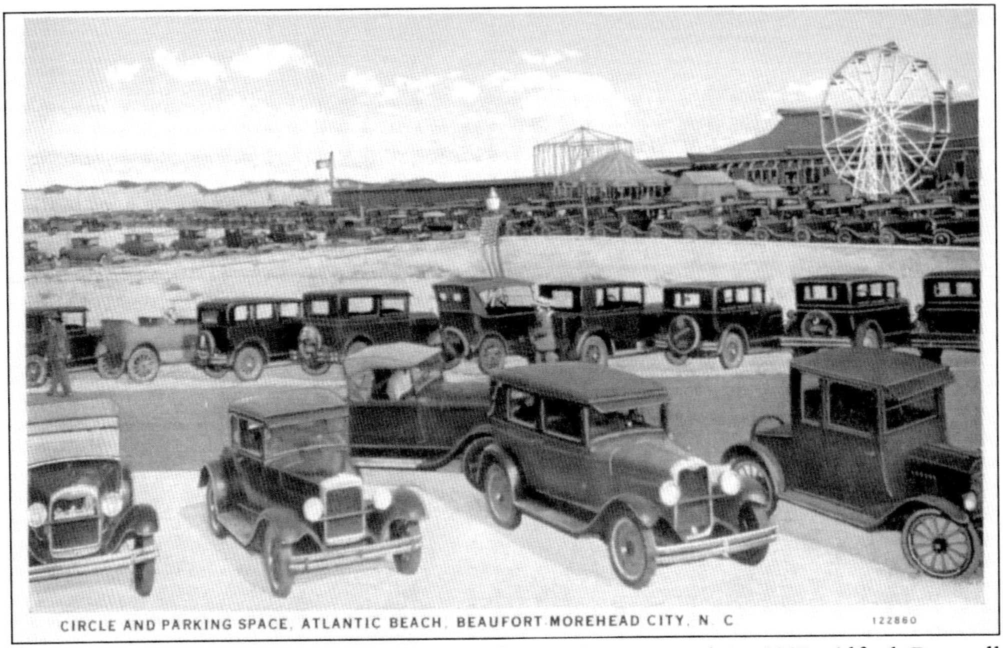

ATLANTIC BEACH. Although Atlantic Beach was incorporated in 1937, Alfred Braswell Cooper is credited with having a vision for developing what many viewed as an island desert into the resort Atlantic Beach became. Starting with a $500 loan, materials bought on credit, and a 25-by-125-foot piece of property, he built the Idle Hour Amusement Center. The Idle Hour, on the right leg of the amusement circle, had a 4-lane bowling alley, which grew to 24 lanes, juke box music, and refreshments. This popular entertainment spot continued to grow when the toll was dropped from the bridge. During World War II, servicemen stationed at Fort Macon frequented the center. It also served as a place to worship on Sundays. (Courtesy of Mickey Weeks.)

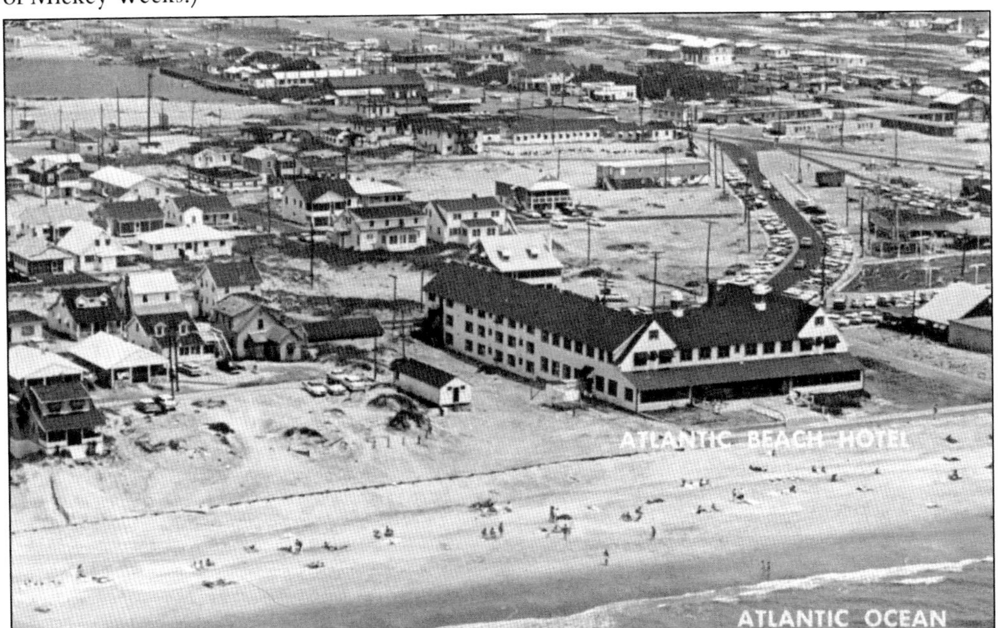

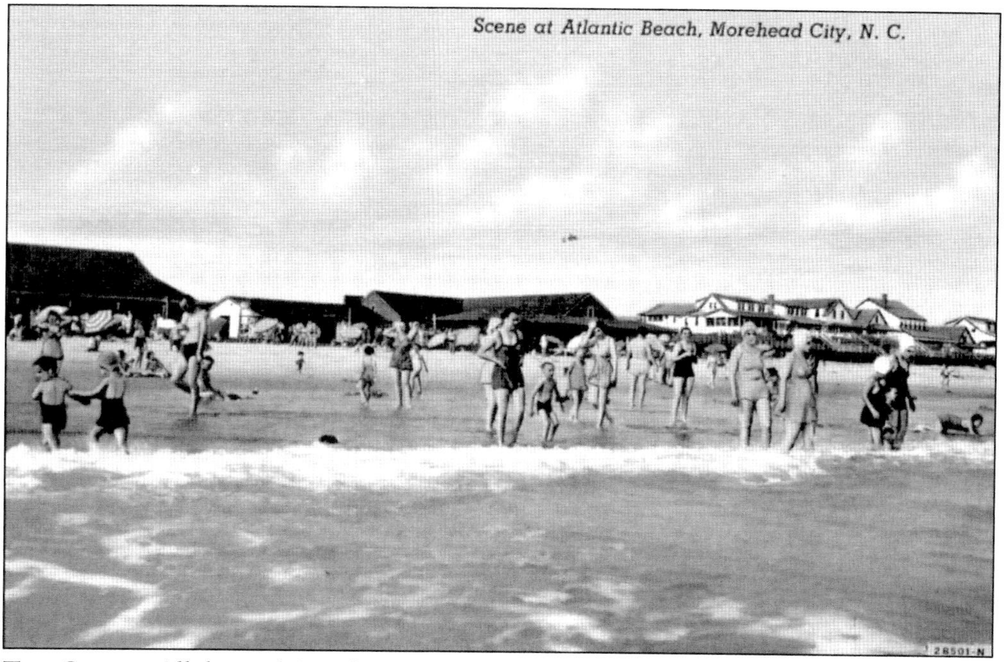

THE CIRCLE. All the stock in Atlantic Beach, Inc., was purchased in 1946 by A. B. Cooper for $40,000. The property consisted of the development extending four blocks east and four blocks west of the amusement circle from the ocean to 200 feet into Bogue Sound. There he built the Surf Club, the three-story Ocean King Hotel, bathhouses, and concessions on the boardwalk. The Rhoda Theatre, named for his wife, was built in 1948 north of the Idle Hour. The 500-seat theater was destroyed in a fire late the same year. Cooper auctioned part of the property in 1948. Approximately 100 lots, 40-by-100 feet each, were sold for $100 apiece. All the properties around the circle except the Ocean King Hotel and Idle Hour properties were sold.

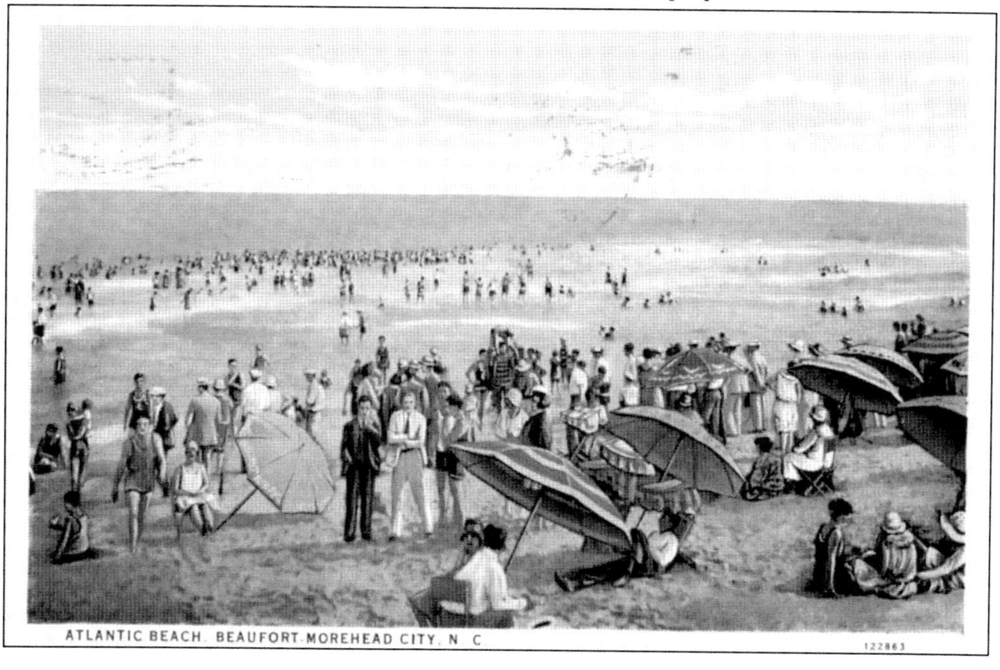

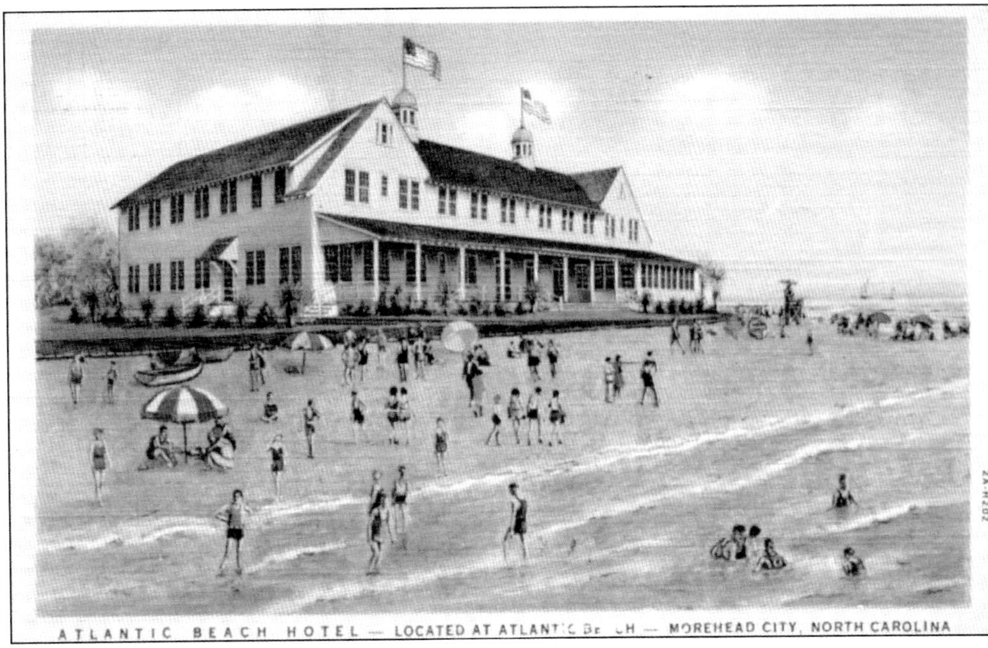

ATLANTIC BEACH HOTEL. The 40-room Atlantic Beach Hotel was built in 1932 just west of the Pagoda by Manufacturers Trust Company. The white-frame green-roofed hotel had a long porch overlooking the ocean. In 1938, Vernon and Walter Derrickson bought and enlarged it to 75 rooms. It opened May 15 for "the season" and operated as a commercial hotel before June 15 and a resort hotel after June 15. The back of the postcard states, "Only place on Atlantic Beach with eating and sleeping accommodations." The hotel was destroyed by fire two weeks after closing for the 1965 season in September. The owner of the hotel was the only person in the hotel at the time and was able to escape and sound an alarm.

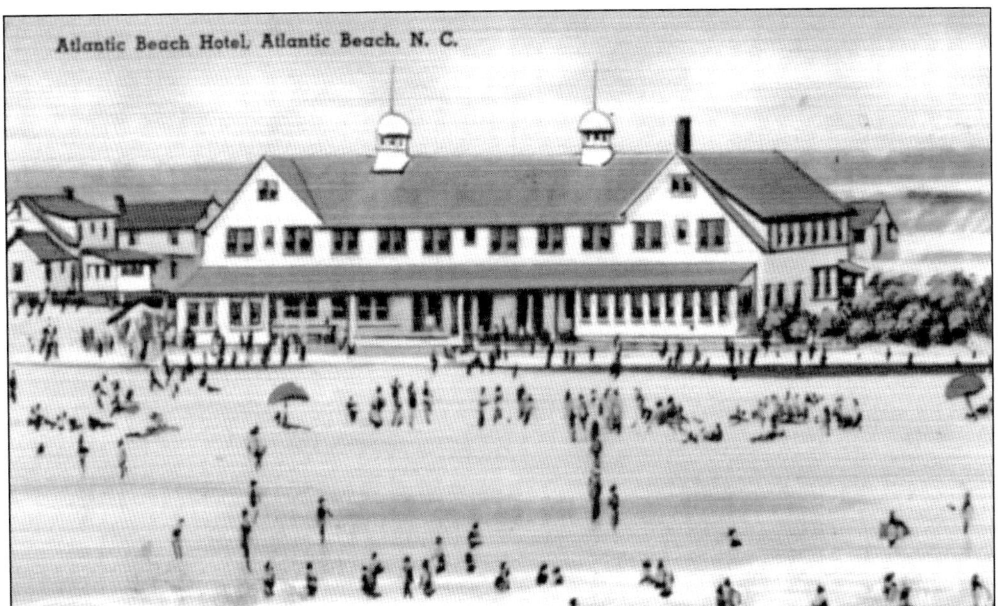

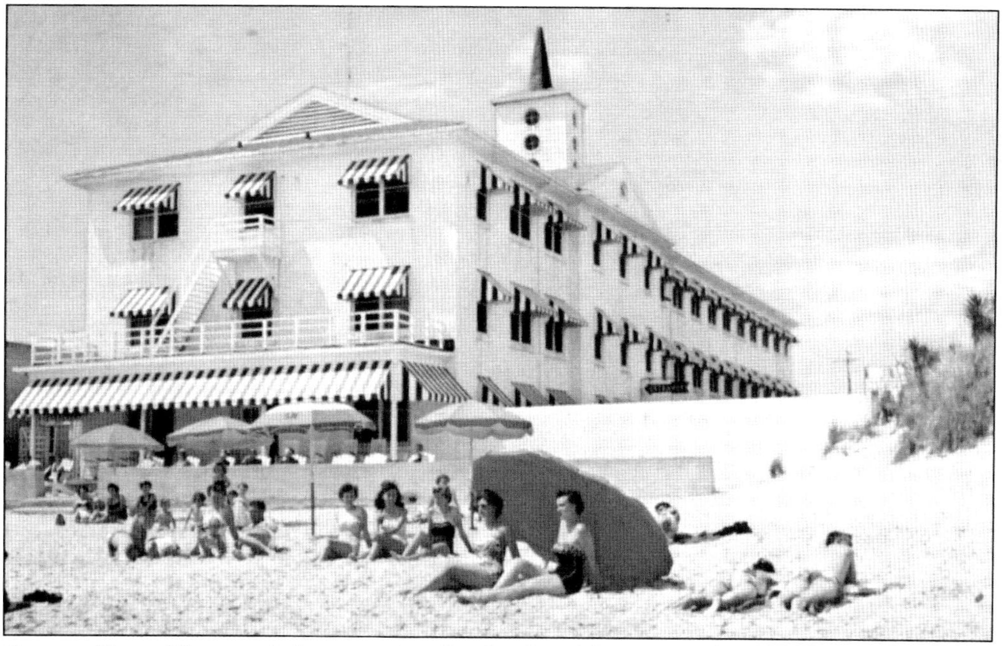

OCEAN KING HOTEL. A few months after buying Atlantic Beach, Alfred B. Cooper built the three-story 70-room Ocean King Hotel just east of the Surf Club on the boardwalk and opened for the 1946 season. In 1954, Hurricane Hazel caused water and structural damage to the hotel. The hotel, restored after the hurricane and ready for the upcoming tourist season, was destroyed by fire early in 1955. Along with the hotel, the fire destroyed the eastern block of the business district. Nine firefighting units from neighboring towns tried to put out the fire but were hampered by lack of water. Atlantic Beach had water for home and business use but not for firefighting. Water to fight the fire was pumped from the sound a third of a mile away and directly from the ocean.

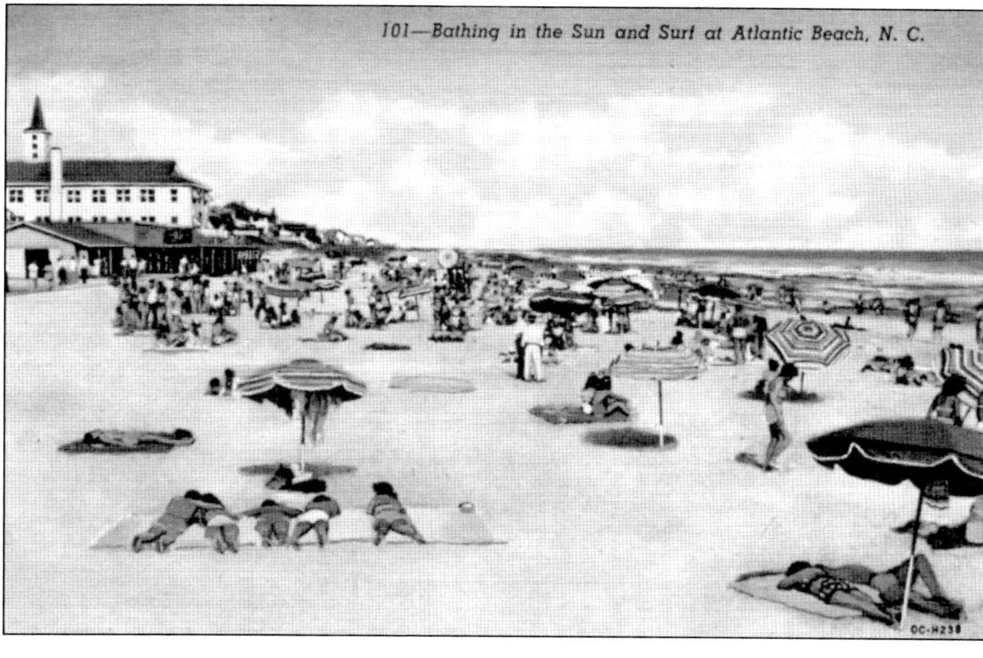

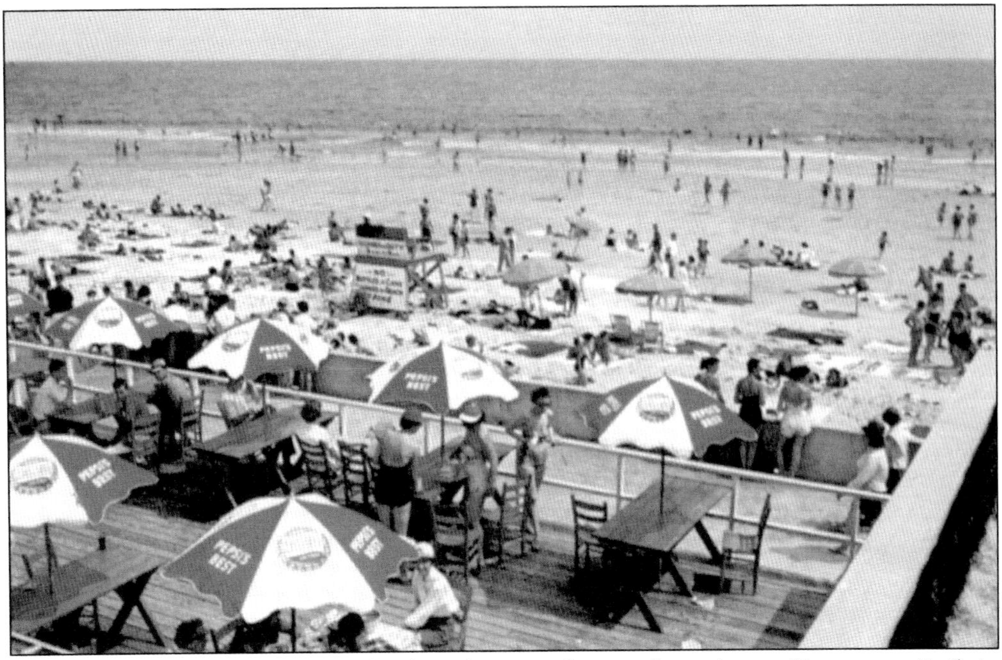

Pavilion. The Pavilion was the third on the oceanfront to have the pavilion name. Built in 1957 with a wooden dance floor, it became a haven for dancers from all around eastern North Carolina. The dance was the beach-bop, which became the shag. Danced to beach music made famous by artists such as the Tams, the Embers, and Maurice Williams and the Zodiacs, the shag is popular on the coasts of North Carolina, Virginia, and South Carolina. In 1995, when the Pavilion was demolished, planks from the club's dance floor were sold for $15 apiece. They each had a brass plaque inscribed: "Wood From Dance Floor Atlantic Beach Pavilion 1957–1995." The postcards show a view of the beach and ocean from the back of the Pavilion.

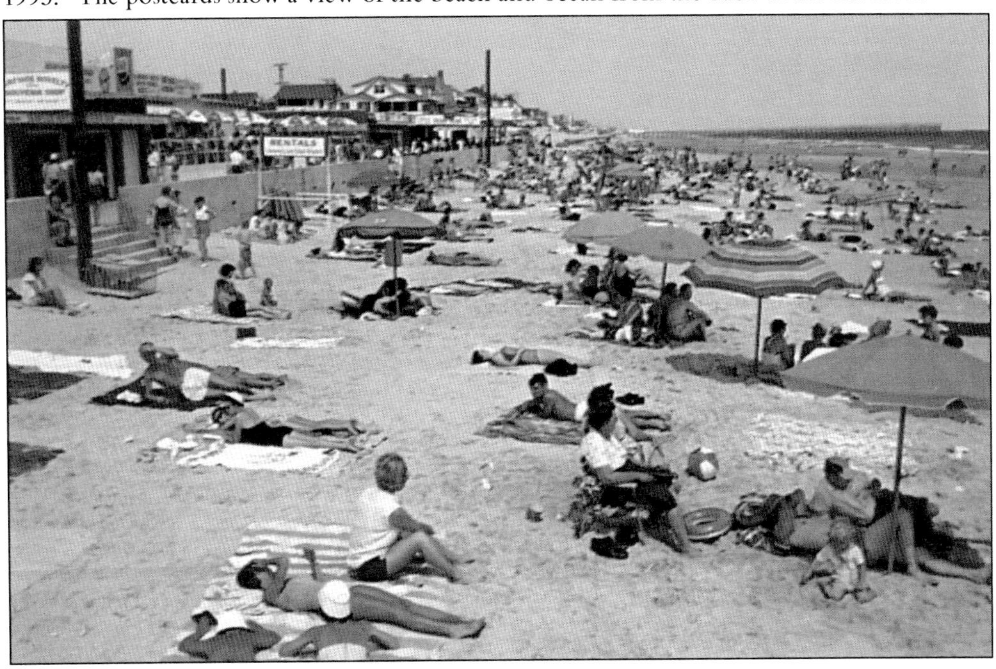

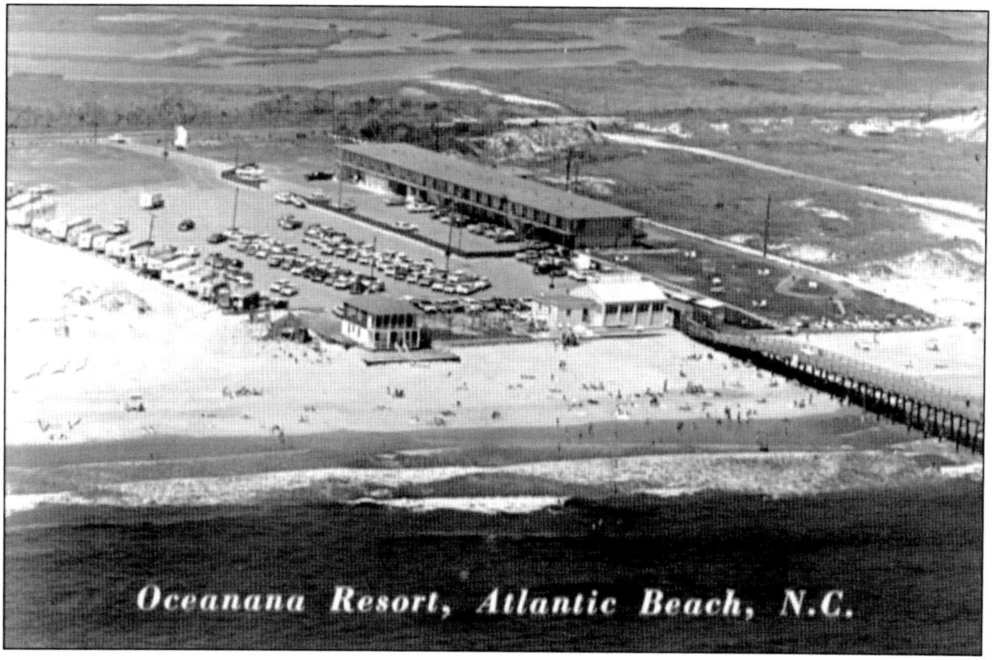

OCEANANA RESORT. The family-oriented resort on Fort Macon Road opened for business in 1959. It was owned by A. B. Cooper who had earlier helped develop Atlantic Beach. Originally he intended to name the resort Oceana, but the sign painter added an extra "na" on the sign and it became Oceanana. The resort had a motel, restaurant, cocktail lounge, and a 1,200-foot fishing pier. In the early 1960s, a playground for children was added. The advertisement on the postcard boasts, "We aren't expensive. . . . We just look that way." It also adds, "We are the only motel on the ocean with a fountain." The fountain is pictured in the bottom postcard.

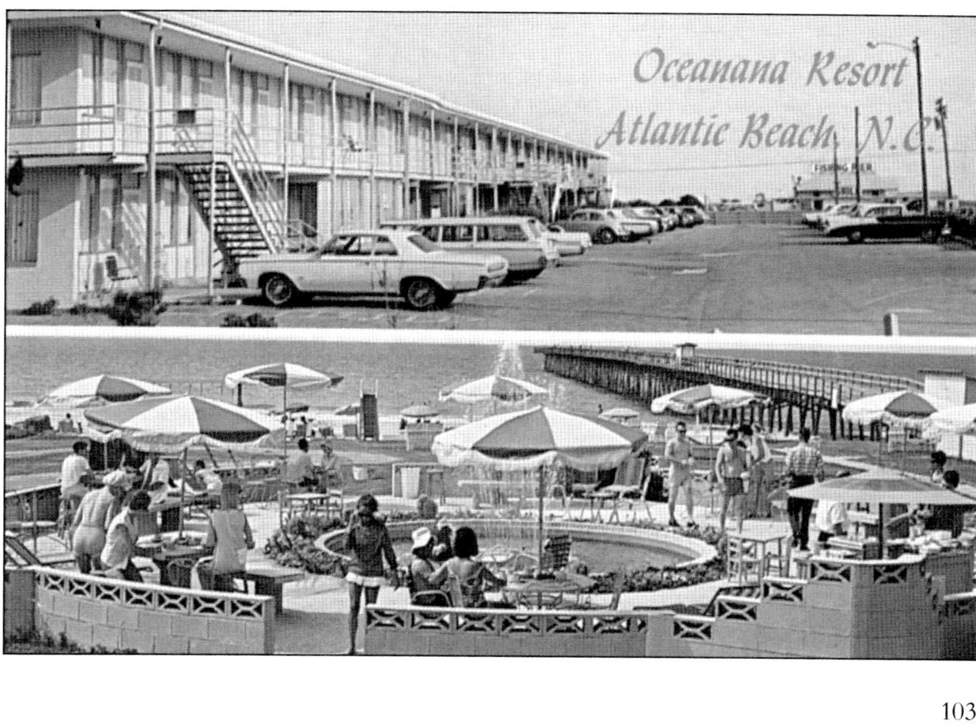

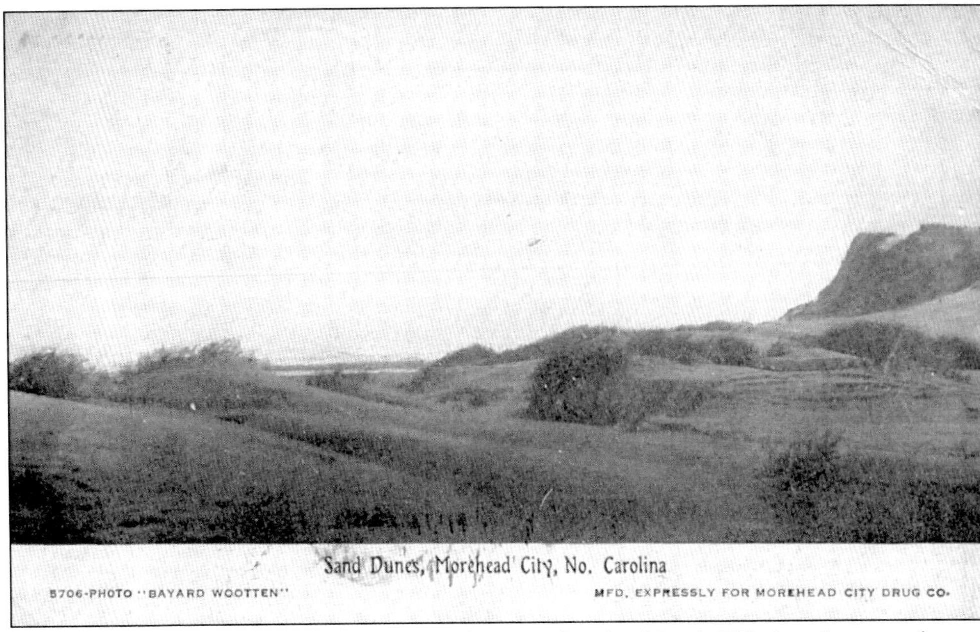

SAND DUNES. Bogue Banks is an ever-changing barrier island. Wind and water changes cause the formation of hills of sand called dunes. Dunes run parallel to the shoreline and are important in protecting development from wind and storm waves. There are very few non-vegetated sand dunes on Bogue Banks, and most are covered with sea oats and other plants that can withstand salt spray. (Courtesy of Gail Barnes.)

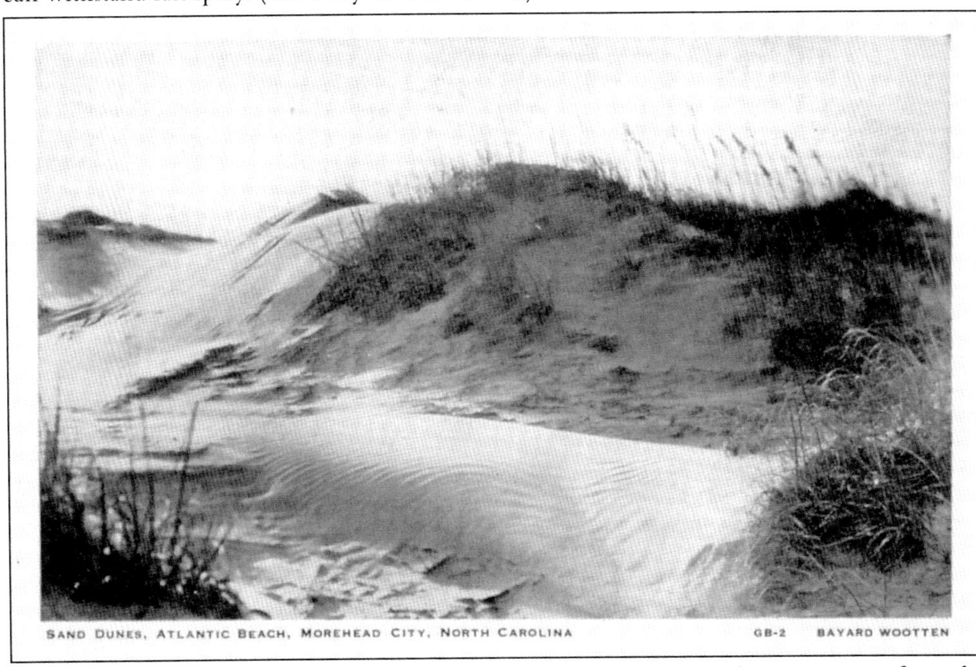

SEA OATS. The postcard shows sea oats growing in the sand dune. The name came from the seeds, which resemble oats. The plant has a strong root system deep in the sand and is able to withstand the salt spray and shifting of sand during storms and hurricanes, helping stabilize the beach from erosion.

TRIPLE S FISHING PIER. The Triple S Pier, also known as the Triple-ESS, was built in 1952 and named for its owner, S. S. Stephenson. This 1956 postcard shows the 1,000-foot wood pier and states that it "is the only fishing pier on the Carteret Coast." It also had a motel and campground. The pier was demolished in 2006 to make way for duplexes.

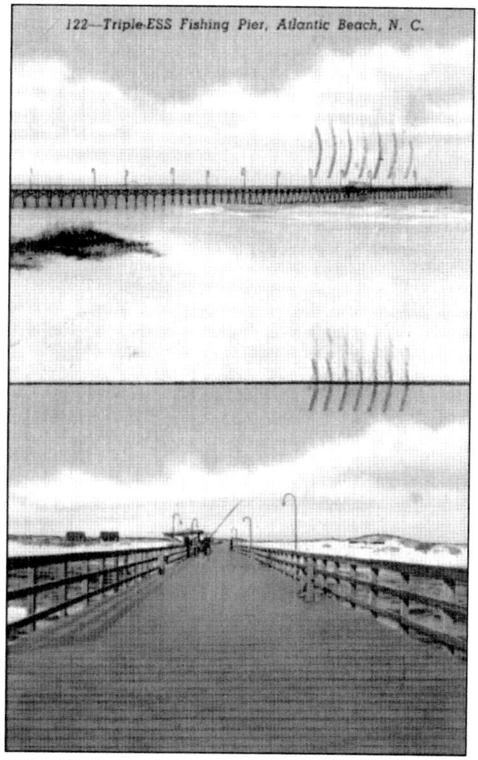

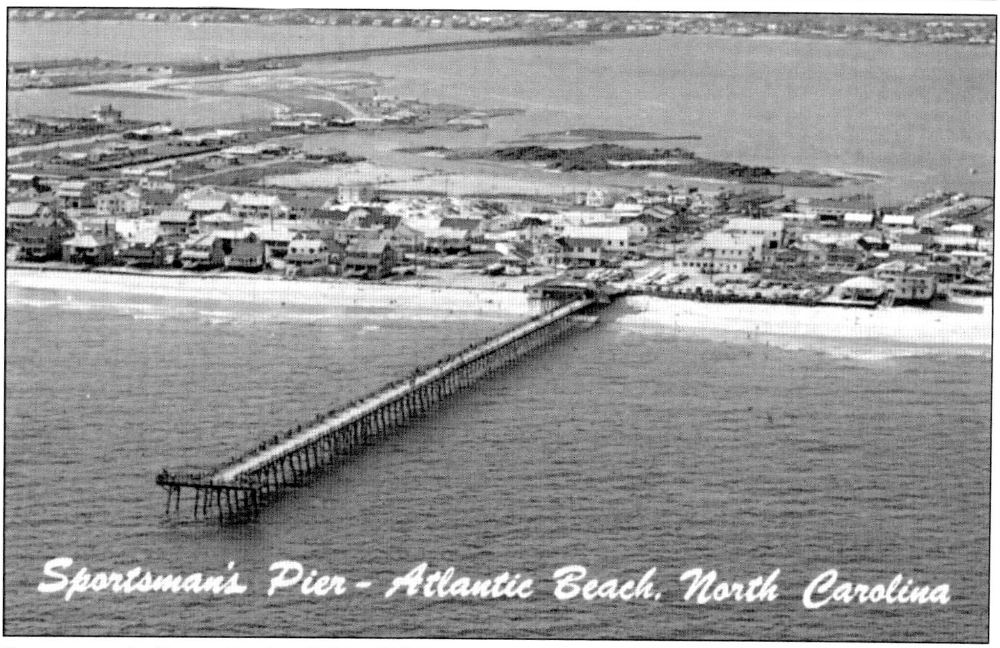

SPORTMAN'S PIER. In the 1950s, fishing piers were built to take advantage of the tourism growth on the beach. Piers gave even a novice fisherman a chance to get out where the action was. The Sportsman's Pier extended 1,135 feet into the ocean and advertised itself as one of the best fishing sites on the eastern coast. A sign at the entrance read, "You should have been here yesterday."

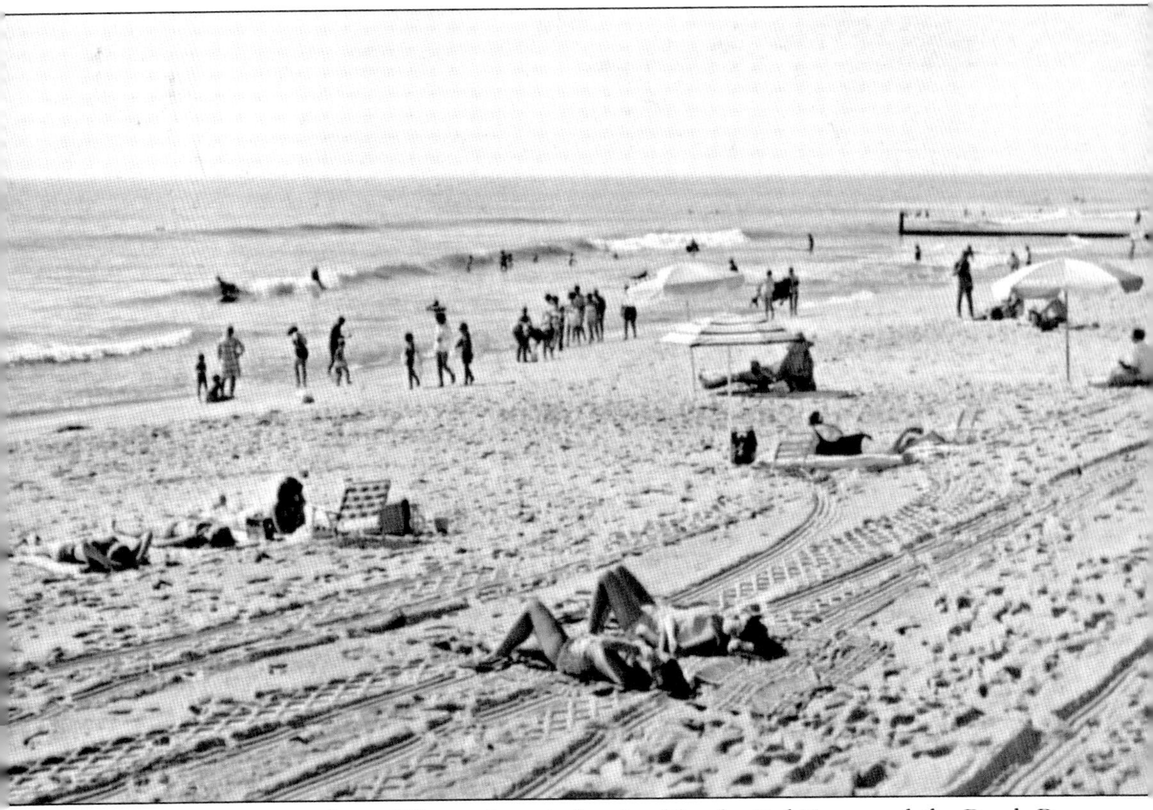

SURFING. Movies such as *Gidget* and musical artists like the Del-Tones and the Beach Boys helped surfing become a national fad in the 1960s. It was natural for Carteret County's beaches to share in that excitement. The area's eight fishing piers provided great breaking surf and became hot surf spots. As amateur surfing took off in Atlantic Beach and Emerald Isle, so did the retail side of the sport. Tommy Morrow started the first surf shop in North Carolina. Atlantic Beach Surf Shop opened its doors to surfers and tourists in 1964. Bert Pearson started selling surfboards in his shoe store in Kinston and soon out of a pickup truck on the beach. He opened Bert's Surf Shop in Atlantic Beach in 1964. Marsh's Surf Shop, another of the Crystal Coast's oldest, was established in 1972 by Bette Marsh. Surfing contests have been held here for nearly as long as surfers have been in the water. Annual competitions continue to be hosted by the Eastern Surfing Association and the Buddy Pelletier Foundation.

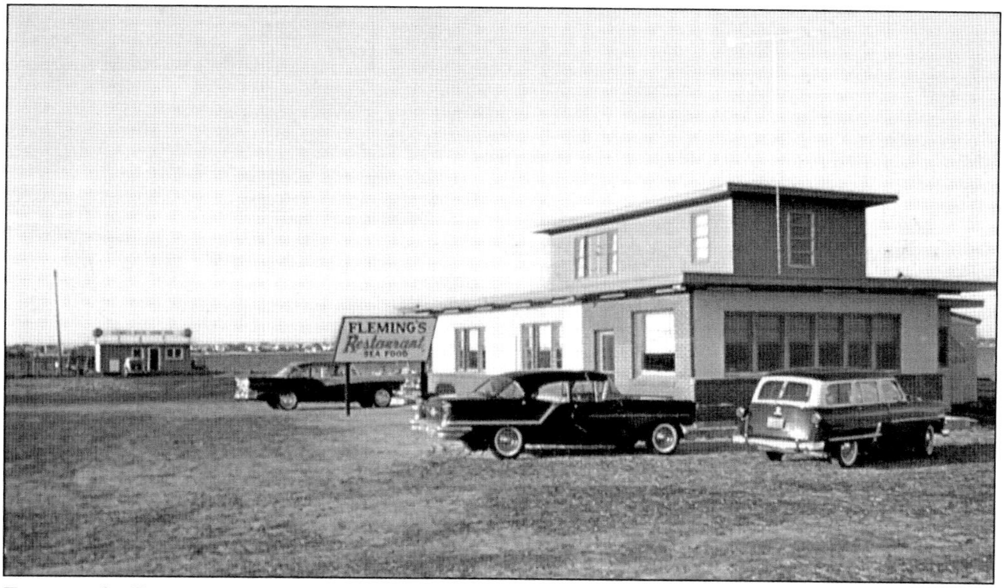

Fleming's Restaurant And Fishing Pier. As the number of tourists visiting the beach increased, more piers, restaurants, and motels were built. Fleming's Restaurant and Fishing Pier were located just off the Morehead City Atlantic Beach Bridge overlooking Bogue Sound. Deepwater fishing was offered from the pier. The restaurant was later located on west Fort Macon Road.

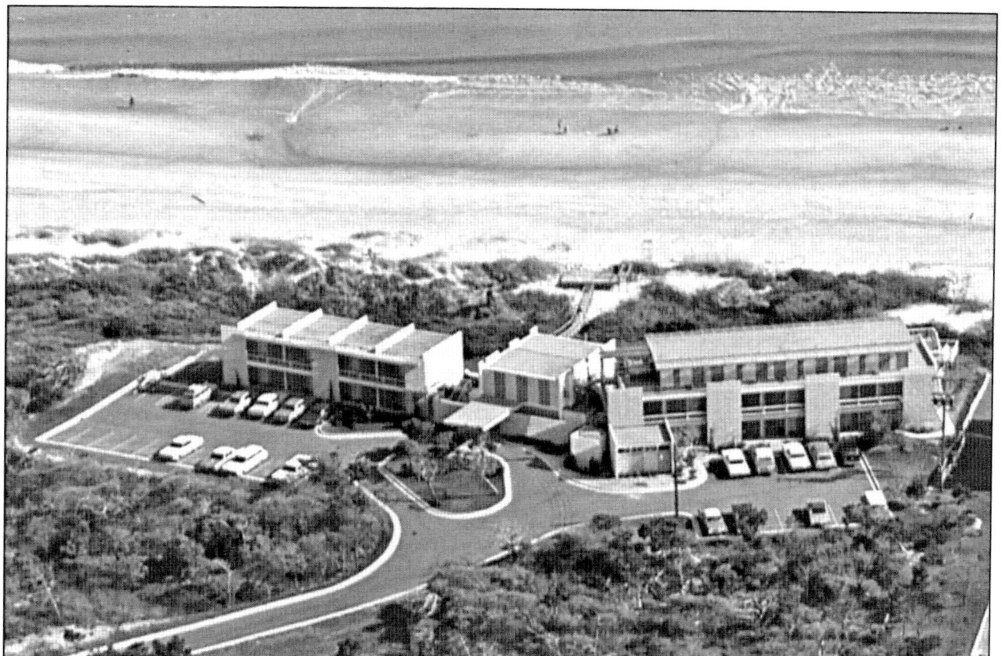

Atlantis Lodge. The Atlantis Lodge is in the middle of a forest of live oak trees on the ocean. Located in Pine Knoll Shores, it was one of the first hotels built on Bogue Banks and opened in 1963. The postcard reads, "Come relax and discover our special magic." The lodge is the site of an annual sand sculpture contest, the "Mile of Hope," which benefits children with cancer.

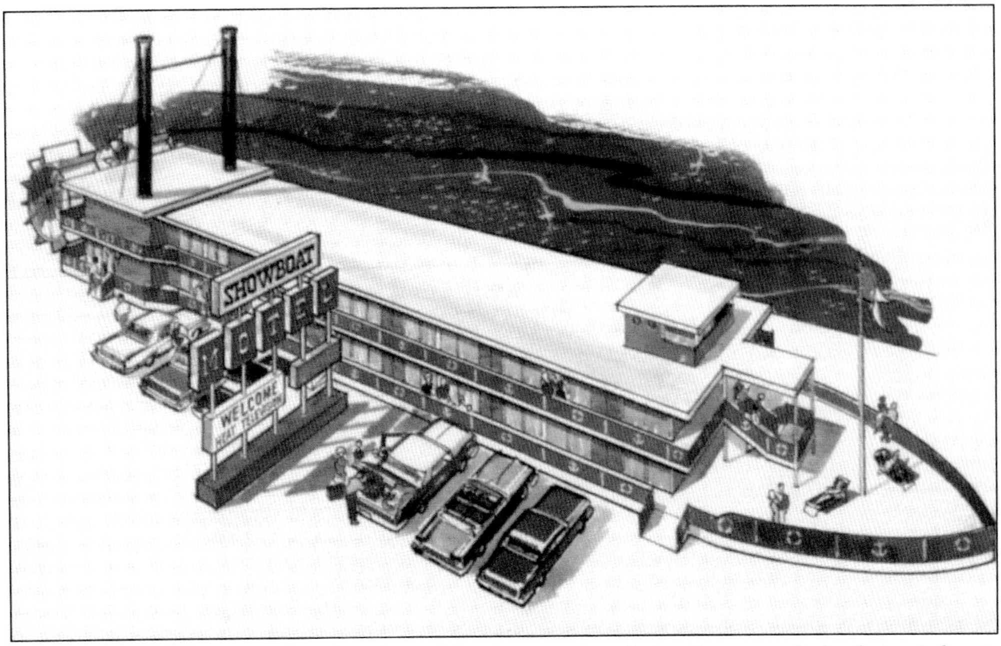

SHOW BOAT MOTEL. The Showboat Motel was one of the first motels built in Atlantic Beach in the 1960s. It was designed to look like a riverboat and featured a paddle wheel. Located on the beach causeway, it overlooks Bogue Sound and at one time was adjacent to Fleming's Restaurant. Archie Fleming owned both the motel and Fleming's Restaurant and Fishing Pier.

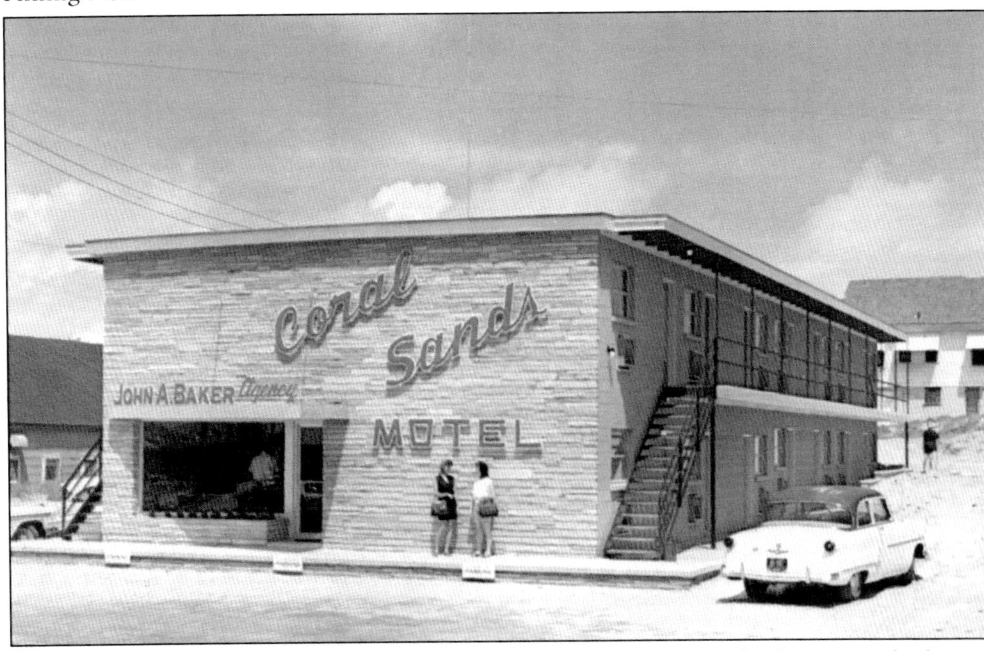

CORAL SANDS MOTEL. The Coral Sands Motel was on the circle of Atlantic Beach close to the Idle Hour Amusement Center. It overlooked the ocean, beach, and amusement center on the circle. The back of the cards reads, "Most centrally located in the heart of Atlantic Beach." (Courtesy of Mickey Weeks.)

Four

FORT MACON

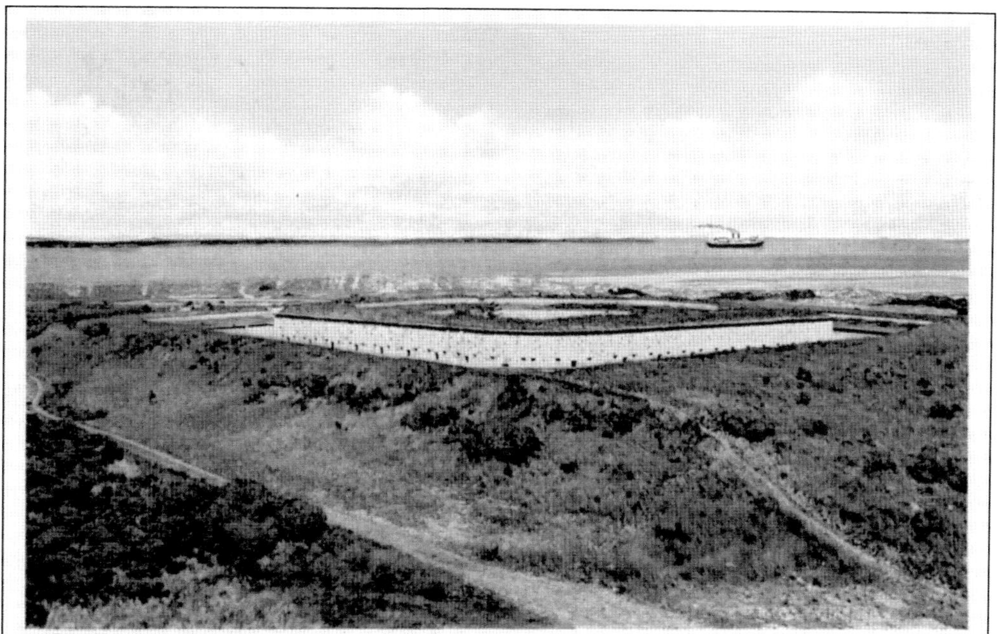

FORT MACON. Fort Macon, the third fort on Bogue Banks, was built on the site of former Forts Dobbs and Hampton as harbor protection. The fort is on the eastern end of Bogue Banks overlooking Old Topsail Inlet. Construction under the supervision of the Army Corps of Engineers started in 1826 and was completed in 1834. Robert E. Lee inspected the fort as a young engineer in 1840.

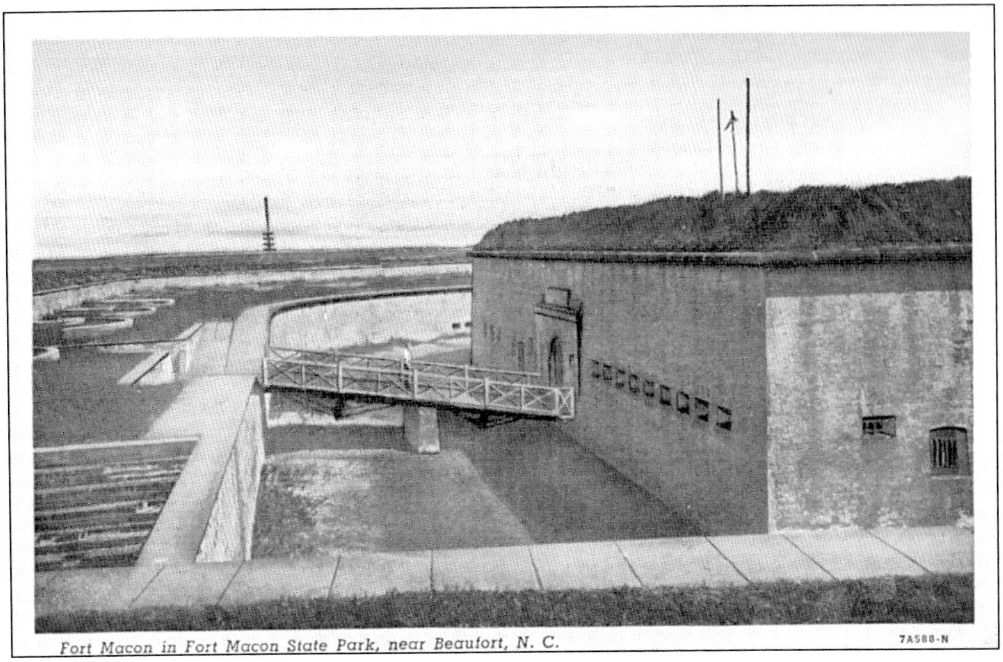

Fort Macon in Fort Macon State Park, near Beaufort, N. C. 7A588-N

THE FORT. Most of the 15 million bricks used to complete the fort were made by local contractors such as Otway Burns of Beaufort. The brick pentagon-shaped fort has a road leading to a bridge that crosses a moat at the fort's entrance. The walls are almost five feet thick, and the outer and inner sections are separated by a moat that entirely surrounds them. Massive oak doors open into the sally port. There are 26 casement rooms for living and working quarters. Five cisterns received rainwater filtered through oyster shells and sand. Two stairways with hand-wrought iron railings (as seen below) lead to the upper rampart. The stairways are supported with brick arches. Cannons faced the ocean and inlet. (Below, courtesy of Gail Barnes.)

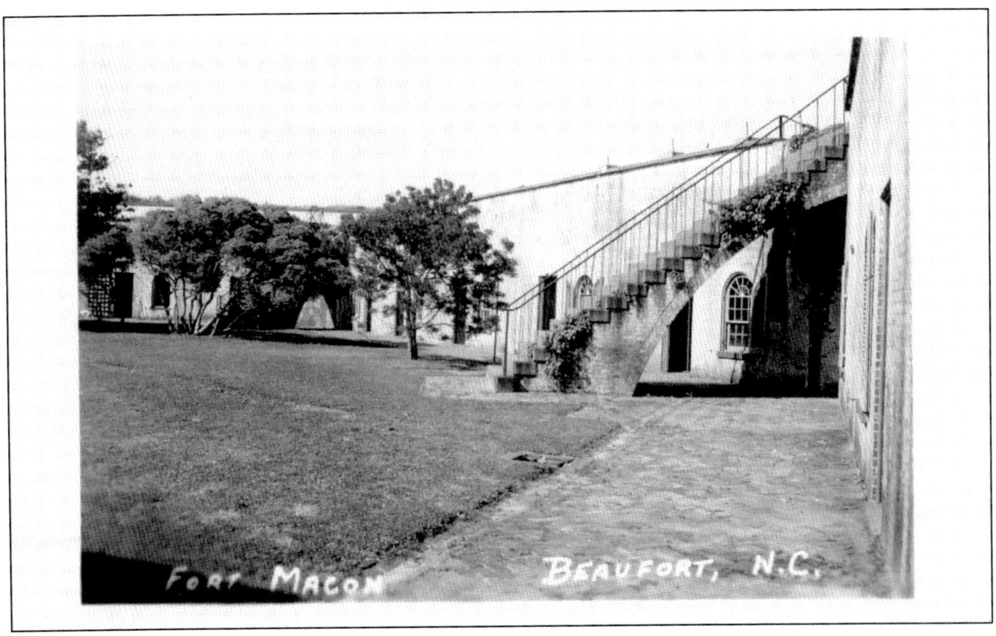

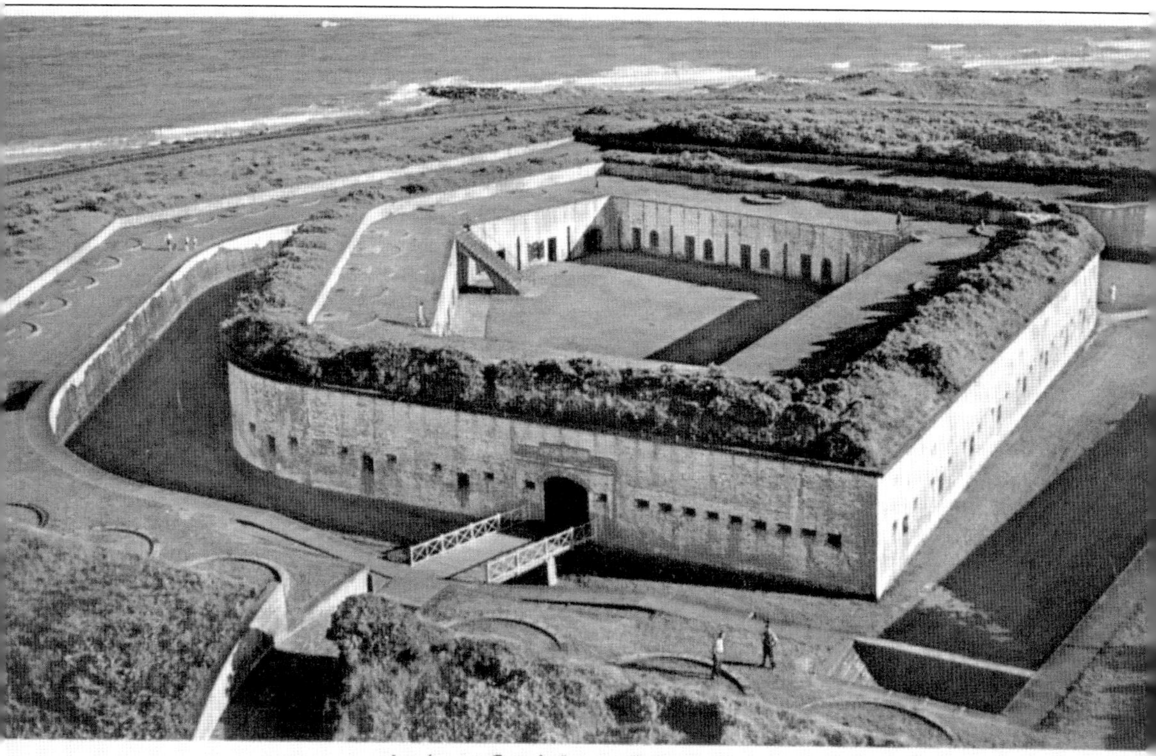

Historic Civil War Fort Macon

Old Fort Macon. Following construction in 1834, the fort was garrisoned for only a few years between 1834 and 1849 and then had a single caretaker until 1861. The Beaufort Harbor Guard, a local militia, took over the fort one month before North Carolina joined the Confederacy in May 1861. It was a Confederate fort for about a year. The fort was designed to protect Beaufort Inlet from attack by sea and had long-range guns. Having been built before mortars were invented, the fort was not prepared for attack by land. Demands for the fort's surrender made by Gen. John G. Parke in March 1862 and by Maj. Gen. A. E. Burnside on April 23, 1862, were refused by Col. Moses A. White. Bombardment began on April 25, when mortars were fired by Federal troops dug in behind sand dunes west of the fort. It was struck by 560 hundred-pound mortars. Eight people were killed and 26 wounded. On April 26, 1862, the fort was surrendered to the Union forces. (Courtesy of Mickey Weeks.)

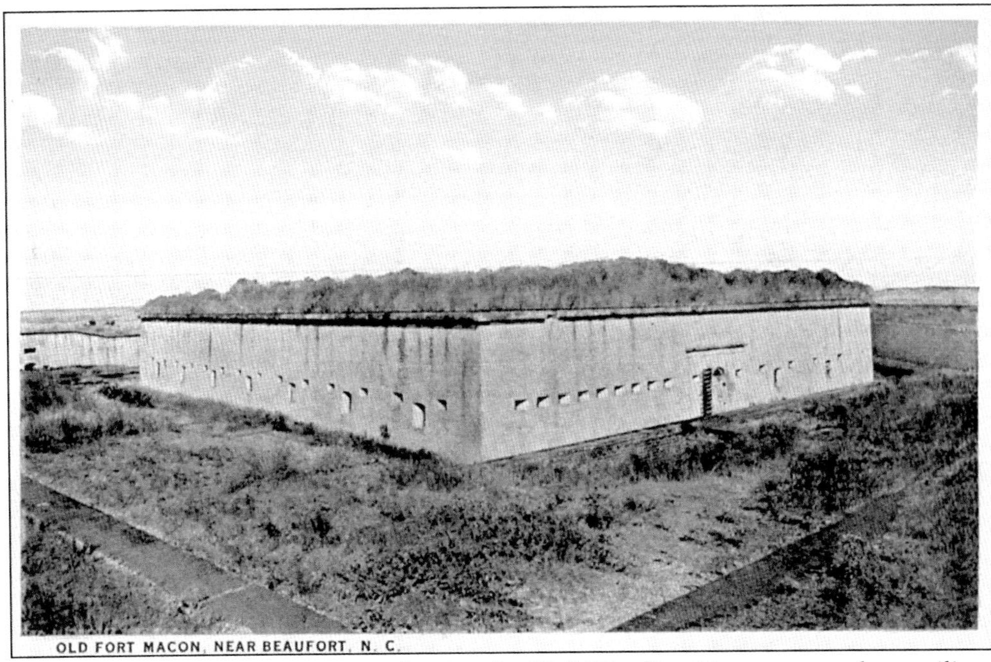

FORT MACON NEAR BEAUFORT. Following the Civil War, Fort Macon was used as a military prison from 1867 to 1876. During the Spanish-American War in 1898, the fort was reactivated and then abandoned again in 1903. Neglected, the fort fell victim to vandals who did much damage. The U.S. government sold the fort and 412 acres to the state for $1. It became the second public park in the state. After the Depression, the Civilian Conservation Corps restored the fort and built a road for visitors. In 1941, the fort was again under military control when it was occupied by the Coast Artillery Units to protect the harbor from German U-boats. After the war, it reverted back to a state park.

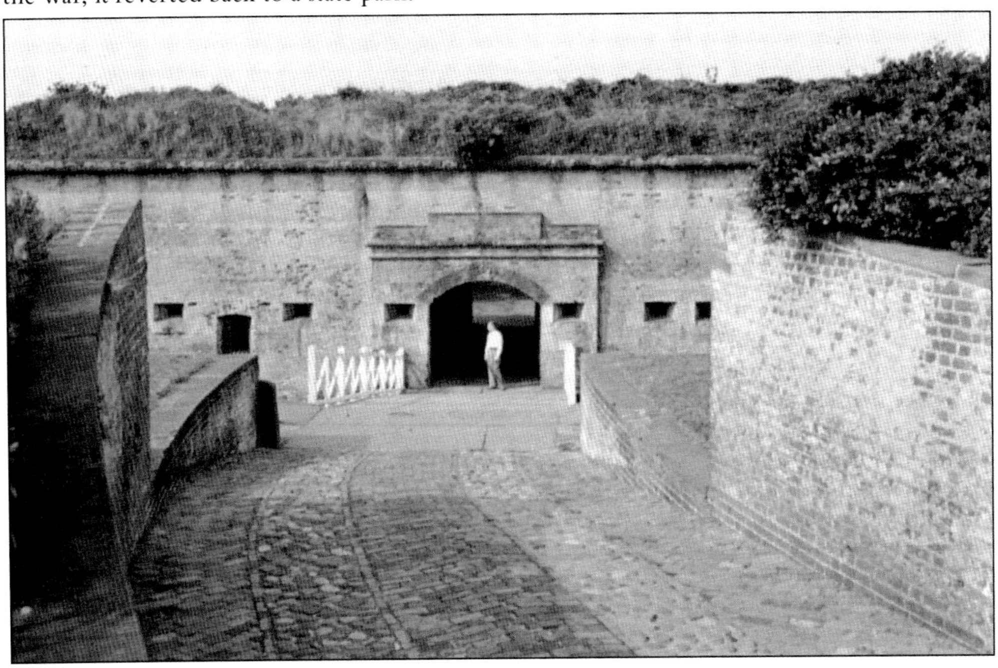

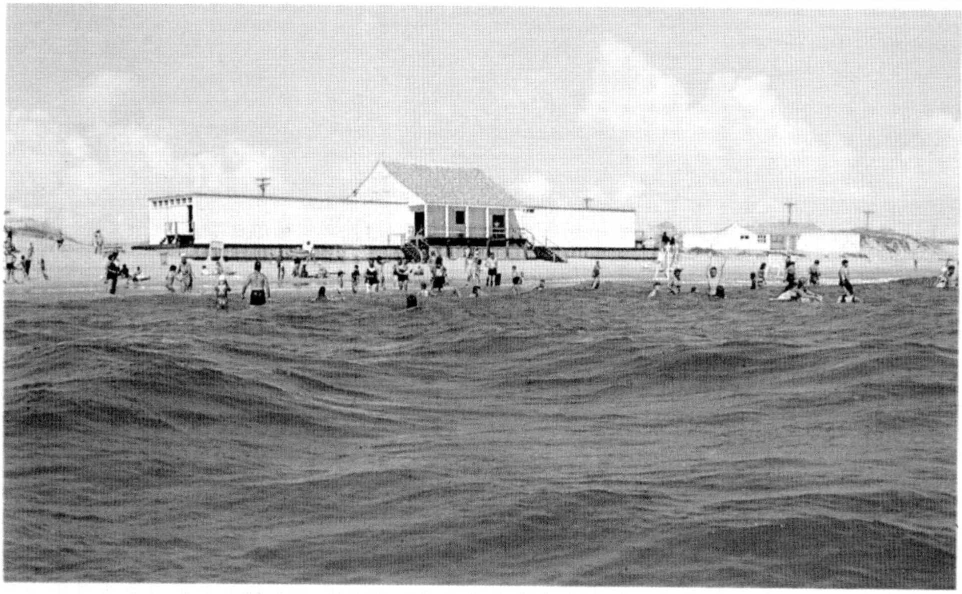

The Popular Beach at Fort Macon State Park

FORT MACON STATE PARK. A free bathing beach without a fence was opened at the state park in 1940. The park is about one mile west of the fort. Prior to this beach, there was a guarded picket fence to prevent people from surf bathing at Atlantic Beach without paying a fee for using the bathhouses. The charge was to pay for "competent lifeguard service." There was a large sand-clay road leading to the parking area. The new public bathing beach had a bathhouse that could accommodate 500 to 750 bathers a day. There was a 6,000-foot-long boardwalk and two shelters with picnic tables and fireplaces. This beach provided lifeguard services. The development was completed and paid for by the Department of Conservation and Development and the Works Progress Administration. (Courtesy of Mickey Weeks.)

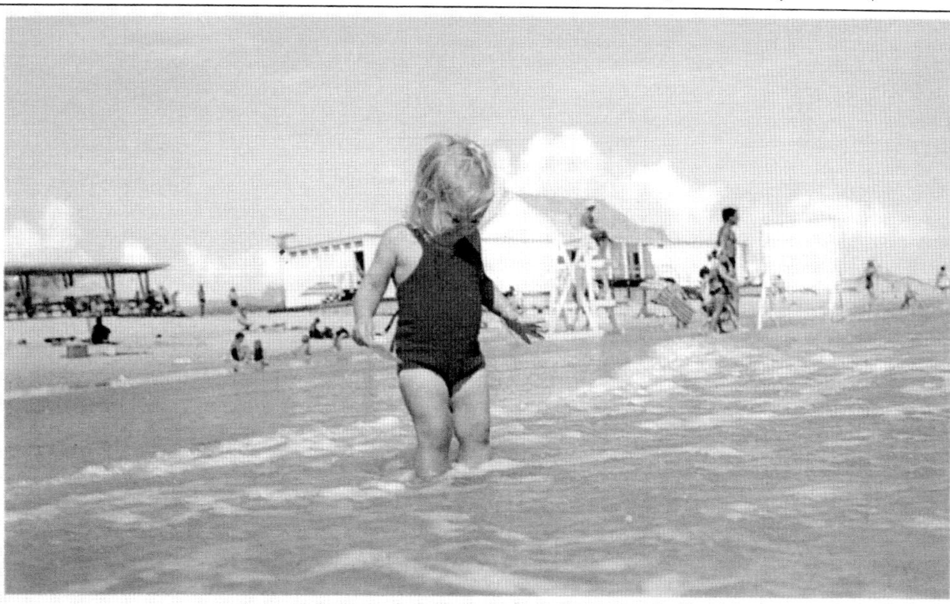

Safe and Beautiful Fort Macon State Park Beach

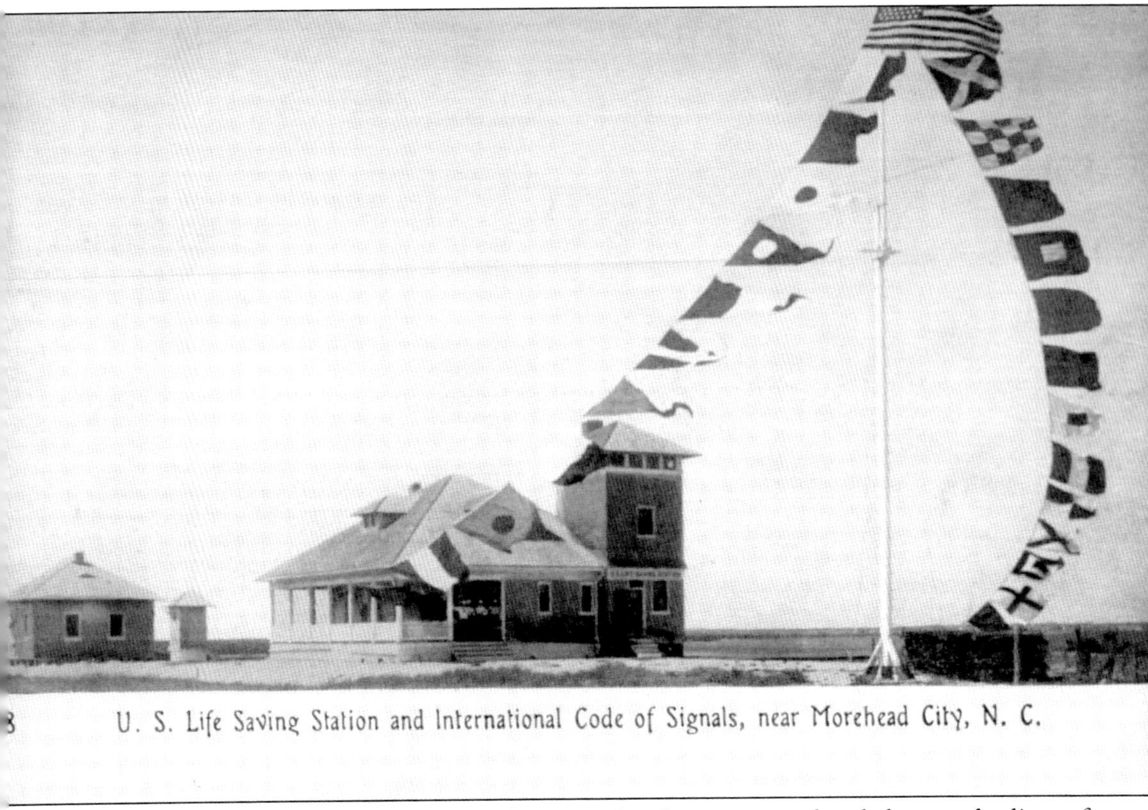

U.S. Life-Saving Station. The Life-Saving Service was started to help save the lives of sailors and passengers of ships wrecked along the coast. Permission was given by the War Department to build a lifesaving station at Fort Macon on the military reservation in 1904. It had one main building, two storage sheds, and a water supply. The Coast Guard was formed when the Life-Saving Service and the Lighthouse Service were combined. A large main building with a watchtower, boathouse, and equipment building were added in 1938. During World War II, a dock area was built by the army. It was turned over to the Coast Guard after the war ended, and the unit was designated as a Coast Guard Base. The Coast Guard has a variety of missions, from helping distressed mariners and maintaining navigational markers to enforcing federal laws. The Coast Guard Base still occupies the same land that it started on. (Courtesy of Mickey Weeks.)

Five

Community Glimpses

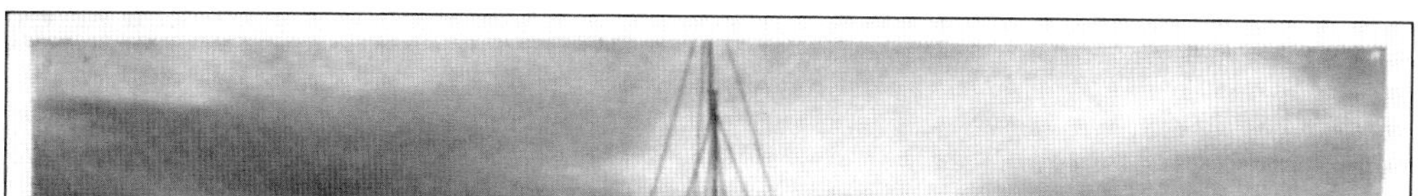

Pivers Island. The small island across Gallants Channel from Beaufort was originally owned by Peter Piver. Piver, an early Beaufort settler, purchased the island for £5 in 1764. He served under the command of Col. Thomas Lovick at the time of the pirate invasions of 1747. After visits by zoologists Theodore Gill and William Stimpson in 1860, Beaufort became a field station for those interested in marine biology.

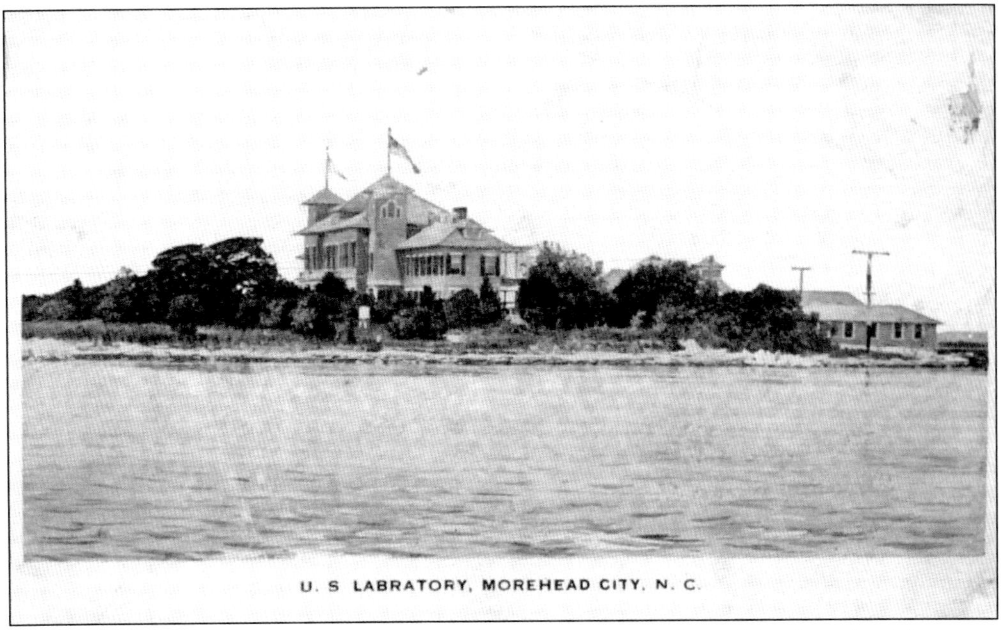

U.S. LABORATORY. The May 1899 issue of *Science* announced that a federal marine laboratory would be established in Beaufort, becoming the second on the Atlantic Coast. The original scientists rented and outfitted the Gibb House on Front Street as the laboratory. A new lab financed in part by Johns Hopkins University was opened on Pivers Island in 1902. Its mandate was to conduct marine biological research and develop methods for raising commercially important fish in captivity. In 1938, it began America's first fish farm, where 15,000 mullets were raised to study the viability of live fish storage. A terrapin hatchery was also in operation. Between 1902 and 1940, nearly 250,000 diamond-back terrapins were raised and released in marshes from Virginia to Georgia to bolster their population.

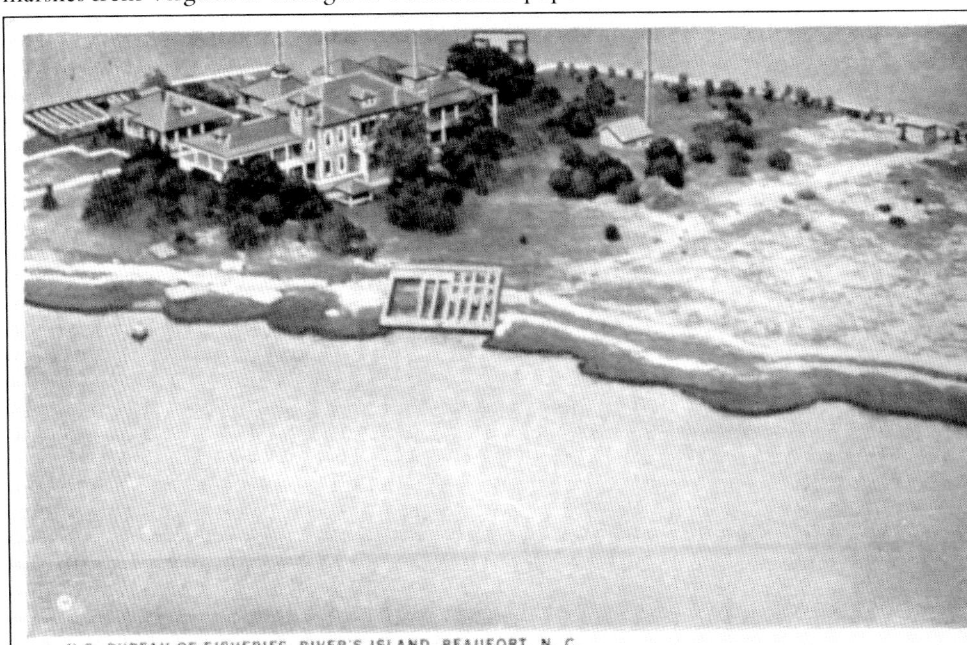

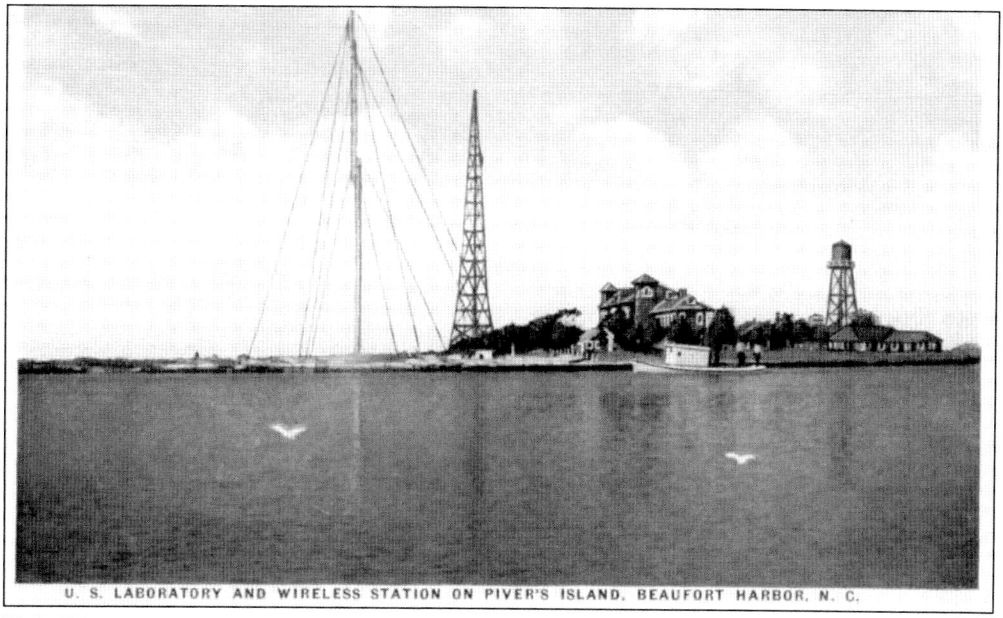

U.S. WIRELESS STATION. In the early 1900s, the navy established a chain of wireless telegraph stations along the Atlantic coast to enhance coastal defense and speed ship rescue. The Pivers Island station was operational in 1904. With the outbreak of German aggression toward England, President Roosevelt called for development of a project that equipped each station and naval base with long-distance telephone service. The station burned April 16, 1920.

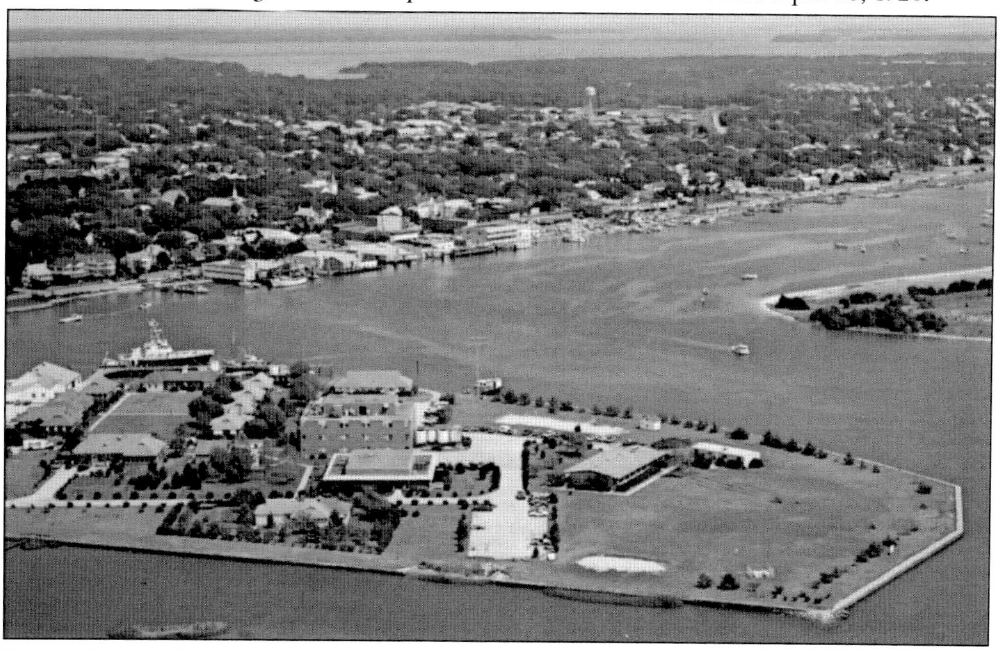

DUKE MARINE LABORATORY. Dr. A. S. Pearce sought the establishment of Duke University's Marine Laboratory on Pivers Island after he found an abundance of marine life nearby. Duke University acquired land on the southern end of the island and erected their first buildings in 1938. Originally it served only as a summer training and research facility. Today it is operated year-round as part of the Nicholas School of the Environment.

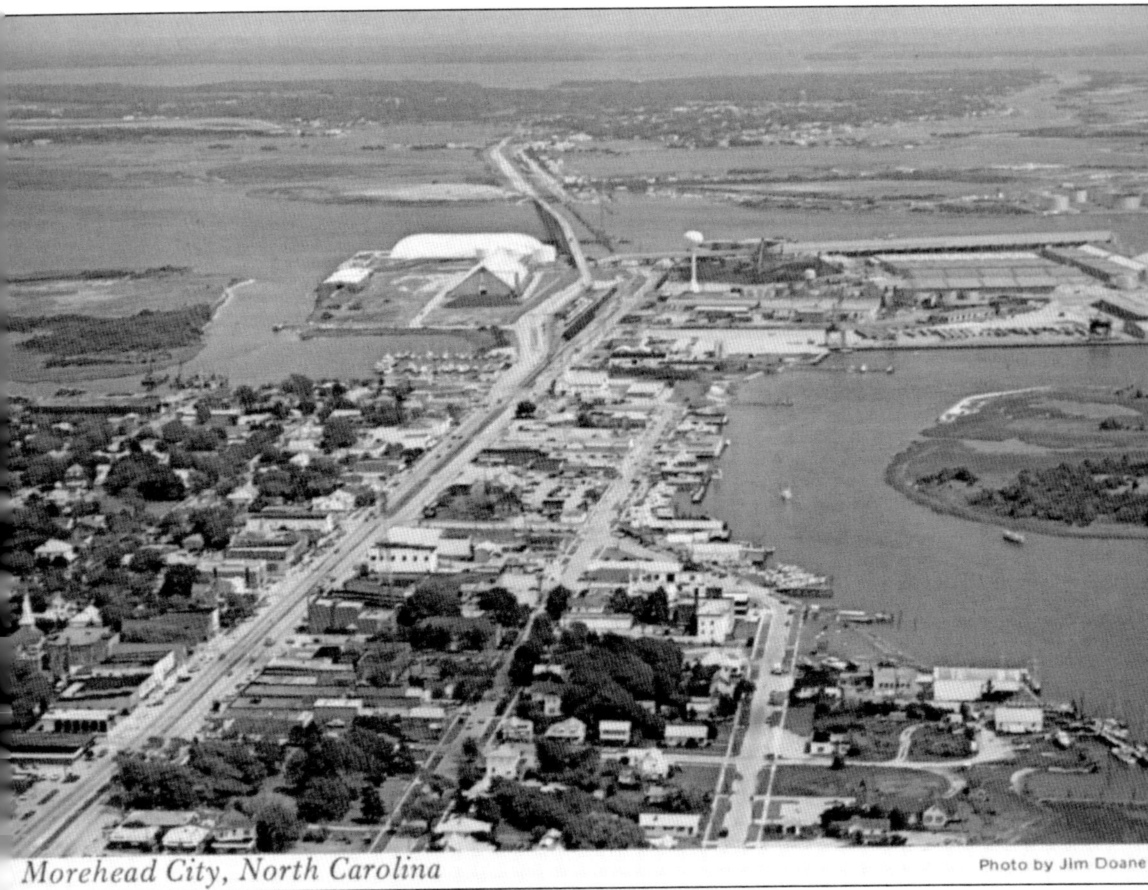

Morehead City, North Carolina

Radio Island. A by-product of the dredging operation that built the Beaufort–Morehead City causeway was the build-up of a small island. Radio Island is situated just inside Beaufort Inlet at the mouth of the Newport River. The island is accessible from the causeway it shares with Pivers Island. A few houses and businesses, like Herman Wetherington's glass shop, sit just off the causeway. Though Wetherington's has been in business on the island since the 1960s, for most of its history, Radio Island has stayed relatively undeveloped. The State Port Terminal owns 250 acres on the west side of the island, part of which has been leased to the privately owned Aviation Fuel Terminal. The U.S. Navy owns 25 acres at the southern end of the island, where it maintains three LST ramps and a large paved staging area. Those facilities are used as embarkation and debarkation points for U.S. Marines stationed at nearby Camp Lejeune and Cherry Point. The public has enjoyed the boat ramp and beach on the Beaufort side of the island.

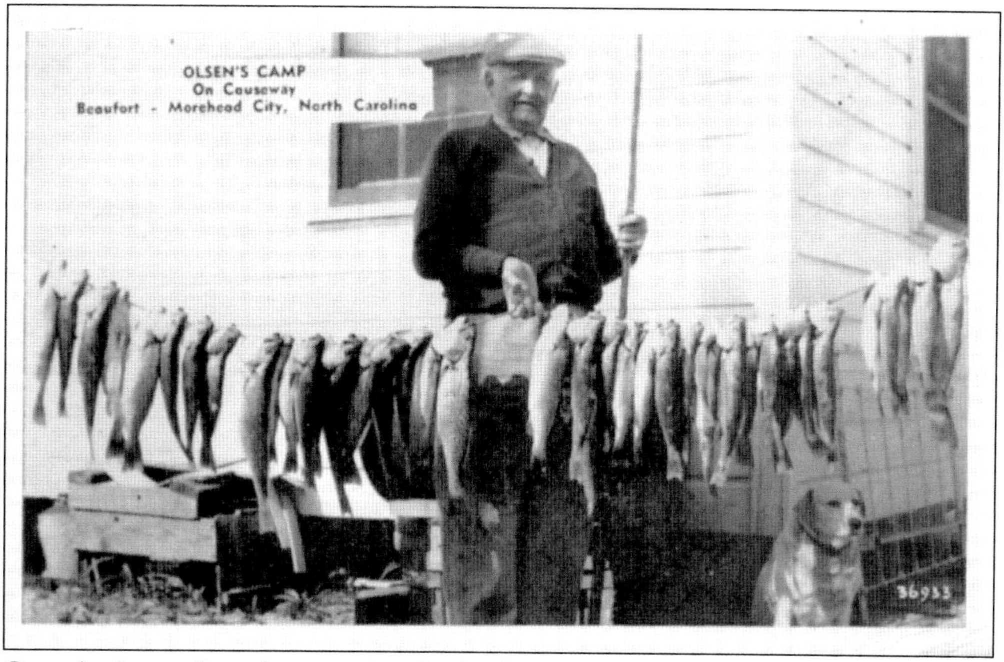

OLSEN'S CAMP. Over the years since its development, Radio Island has become home to a number of fishing camps and small fishing piers. Olsen's Camp offered cabins, boat rentals, fishing tackle, and bait. This postcard indicates that in April 1947, Mr. Olsen caught 220 fish in one three-day period. (Courtesy of Mickey Weeks.)

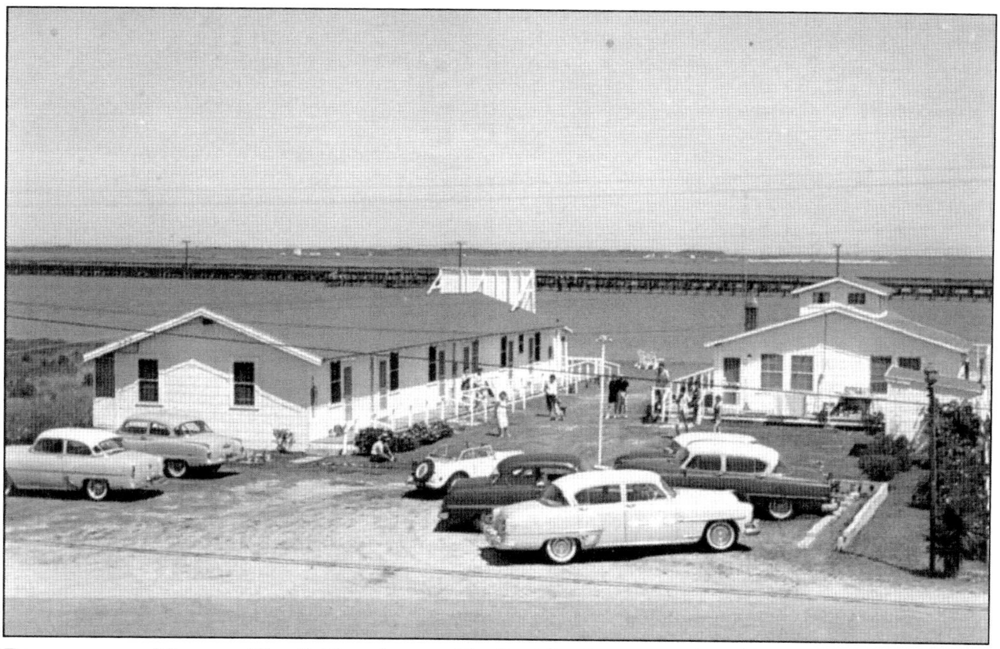

BRIDGEVIEW MOTEL. The Bridgeview on Radio Island promoted itself as an all-family motel. It rented one- and two-room efficiency units with private baths and kitchen facilities. The facility offered a clean private beach on the Newport River. The motel also arranged guided hunting and fishing trips for its guests. (Courtesy of Mickey Weeks.)

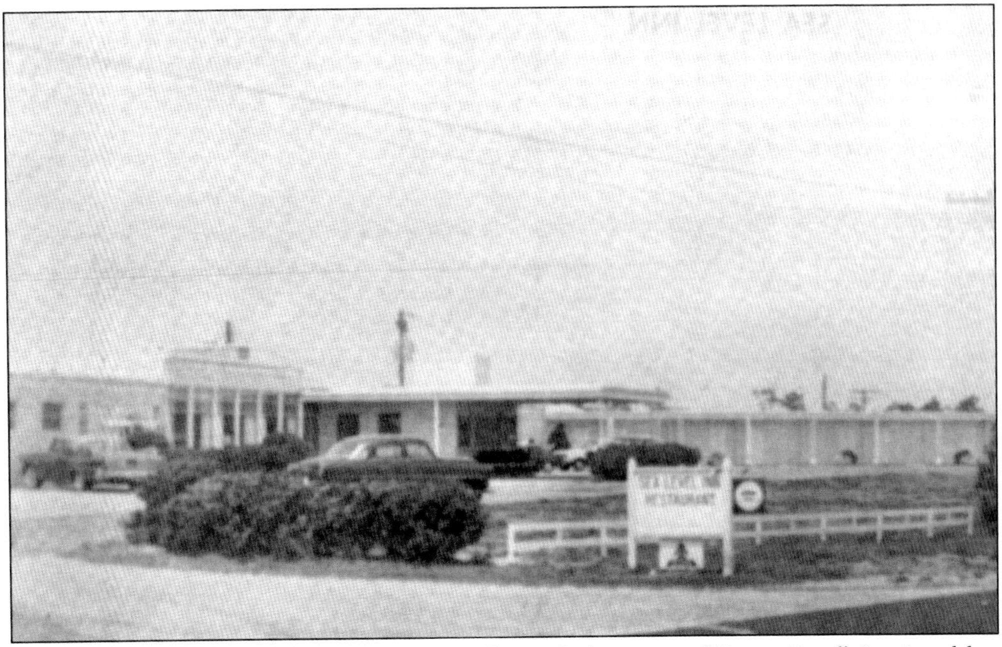

Sea Level. One of the 13 small villages collectively known as "Down East," Sea Level has one of the lowest elevations in North Carolina. Historically isolated by its geography and lack of serviceable roads, Sea Level finally received a post office in 1947. The Sea Level Hospital was established in 1953 to serve the residents of Down East who were far from the county's only other hospital, located in Morehead City. In 1976, the Sailor's Snug Harbor was relocated to Sea Level. It was originally founded in 1801 on Stanton Island by Capt. Robert Richard Randall, a Revolutionary War hero. He envisioned a safe place for retired seamen. The facility now provides for all retirees. Sea Level Inn overlooking Nelson Bay offered a dining room and 24 air-conditioned and heated motel units.

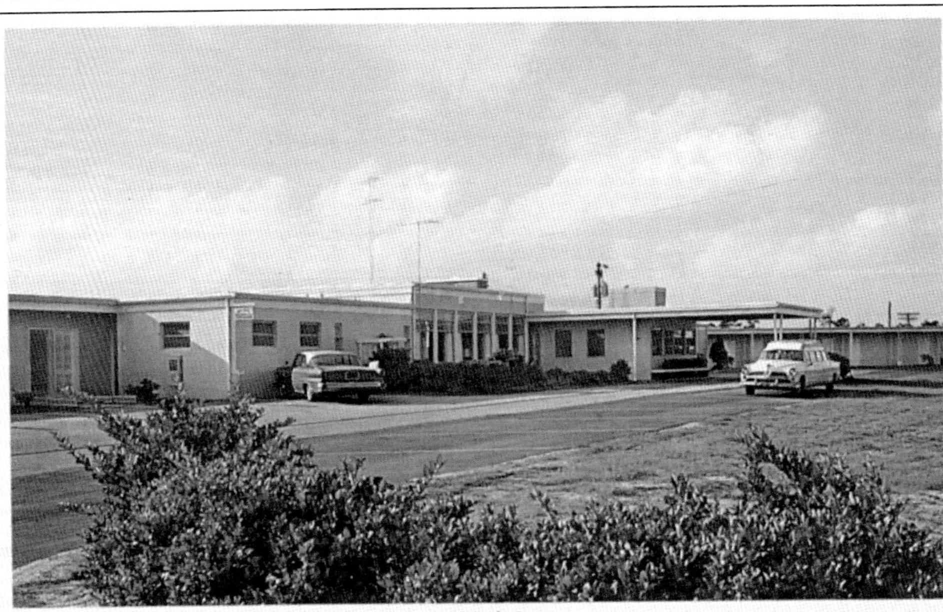

Sea Level Inn

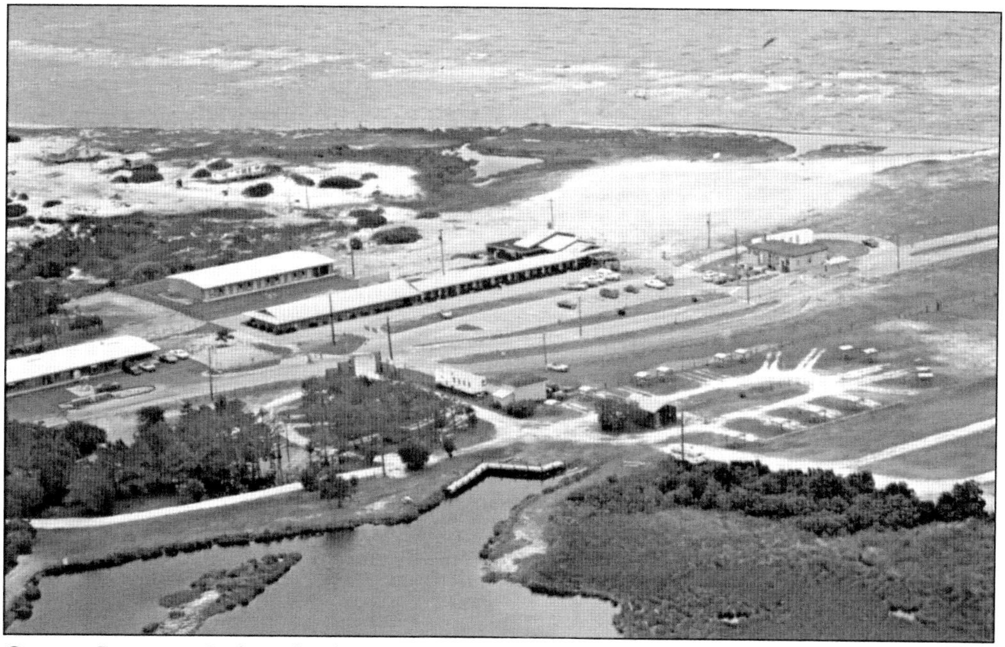

CEDAR ISLAND. Cedar Island is the easternmost community in Carteret County. Local legend holds that it's the actual home of the "Lost Colony." The community of 350 was first settled in the 1700s by whalers and fishermen. Fishing is still the main occupation today. The island contained two settlements, Roe in the north and Lola on the east, until 1960, when the government built a naval radar station on the eastern end of the island. That area is now part of the 14,480-acre Cedar Island National Wildlife Refuge. The North Carolina Department of Transportation operates a ferry terminus (above) on the island. The two-and-a-half-hour ferry ride across the Pamlico Sound links Cedar Island with Ocracoke Island in Hyde County. Driftwood Motel, Restaurant, and Campground are located near the ferry. (Courtesy of Mickey Weeks.)

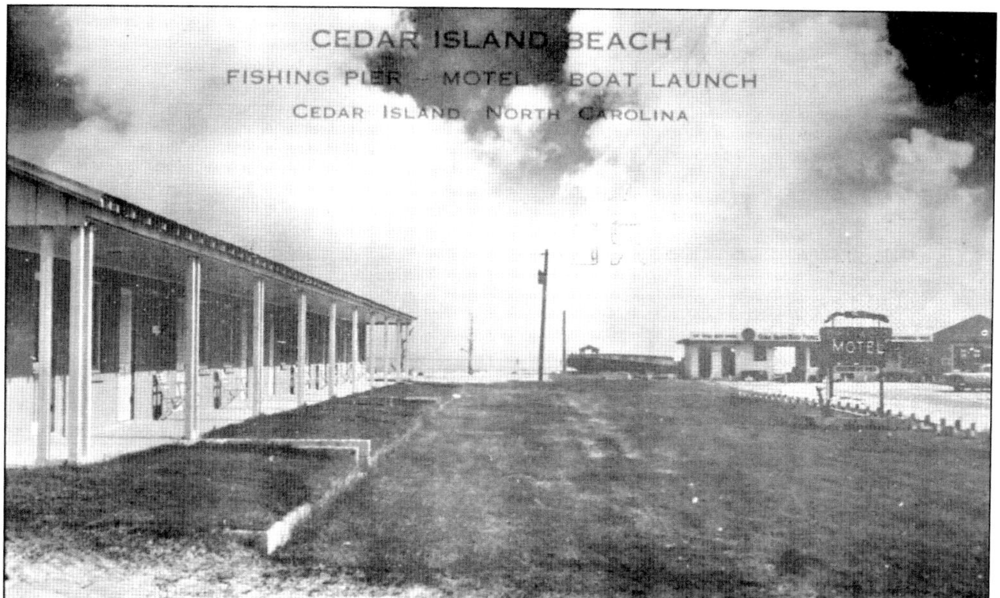

SALTER PATH. Salter Path had its beginning as a fishing village west of Atlantic Beach between the Atlantic Ocean and Bogue Sound. As schools of mullet ran close to the ocean shore, people from villages on Bogue Banks would go to the beach near Riley Salter's home to catch the fish. Mullet were caught in long nets and put in baskets, then washed in the ocean and salted down in barrels. The barrels were carried down a path to the ocean to be traded for other food staples when a boat came from Hyde County. The path, known as Salter's Path, became permanent after it was worn down over the years. Many settlers built their homes without a deed to the property, and the area became known as a squatter's village. The residents were sued in 1923 by Alice Hoffman, and the court restricted the village to 81 acres with ownership given to the village. In 1979, residents were given the right to have a title to their own property.

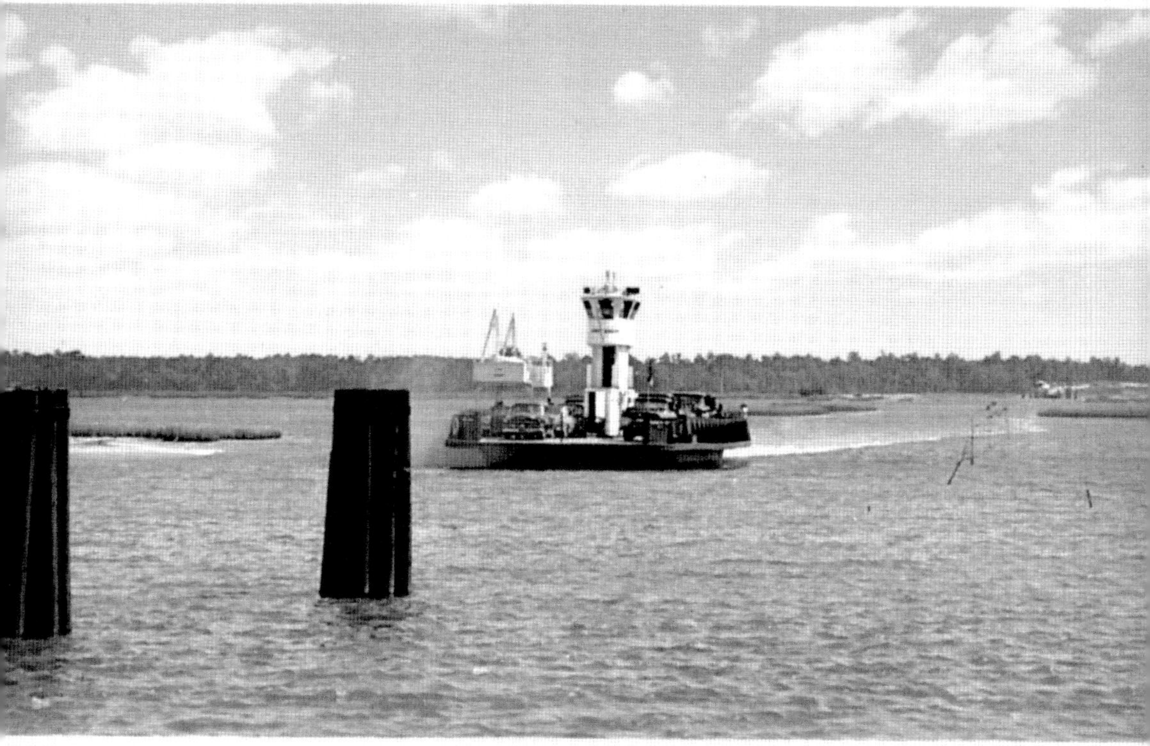

Bogue Sound Ferry

EMERALD ISLE AND BOGUE SOUND FERRY. Before the B. Cameron Langston Bridge was built in 1971, the only access to the western end of Bogue Banks was by driving across the bridge at Atlantic Beach or by ferry. The Bogue Sound Ferry (shown) was a free car ferry service between Cape Carteret and Emerald Isle. After the bridge was built, Emerald Isle became one of the fastest-growing areas in the county. Emerald Isle was originally owned by Henry Fort from Philadelphia, who had planned for it to become a giant resort similar to Atlantic City, New Jersey. His plan came to an end when a permit to build a bridge from the mainland to the island could not be obtained and the Depression occurred. In 1954, Fort's daughter sold this western part of Bogue Banks. Emerald Isle was developed and incorporated in 1957.

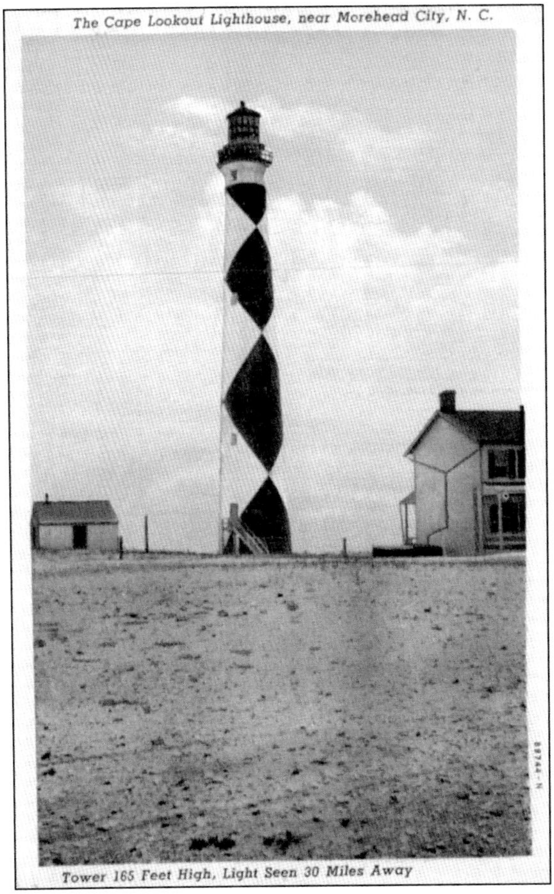

Cape Lookout. Shoals, known by sailors as "Horrible Headland" ran out 10 miles into the cape, making sea navigation treacherous. The cape itself offered the best-protected anchorage between Maine and Georgia. Spanish privateers used it as a hiding place in the 1740s. Captain De Cottineau anchored the French frigate *Ferdinand* there in 1778 and built a fort to protect the harbor. The first lighthouse, erected in time for the War of 1812, was painted with red and white stripes. The current one, built in 1859, received its black and white diamond pattern in 1873. The village of Diamond City was established by whalers in 1885. Once home to 500 people, it was abandoned because of hurricanes. Many families floated their houses on barges to Beaufort, Harker's Island, and an area in Morehead City they named "Promised Land."

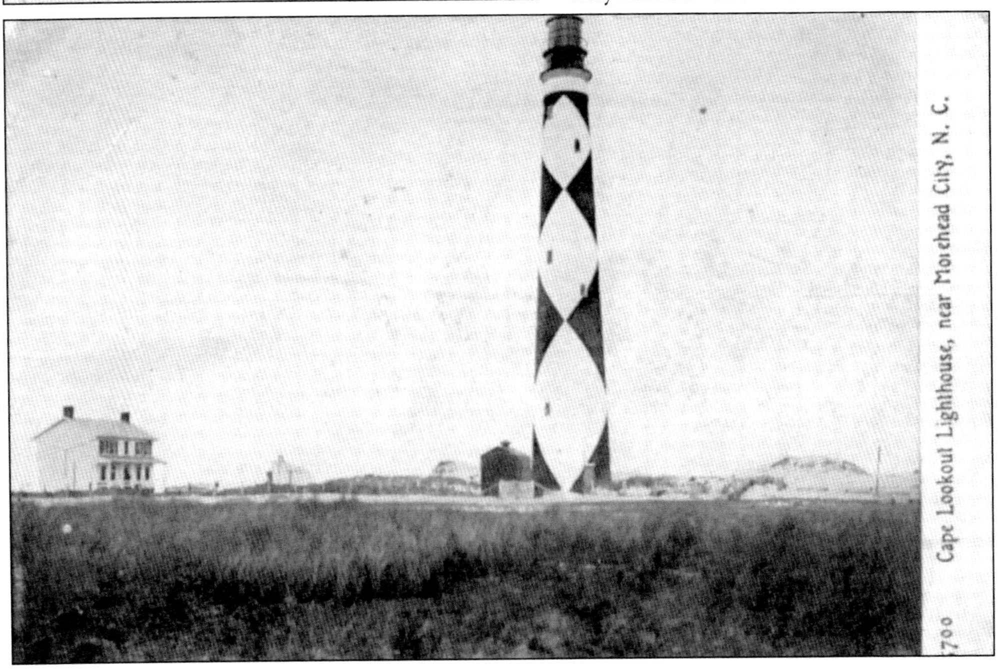

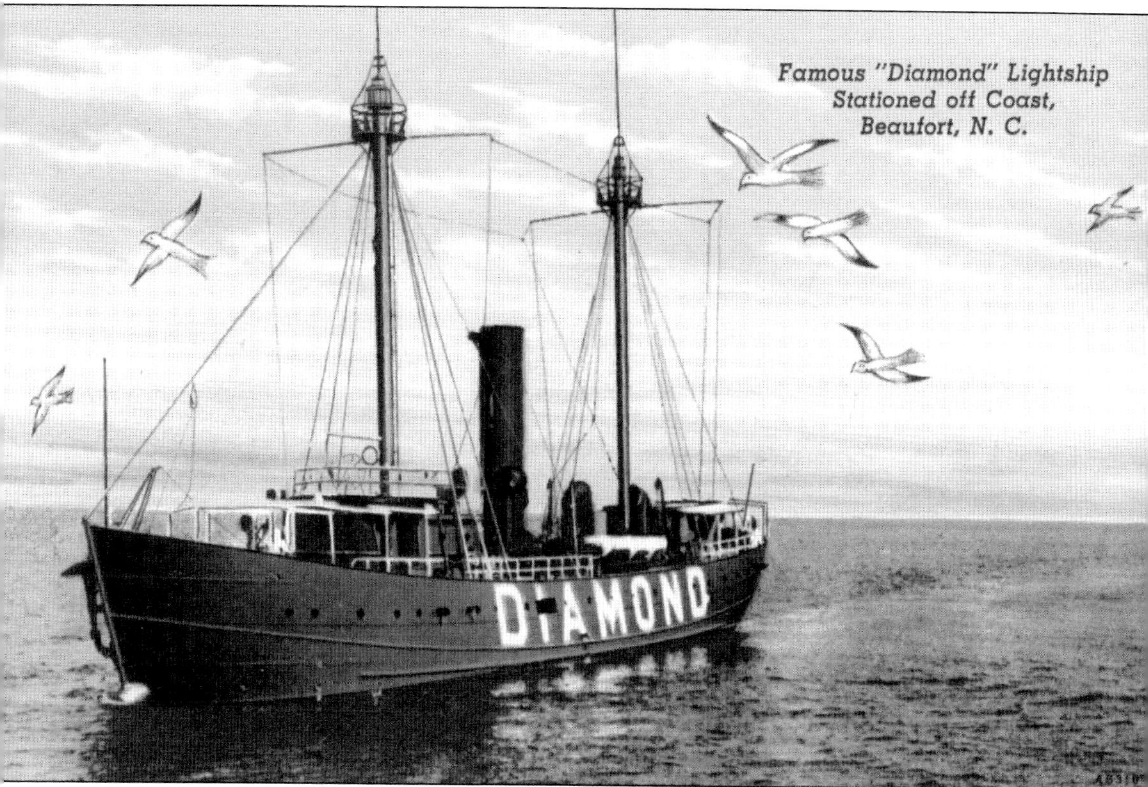

DIAMOND LIGHTSHIP. North Carolina's coast is often referred to as the Graveyard of the Atlantic because more than 600 ships have wrecked there since the 16th century. The northbound Gulf Stream and southbound Labrador currents create speedy highways for ships. Near Cape Hatteras, however, the shipping lane is forced close to the shoreline, where the shifting sands of Diamond Shoals have claimed many victims. In 1824, a lightship was placed at Diamond Shoals to protect shipping. Seven vessels served that role, braving dangerous storms until being permanently replaced in 1966 by a light tower. In 1918, *Lightship V71* reported sighting a German U-boat. The message was intercepted by the submarine, which sunk the lightship after giving the crew time to abandon ship. No other place on earth has had as many lightships guard its shores as North Carolina. Fourteen lightship stations have protected the state's inner sounds and outer banks. A lightship served at Cape Lookout Shoal from 1905 until 1933, when it was replaced by a bell buoy. (Courtesy of Mickey Weeks.)

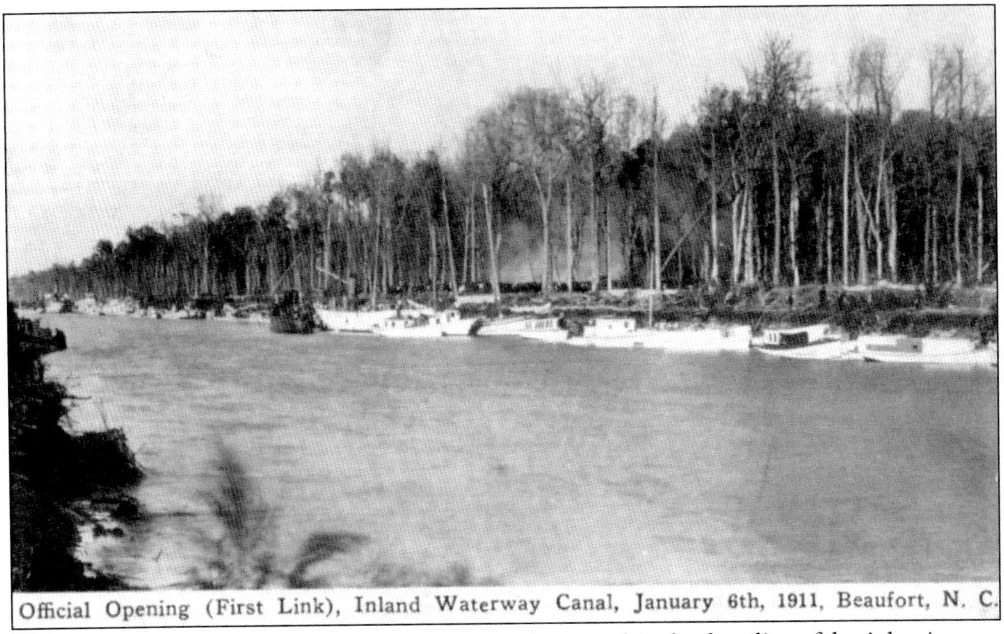

INTERCOASTAL WATERWAY. The bays and sounds lying within the shoreline of the Atlantic coast were indispensable arteries of communication and commerce for early settlers. Connecting them by canals increased their usefulness. In the early 1800s, Congress began this process, culminating in a Boston-to-Beaufort route in 1911. The digging of the five-mile canal connecting Adams and Core Creeks linked the area to the Dismal Swamp Canal and Norfolk, Virginia.

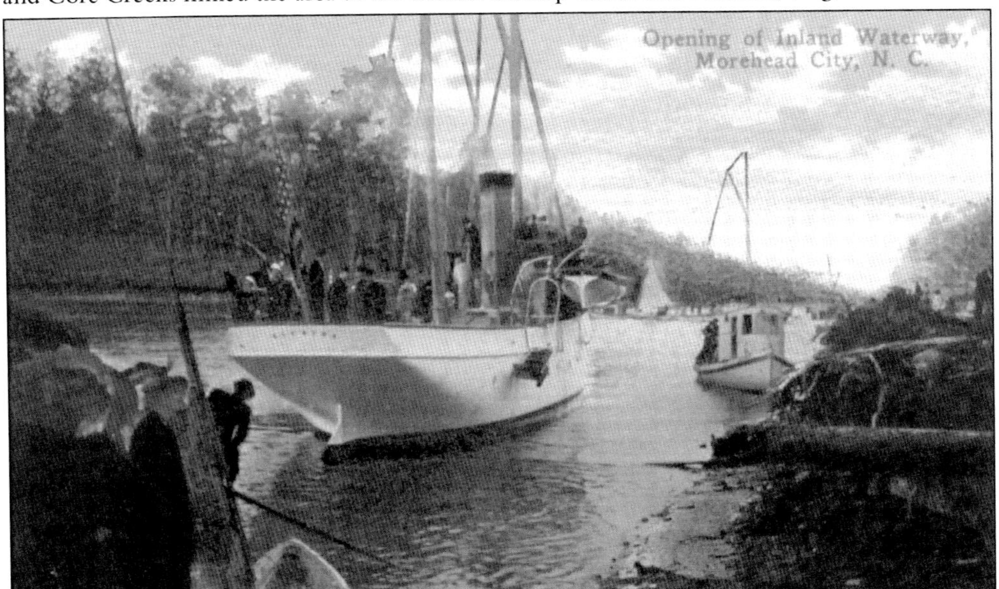

OPENING CELEBRATION. In November 1910, the Newport and Neuse Rivers were connected when dredge boats finished digging through five miles of dry land. An official opening celebration in honor of the Beaufort-to-Boston route was held January 6, 1911. One hundred boats and 2,500 people watched the parade featuring Coast Guard cutter *Pamlico*, torpedo boat *Dupont*, and converted cruiser *Elfrida*. North Carolina senator F. M. Simmons was the master of ceremonies.

Bibliography

Alford, Ben R., et al. *Morehead City Centennial Jubilee Book*. Morehead City, NC: The Centennial Committee, 1957.

Beaufort News, Beaufort, North Carolina.

Carteret County News-Times, Morehead City, North Carolina.

Davis, Pat Dula and Kathleen Hill Hamilton, eds. *The Heritage of Carteret County North Carolina Volume 1*. Beaufort, NC: The Carteret Historical Research Association, 1982.

Doughton, Virginia Pou. *Tales of the Atlantic Hotel*. New Bern, NC: Griffin and Tilghman Printers, Inc., 1994.

Dudley, Jack. *Beaufort: An Album of Memories*. Morehead City, NC: Coastal Heritage Series, 2004.

Hill, Fred, ed. *Historic Carteret County, North Carolina 1663–1975*, Beaufort, NC: The Carteret Historical Research Association, 1975.

Kell, Jean Bruyere. *The Old Port Town Beaufort, North Carolina*. Beaufort, NC: Self-published, 1980.

Little, M. Ruth. *The Beaufort National Register Historic District Comprehensive Survey*. Raleigh, NC: Longleaf Historic Resources, 1997.

———. *The Historic Architecture of Morehead City: North Carolina's First Coastal Railroad Resort*. Morehead City, NC: Downtown Morehead City Revitalization Association, Inc., 2003.

Morehead City Woman's Club. *A Pictorial Review of Morehead City History Through 1981*. Greenville, NC: Terrydale Printing Company, 1982.

———. *Yesterday & Today "A History of Morehead City."* Greenville, NC: Griffin and Tilghman Printers, Inc., 1998.

Russell, Nancy Duffy. *Beaufort Scrapbook*. Beaufort, NC: North Carolina Maritime Museum, 2005.

Willis, Neal. *Beaufort by the Sea; Memories of a Lifetime*. Kearny, NE: Morris Publishing, 2000.

———. *Book Three*, unpublished work.

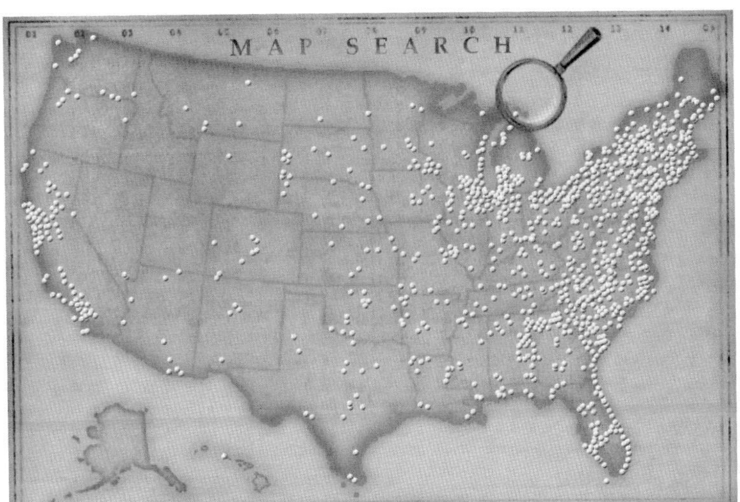
MAP SEARCH